CAROL BOWEN has a degree in Home Economics from the University of Surrey. She has been a freelance cookery writer, food consultant and broadcaster since 1979, having previously worked for *Good Housekeeping, Homes & Gardens* and Birds Eye (as Head of Consumer Affairs). Carol has contributed frequently to national newspapers, magazines and radio programmes including a regular spot with Michael Aspel on Capital Radio and a cookery programme 'What's Cooking?' on Piccadilly Radio in Manchester. On television she was cookery consultant and guest on the X-Cel Diet for TV-am with Diana Dors, and made a guest appearance on the BBC's *Snowdon on Camera* on food photography. To date she has written over fifty cookery books including *Versatile Vegetables* (Octopus) which won the 1984 Bejam Cookery Book of the Year Award. She is passionately committed to good, healthy food and cooking. Carol Bowen is married and lives with her husband and two children in Surrey.

BOB SHERMAN is a self-taught gardener with thirteen years experience of growing organically. In 1986 he became deputy head gardener to the Henry Doubleday Research Association at the National Centre for Organic Gardening, Ryton Gardens. Since then he has been a frequent contributor to gardening and conservation magazines and co-presented the first two series of Channel 4's popular television series 'All Muck and Magic?'

The GREEN *Gardening and Cooking Guide*

Bob Sherman & Carol Bowen

Pan Books
London, Sydney and Auckland

Acknowledgements

CAROL BOWEN

For valuable information and guidelines for some recipes
I should like to offer my grateful thanks to the Danish Dairy
Board, Heinz, Sunpat, Outspan, Tabasco, British Meat, Green
Giant, Flour Advisory Bureau, Sea Fish Industry Authority,
British Cheese Board, Colmans, Wells Drinks, Gales Honey,
Californian Raisins, CMA (UK) and Kiwifruit Information
Bureau.
I must also thank Bob Sherman for his enthusiasm, supplies of
unusual organic vegetables and seeds, invaluable advice and, not
least, friendship while putting together my share of this book.

BOB SHERMAN

My share of this book would never have been possible without the
instigation of Carol Bowen, who gave me an opportunity that
I could hardly refuse. I also owe thanks to the Henry Doubleday
Research Association, and to my colleagues there who offered me
advice and encouragement whenever I needed it. I must also
thanks Miles and Louise and their family for occasionally giving
me a corner of their house and a desk. Most of all I would like to
thank my wife, Christina, who sorted through my muddled text
and typed and retyped every page.

First published 1990 by Pan Books Ltd
Cavaye Place, London SW10 9PG

9 8 7 6 5 4 3 2

© Bob Sherman and Carol Bowen 1990
Illustrations © Rob Dalton 1990
ISBN 0 330 30804 1

Photoset by Parker Typesetting Service, Leicester
Printed in England by Clays Ltd, St Ives plc

Contents

Introduction

There is no longer any need to explain or justify organic gardening. Nowadays even the remote ramparts of Westminster ring to 'green' rhetoric and eloquence free from artifical flavouring or colouring. It is hard to believe that any gardener – drawn out into the fresh air to take part in the natural rhythms and rituals of the seasons – should not be an environmentalist and a conservationist. Most of us now 'think green' but not nearly enough of us 'act green'.

It is easy to feel overwhelmed at the relentlessness of the apparently steady march towards planetary suicide. Awareness of impending disaster has, however, grown enormously in the last decade and our precious life-sustaining earth is still not yet beyond recovery. But what can we, as individual gardeners tending relatively small plots, do? The size of most British gardens is less than 500 square yards but, in total, gardens cover more than a million acres. Here, then, is an active contribution all of us can make. Instead of adding to the pollution of land, air and water, we can embrace a new approach to gardening that acknowledges responsibility for the immediate environment and shows care and consideration for all the life that shares that space. Once you have nurtured, harvested and tasted your own organically grown produce, you will never be satisfied with anything else.

Organic gardening is not a step backwards into a sepia-tinted utopia. Such a time never existed. Nevertheless the wisdom of the past should not be thrown away. The soils bequeathed to us before the chemical revolution by countless generations of gardeners and farmers were carefully fattened and fed on organic matter to become full of natural potential energy. Such healthy soils feed plants without the need for short-term inputs of miracle powder. Garden hygiene, observation, rotation of crops and good timing are all principles that we should not hesitate to adopt. But we have learned new tricks and gained much new insight in recent years. A bacterium found in soil in America, now in widespread use as a control of caterpillars, is harmless to all other creatures. Stronger strains of this bacterium have since been discovered, and there are other such organisms which we can harness to work with us – and many more perhaps yet to be found. New varieties and root-stocks give plants inbred strength and resilience against a host of pests and diseases, and new materials that need no sprayer to apply them are available to protect crops or smother weeds.

Although the imbalances in nature created by man's lifestyle and land use have turned some pests into plagues and some diseases into epidemics, it is easier in many ways to garden organically now than it has ever been. It is not simply a matter, however, of changing brands, of replacing chemicals with natural products. While this alone would contribute a great deal to reducing pollution levels, it does not constitute sound organic practice – this begins with creating and maintaining an environment below ground healthy enough to sustain life indefinitely, and an environment above ground sufficiently varied to invite a wide range of beneficial and attractive creatures to maintain the balance between pest and predator.

While it may take two years or more to achieve this, subsequently the benefits will be seen in a garden that is healthy, vibrant with life and safe. It will need less maintenance too, and the fascination of observing the wildlife in this haven may lead to a greater tolerance of damage – much of which is superficial – a greater degree of peace of mind and a great deal of enjoyment.

*From
Organic
Plot . . .*

1. *Looking After Your Soil*

A handful of soil does not reveal its secrets by its colour. That apparently lifeless lump of dirt is actually a living community, teeming with microscopic organisms, bacteria, fungi and larger creatures such as worms, slugs and beetles. These are vital to sustaining a healthy soil through their action on organic matter (see p. 4). The clay, silt, sand and, in some cases, peat, which in combination make up the physical composition of our soils, were created by different prehistoric geological activities. While the structure and health of a soil can be improved, its texture will never alter.

Soil Particles

Soils are mixtures of different particles including humus and are described as clays, silts, sands, peats or loams.

CLAY The tiny, plate-like particles of clay bond very tightly together, making them airless and badly drained. On the other hand they hold good reserves of minerals and are naturally fertile.

SAND Sand particles are tiny pebbles which, therefore, have plenty of air spaces between them and drain very freely. Nutrients are often in short supply and leach away rapidly.

SILTS These are similar to sand in structure but smaller – not nearly as small, however, as clay particles.

PEAT In certain parts of Britain and Ireland, mosses and sedges have broken down very slowly under very wet conditions. The result is a dark, very acid substance, virtually devoid of minerals. With careful management such soils can be very productive.

LOAM This term indicates a mixture of particles and applies to most soils. Thus a sandy loam is essentially sandy in nature, but contains silt and clay also.

HUMUS is the general term given to organic matter in various stages of decay that, amongst other effects, bonds soil particles into crumbs.

Soil Analysis

Taking over a new garden can be a lottery. Simple observation of plant growth will give you some idea of the health of your soil, but tests can be done to provide a more accurate picture. A detailed organic analysis of your soil can be obtained from Elm Farm Research Centre (see list of useful addresses), but there is one test you can do yourself.

The Acid Test

Cheap kits are available which enable you to find out how acid or alkaline your soil is. This can affect the availability of plant nutrients and will determine how your soil should be managed. Acidity is measured as pH on a scale from a very acid 4.5 or less to about 8.0, which is alkaline, with 7.0 indicating a neutral soil. Fruit and vegetables prefer a slightly acid soil between 6.0 and 7.0, where nutrients are slowly dissolved to become available as plants need them. Under very acid conditions minerals are released too quickly and may be leached out or rise to toxic levels. In addition earthworms cannot survive in these conditions and the activity of soil micro-organisms is greatly diminished. This is how the highly acid peat bogs – which are essentially pure humus – can remain virtually unaltered for centuries. Very alkaline soils are high in calcium, which can lock up some plant nutrients by its bonding action. Deficiencies of iron, magnesium and even potash are not uncommon in alkaline soils, not because they are necessarily absent but just temporarily unavailable.

The pH of soils which are well managed will change and should be regularly monitored with your kit. Acid soils can be corrected by using lime. The best forms of this are dolomite (containing additional magnesium) or ground limestone; these are both natural rock and so dissolve more slowly and have a longer-lasting effect. The most commonly available form is hydrated garden lime, which is highly soluble and quickly spent. As a rough guide, a sandy soil with a pH of 6.0 will need 270 gm/m^2 (8 oz/yd^2) to raise the pH to 6.5. A silt loam will need twice as much and a clay soil three times as much. It is generally advised that lime and manure should not be applied at the same time. Provided that the manure is reasonably well-rotted, however, and is worked into the soil before liming, there is little likelihood of nitrogen loss.

Lowering pH is extremely difficult and cannot be achieved quickly. Both compost and leaf-mould can be quite alkaline but peat, lawn mowings and manure would all have a slightly acidifying effect. Under no circumstances should alkaline soils be limed.

Soil Food

Whatever your soil type, it needs organic matter. This is decayed plant and animal remains on which soil micro-organisms feed to release the minerals that plants require. Its other magical effects include bonding soil particles to improve soil structure, aeration and drainage; darkening light soils to make them warmer; acting as a sponge to absorb water as a reserve for when times get hard and dry; retaining surplus minerals which might otherwise be washed out in heavy rain.

Organic matter for the soil can be bought as manure, laid on the surface in the form of straw or hay mulches, or made into an ideal soil food by composting garden and kitchen residues. The compost heap is the heart of the organic garden; it is a means of speeding up a natural process by harnessing the activities of bacteria, fungi and ultimately worms and other creatures into a concentrated frenzy of activity.

4

The Compost Heap

The quality of your compost and the speed of decomposition will depend on the container, the ingredients and the time of year. Any pile of debris will eventually rot down given time, but the process can be greatly improved by using a good container.

The container

There are many commercially available compost bins of varying types, but bins are easy to make and need only basic materials and unsophisticated tools. The ideal bin drains well, is not too small, has good insulation and is weatherproof.

A solid-sided wooden box of a minimum cubic metre or cubic yard in size is ideal for this. Smaller bins can be used, but tend to lose heat more rapidly. Prunings, cabbage stumps and other stemmy material at the base will provide drainage, a lid keeps out the rain and drying sun and an old carpet on the surface will retain heat. Timber used for the box should not be treated with creosote, which is harmful to the micro-organisms in the heap.

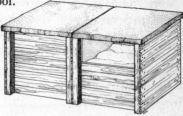

New Zealand box

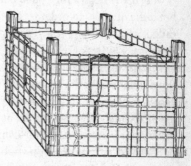

DIY compost bin (wire mesh & cardboard)

A cheaper version of this can be made from wire mesh supported on posts. Such a structure (and any bought container with mesh or slatted sides) should be lined with cardboard to improve insulation and prevent the sides from drying out.

It is a good idea to have at least two bins, so that one can be rotting while the other is being filled and so that the heap can be 'turned' (see p. 7).

The ingredients

The flavour and nutritional value of a meal relies on the right combination of ingredients. In the same way, a heap is improved by containing a variety of materials in the right combination. The two important elements are carbon, in the form of tougher, stalky material; and nitrogen, in the form of soft, sappy plants such as grass or young weeds. Lawn-mowings on their own will deteriorate into a black slime and a pile of prunings will take years to decompose. It is hard to give exact quantities for these and only trial and error will give you the experience to know what combinations work. More carbon than nitrogen is required and the ingredients need to be mixed well. Moisture is also essential; the heap should not be waterlogged but evenly moist.

N.B. It is important to exclude any virus-infected or diseased material. Although the heat of a good heap will kill many pathogens, enough may survive to contaminate future crops.

Activators

A well-made heap with a good balance of materials should become hot quite quickly. In order to speed this process certain products called 'activators' are sold, most of which tend simply to be chemical sources of quick-acting nitrogen. Some organic activators are available either in the form of a powder containing bacteria and fungi to inoculate the heap or as a herbal preparation. But in any case activators are freely available in or near most gardens. Lawn-mowings and young nettles are both rich sources of nitrogen and urine is far better used on the compost heap, where its nitrogen can be recycled, than flushed down the drainage system and possibly out to sea. Comfrey (see p. 14) is another excellent source of nitrogen and therefore a good activator.

Shredders

Shredders are noisy and not particularly cheap. They do, however, allow you to compost almost all garden refuse and greatly reduce the need for choking bonfires, which waste as many valuable nutrients as they send carcinogens into the atmosphere. Shredding cabbage stumps and prunings increases the surface area available for micro-organism activity. Such shredded waste often heats up by itself and, mixed with lawn mowings or urine, makes an excellent weed-free compost.

Compost Tumblers

The initial heating process can be speeded and sustained by using a compost tumbler. Regularly stirring air into the tumbled contents helps to keep the temperature high until the first decomposition stage is complete. After three or four weeks (except in winter), a substance results which is suitable as a surface mulch but benefits by further maturing either in a loose carpet-covered heap, a worm bin (see p. 8) or a compost bin.

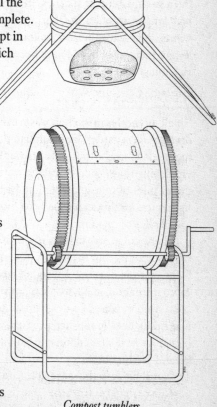

Building the Heap

1.   The base layer of the heap should consist of cabbage stalks or other stemmy wastes. It is worth saving these for the next heap.

2.   It is better to fill half a bin at a time, saving ingredients in sacks or an empty bin until you have sufficient, rather than adding dribs and drabs as they become available.

3.   Chop up stems, large leaves and roots or put them through

Compost tumblers

7

a shredder. Thoroughly mix the ingredients, adding lawn mowings (with restraint) or other high nitrogen activators (see above), and fill the bin. Wet the ingredients if they seem too dry.

4.   Cover the heap with a square of old carpet, hessian bags or cardboard and finally fit a lid.

5.   The heap will break down more evenly and speedily if it is turned. Gardeners' hands can be horny and insensitive but are usually good enough to gauge when a heap has cooled; alternatively use a soil thermometer. At this stage it can be turned out into the empty box beside it. This stirs in more air needed by the bacteria to continue working, and the heap heats up a second time.

In summer compost can be made in four to six weeks but will take longer in cooler weather, while little breakdown takes place in winter. It is ready to use when most of the original contents are no longer recognisable and have become the colour and texture of a rich moist cake.

Worm Compost

Small quantities of kitchen waste can be awkward to recycle if you do not have a garden large enough to produce adequate compost materials to mix with it. The answer to this is worm composting, employing the striped brandling worm, which naturally lives in or under piles of rotting vegetation. Fishing shops sell them as bait for fishermen, or they can usually be found in old piles of manure.

There are many versions of worm boxes recommended, but the simplest is made from a plastic dustbin. A wooden box gives more insulation, and a wooden box on legs allows you to wheel a barrow underneath and riddle out the finished product. All containers will need drainage, a tight-fitting lid and starter bedding.

1.   Drill holes in the sides of the dustbin about 15 cm (6 in) from the base in a ring with 15 cm (6 in) between holes. Fill the

Worm bin

8

bottom of the bin with gravel to a point just above the holes and
cover it with a wooden board or sheet of thick-gauge plastic
perforated to allow drainage.

2.   Put in a layer of bedding about 10 cm (4 in) deep. This can be
shredded newspaper, sawdust, old compost, manure or peat to
which is added calcified seaweed to give essential calcium to the
worms. Introduce a handful of worms and leave them a few days to
settle in. Cover them with bubble polythene, old carpet or sacking.

3.   Kitchen waste can now be added either to the surface or in a
scooped-out hollow down one side. Worms need protein, which can
be added in the form of wholemeal flour or fish-meal if it is not
present in the kitchen waste.

4.   Add calcified seaweed occasionally to keep the contents from
becoming too acid, and avoid excessive quantities of citrus peel. As
the waste is worked through more can be added, but not too much
at a time.

5.   Stir contents now and then to add air and keep material moist.

6.   Worms will be most active when the temperature is between 13
and 25°C (55–75°F) and may need shading in summer and
protection in winter, when they are best housed in a greenhouse or
insulated shed.

Small white, threadlike worms may appear in the bin. These are
enchytraids, which perform the same function but more slowly and
in more acid conditions.

It may take six months for the worms to convert a full box of
kitchen waste to the very rich, dense black end product. At this
stage put a fresh layer of waste on the surface and after a few days
scoop it off with as many worms as possible to start a new bin. The
remainder is so high in nutrients and bacteria that it is best used as a
fertiliser for scattering round plants or working into seedbeds.
Alternatively it can be mixed half and half with peat to make a
potting compost.

Trench Compost

Very little decomposition takes place in winter, but kitchen waste
continues to accumulate and a good way to deal with this is trench

composting. Dig a trench 25 cm (10 in) deep and a spade's width where the runner-beans are to grow next year. Tip the kitchen waste into the trench as it is available until the trench is half full. Scatter some lime or calcified seaweed over it, add a sprinkling of soil to cover and continue to fill the trench with waste. When full, lime it again and heap the soil over the top where it will slowly sink. This process is repeated with a second trench for the other row of beans, with 45 cm (18 in) between the centres of the trenches. By the time the beans are planted, the contents will have rotted.

Leaf-mould

Autumn leaves are a greatly wasted resource; every year councils dump tons of street leaves on municipal tips to waste their qualities on tin cans and bedsprings. Some councils will deliver loads to allotments and householders so it is always worth asking. Leaves have little nutrient value but are excellent as soil improvers. Small quantities can be stored in plastic bags where they will slowly rot over a period of two years, at which stage they can be used. Larger quantities can be left in rough heaps or enclosed in wire mesh to prevent them blowing away. Leaves decay by a fungal process which differs from composting, so it is preferable to keep them separate from the compost heap.

Two years can seem a long time to wait, especially if space is limited in your garden. The process can be greatly speeded either by shredding the leaves or by mixing in lawn-mowings in May or June (at the rate of 1 part mowings to 4 parts leaves) or both.

Rotted leaf-mould is best applied as an autumn mulch to protect bare soil over winter. It is particularly good for creating a fine tilth on heavy soils where seeds are to be sown. Alternatively it can replace peat as an ingredient in home-made potting compost if it is well-rotted, sieved and, ideally, sterilised.

Manures

You will be doing very well if you can produce enough compost to supply your garden; it is more likely that you will need to buy in animal manure. Horse and cow manure are both excellent, but may arrive fresh or partially decomposed. If applied to the soil in this state they are likely initially to deplete the nitrogen from the soil as it is taken up to complete the breakdown of the manure. In addition farmyard manure is likely to contain residues of weedkillers, hormones and other contaminants. Composting the manure under a polythene sheet will help to reduce the chemical contamination and complete the decomposition process.

Horses are often stabled on wood shavings or sawdust. Manure in this combination needs longer decomposition to ensure that the high carbon levels in the wood are reduced to a level which will not 'rob' nitrogen from the soil.

Poultry manure is extremely high in nitrogen and can 'scorch' plants; it is best used as a compost activator. Farming of pigs and poultry is not what it once was and you may want to be aware of the source of such manures, especially since feeds used for intensively farmed pigs and poultry may contain unacceptable chemicals.

Green Manures

Not all animal manure comes in glutinous black lumps. There are also green manures, which are crops grown for no other purpose than to dig in to the soil. Vacant, bare plots are at the mercy of the elements. From spring until the onset of winter the soil is warm enough for biological activity in which nutrients are released from organic matter into soil water. If there are no plant roots to take up those nutrients, the next downpour will carry them away for ever. The extensive root system of these green manures also helps to stabilize soil structure, while their leaves and stems protect the soil surface from the hammering of heavy rain and smother out unwanted weeds. Some green manures are members of the pea family (leguminous) and live in symbiosis with bacteria that cause nodules on their roots. These bacteria fix nitrogen from the air, so extra nitrogen becomes available for the following crop after the green manure is buried.

There are several instances where green manures are particularly useful. Every garden has bare soil in winter; a hardy green manure will protect it through the worst period of the year and can be dug in during March before the ground is needed. It is not advisable to sow seed directly after such a crop but transplants suffer no difficulties. There are often gaps in the rotation between crops in spring and summer which a fast grower like mustard can bridge. Finally, you may want to rest some land or wish to improve some newly broken land before attempting to crop it. A long-term leguminous green manure will fulfil this role.

Green manures should be dug in before they become tough and stemmy. If they do so, they are best cut and composted so that only the roots are incorporated. Allow two weeks of decomposition after incorporating a green manure before planting up the site.

Mulches

Most microbiological activity takes place in the top 10–15 cm (4–6 in) of soil. Organic matter applied to the surface as a mulch stimulates this activity and encourages earthworms to aerate and enrich the soil as they tunnel up and down fetching this material into their burrows. Unrotted materials such as hay and straw (ideally organically produced and free of weedkiller residues) laid thickly round fruit will last a whole season or more, suppressing weed growth and holding moisture in the soil. Lawn-mowings are useful between rows in dry weather.

The ideal time to apply a mulch is when the soil is warm and moist. Covering a sodden or frozen soil will tend to keep it in that condition for some time, causing a slower start if cold and rotting roots if too wet.

Not all mulches are made of organic matter. Black polythene and woven strawberry mulch are useful for long-term crops such as strawberries to suppress weeds and retain moisture, but do not have the soil-building qualities of organic matter. The woven mulch has the advantage of allowing moisture to penetrate.

SUITABLE ORGANIC MATERIALS: Compost, manure, leaf-mould, lawn-mowings, straw, hay, newspaper or cardboard (topped with hay or straw), peat, comfrey leaves (see p. 14).

Some Recommended Green Manures

Crop	Hardy	Sow	Rate	Dig in	Notes
Nitrogen Fixers					
ALFALFA	Yes	Mar–Aug	15 g/m² ½ oz/yd²	After whole season	Deep-rooting; suitable for long term. Can be cut several times for composting. Fixes nitrogen only if sown together with special inoculum.
FENUGREEK	No	May–early Aug	25 g/5 m² 1 oz/6 yd²	Before flowering (about 8–10 wks)	Semi-hardy.
ESSEX RED CLOVER	Yes	April–July	25 g/8 m² 1 oz/10 yd²	Any time in summer or leave till spring	Suitable for long term.
TARES	Yes	April–early Aug	25 g/2.3 m² 1 oz/4 yd²	In summer, or leave over winter	Excellent weed suppressor.
Others					
MUSTARD	No	Mar–end April	25 g/5 m² 1 oz/6 yd²	Before flowering (4–8 wks)	Very fast in summer. Avoid clubrooted soil – a brassica.
PHACELIA	No	Mar–end Aug	25 g/3.5 m² 1 oz/4 yd²	Before flowering (4–8 wks)	Can be left to flower for bees.
GRAZING RYE	Yes	Mar–mid Oct	32 g/m² 1 oz/yd²	When flower stalks begin to form – usually Mar/April	Best for winter ground cover. Good weed suppressor.

Other Sources of Organic Matter

PEAT is a useful soil conditioner and will make an excellent seedbed when worked into the top few centimetres. Mineral content is low. Peat is one of the world's vanishing resources and can be adequately replaced by leaf-mould.

PULVERISED BARK The ornamental bark mulches are best kept away from vegetables, where they may get worked into the soil and cause nitrogen robbery. Composted finer grades are available which are designed specifically for soil improvement and should give careful instructions as to quantities on the bag. Useful on heavy soils.

MUSHROOM COMPOST is rarely of organic origin and is likely to contain residues of the pesticides used against fungus gnats as well as a high lime content, which would not benefit an alkaline soil. It is best avoided.

Concentrated Bagged Manures

There are a growing number of concentrated manures available based either on wormcasts, cow manure, poultry manure or other composted materials. Some of these may be derived from morally questionable methods of intensive farming and contain, in addition, unwanted hormones and chemicals as a result. Any product that carries the Soil Association symbol of approval is guaranteed to be acceptable.

These products lack the bulky nature of garden compost or manure, but are a useful means of feeding soil in small gardens where large piles of rotting dung might leave little room for gardening. The additional use of green manures is advisable if this is the only compost or manure that you are using.

Comfrey (*Symphytum* × *uplandicum*)

Russian comfrey, an improved hybrid derived partly from our native wild species, is a valuable plant. The nitrogen and potash which it mines from deep in the sub-soil is almost immediately available in its cut leaves, as they have little fibre and rot quickly without taking nitrogen from the soil. Leaves should be allowed to wilt for 24 hours, or at least overnight, before being laid in potato or bean trenches or round the haulms of growing tomatoes.

If you have space it is well worth growing a patch of comfrey. Six plants will yield an annual crop of about 50 kilos (110 lb) from four cuts, starting in April. Leave 8–10 cm (3–4 in) of leaf stalk to avoid cut leaves rooting in the soil. Russian comfrey does not set seed and is bought as root cuttings, which should be planted 75 cm (2½ ft) apart in a permanent bed between April and September. Choose the site well, as comfrey is hard to remove once it is established. Give the patch an annual dose of manure if possible, which can be in a fairly crude and semi-rotted state.

Russian Comfrey

SYMPHYTUM × UPLANDICUM

Liquid Manures

The most efficient use of cut comfrey leaves is as a liquid manure. A plastic barrel with a lid will make a suitable container; raise it on bricks or blocks to allow a collection bucket to stand under a hole drilled in the bottom. Simply

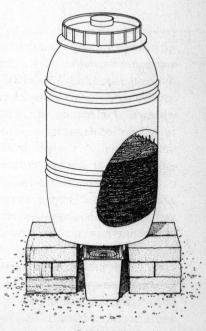

Comfrey barrel

15

stuff the barrel with dry cut leaves with no added water and replace the lid. After two to three weeks a black concentrate will drip out into the container. Diluted with 20 parts of water, it makes a feed for tomatoes and pot-grown plants comparable with any commercially available concentrate.

Spring-harvested nettles packed into a barrel and fermented in water also make an excellent if not entirely fragrant feed, diluted 1:10.

Various good organic proprietary liquid feeds are available based on seaweed preparations or manure. A bag of manure or proprietary concentrated manure suspended in a barrel of water will make a brew which can be used neat after at least ten days of soaking.

Fertilisers

A gardener who feeds his soil well will not need to wander round his plants scattering handfuls of this or that fertiliser. The regular addition of organic matter and lime, where appropriate, will keep nutrients at an adequate level. If, however, you take over a garden which has been badly managed, or have to start from scratch with what was a building site only months previously, there may be some problems. Some soils also tend to 'lock up' nutrients or be naturally deficient. Iron, for example, is often unavailable in alkaline soils and molybdenum deficiency is normally only found in acid soils.

The major minerals needed by plants are nitrogen, potassium and phosphorus. Nitrogen controls leaf and stem growth and a deficiency will show as yellow, small leaves and stunted growth; phosphorus influences the growth of shoot tips and roots, and plants that are short of it will be stunted with a blue/green colouring to the leaves; potassium (or potash) is important to fruiting and flowering and a shortage will cause scorching to leaf edges and poor fruiting. Sulphur, calcium and magnesium come next in importance and the remainder – including iron, copper, zinc, molybdenum, manganese and boron – are referred to as 'trace elements'. They

are needed in minute but vital quantities, but an excess of them –
for example, caused by copper fungicide applications – can be fatal
to plants. Soils fed with organic matter are seldom deficient in trace
elements.

The organic fertilisers used to correct deficiencies are not as
quick-acting as soluble chemicals but will be available over a much
longer period. They are derived from plant or animal origins or are
forms of crushed rock. A list of the most useful fertilisers follows:

BONEMEAL Slow-acting source of phosphorus with some nitrogen.
Useful for encouraging rooting of newly-planted fruit.

BLOOD, FISH AND BONE A combination fertiliser with nitrogen
available quickly from the blood and more slowly from the rest,
with phosphorus but little potassium. Avoid brands with added
chemical potassium.

HOOF AND HORN Slow-release nitrogen. Useful for blackcurrants
if their vigour wanes.

SEAWEED MEAL Dried, ground seaweed supplying a good balance
of nitrogen and potassium with some phosphorus and trace
elements. Also helps improve soil structure.

CALCIFIED SEAWEED A source of calcium, magnesium and a full
range of trace elements. Can be used instead of lime. Its
structure stimulates soil bacteria. Also useful in potting mixes
and worm boxes. Use to correct trace element deficiencies.

SEAWEED SPRAYS Substances applied as sprays to leaves are
absorbed by the plant more quickly. Seaweed foliar feeds are
useful to remedy trace element deficiencies and for general plant
health.

ROCK PHOSPHATE This pulverised rock releases its phosphate
very slowly.

ROCK POTASH Another ground rock, containing potassium. Its
value is not entirely certain.

GROUND LIMESTONE Naturally-occurring limestone ground to a
flour to provide long-lasting calcium and raise the pH of acid
soils.

DOLOMITE An alternative natural rock flour to limestone with
additional magnesium.

GYPSUM A natural source of calcium sulphate, used principally with dolomite to condition clay soils.

WOOD-ASH Frequently used as a source of potassium, which it certainly contains until it becomes wet. The potassium is in a highly soluble form and washes out quickly. It is best mixed sparingly into compost heaps, where its potassium will be saved for recycling.

2. Pest and Disease Control

P ests and diseases are in the eye of the beholder. The unwanted organism is simply carrying out its natural function because the conditions are right. Few gardeners want to grow fruit and vegetables exclusively for the birds and insects to eat, but there are ways of arranging the garden so that conditions are not right for diseases and unwelcome pests are excluded or kept to a tolerable level. A pest and disease control programme that relies entirely on spraying can do more harm than good by eliminating natural predators, and there is much that we can do before dusting off the sprayer.

Diseases

Plant diseases are either fungal, bacterial or viral. All plants are potential hosts to a virus, but several have inbred or natural resistance. Sap-sucking insects are often the culprits in spreading viruses, which can manifest as mottling, spotting, distortion and nearly always poor growth and cropping. Keeping these insects under control will reduce the odds of infection, but it only needs one to do the damage. Fungi and bacteria are responsible for the other rusts, rots, mildews and moulds. Often these need fairly specific conditions to grow, which is why they do not appear every season.

The best defences against disease are vigilance and foresight. Spotting a disease at an early stage of development may help you to nip out the infection before it takes hold. Any virus-infected plant should be removed immediately and burnt. Never compost diseased material, as some of the pathogens may survive the heat and few of us make perfect heaps anyway. Plants which are given good growing conditions are less likely to succumb to disease. Typical conditions that favour infection are waterlogged soil, too close spacing and very still and humid air. There are very few useful organic sprays to combat disease, so the best defence is undoubtedly prevention.

Pests

Balanced Environment

Not everything that crawls, flies or jumps is an enemy. We can enlist the aid of many creatures if we give them the right conditions to breed and feed. Both large and small creatures play an important role in maintaining the balance of nature, and it is the imbalance that we create in our manipulation of the environment which causes so much trouble. The more varied a habitat we can create, the more likely we are to gain the beneficial presence of predatory and parasitic creatures.

Birds, Bats and Beasts

The simple provision of a pond enormously increases the diversity of life in the garden. Birds will come to bathe and drink. A delight to watch in themselves, they have the added advantage of being major consumers of flies, moths, caterpillars, grubs, slugs, snails, weevils and aphids. They can also see them better than we can.

Frogs, toads and newts can be introduced as spawn. They will generally return to the pond of their birth to breed and – provided that there are no fish in the pond to eat the tadpoles – over the years will build up a formidable population of slug and insect hunters that come a lot cheaper than a packet of slug pellets. The most likely creature to suffer from the effects of slug pellets is the ever-popular hedgehog, whose varied diet includes a substantial number of slugs. A hedgehog is unlikely to be permanently resident, but the fewer we kill the more chance we have of benefiting from their visits.

Toads like to take refuge in cool nooks and crannies. A dry-stone wall with plenty of crevices is a perfect habitat for these, as well as slug-hungry slow-worms, spiders and beetles.

One should not forget or underestimate the value of bats, since many garden pests operate at night. The cabbage moth is among a vast horde of nightfliers whose caterpillars or larvae feed on our fruit and vegetables. A bat can gather thousands of moths in a night but their numbers are in decline. We can help them by providing them with roosts and shelter in the form of a bat box fitted under the eaves of the house on an east- or west-facing wall, or in a tree.

Flowers

Some insects are only beneficial in the larval stages, their parents being nectar-feeders. Usually these insects have short tongues and are looking for two things in your garden – a good larder of aphids for their young, and open-petalled flowers. Over the years, the Henry Doubleday Research Association has established a number of good attractant plants, some herbaceous perennials, others annuals (see list, below). Principal guests at this feast are the wasp-like hoverflies of which there are a bewildering number of varieties, many of which have aphid-eating larvae. Lacewings are also beneficial in this way.

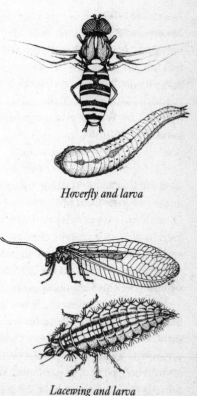

Hoverfly and larva

Lacewing and larva

Attractant plants

FOR LADYBIRDS nettles – early food supply of aphids.

FOR BEETLES ground-cover plants such as ivy, periwinkle,
cranesbill, Lamium, *Rubus tricolor* (also flat stones and tiles).

FOR HOVERFLIES AND LACEWINGS *Limnanthes douglasii*,
Convolvulus tricolor, *Nemophila insignis*, sunflower, buckwheat,
Achillea spp., fennel, *Phacelia* spp., roses, parsnip & carrot
(transplant and allow to flower), *Cichorium* spp. (incl. vegetable
chicory), *Scorzonera*, *Anaphallis* spp., dandelion.

Beetles

Most people are familiar with
ladybirds. Not all ladybirds are red
and not all eat aphids, but the
majority do. Not only do the adult
ladybirds feed on aphids but so do
their larvae. We can give ladybirds a
good start by growing a patch of
nettles; these will be host to the
earliest aphids, which in turn can
feed the first hungry, sleepy ladybirds
as they emerge from hibernation.
Once aphids appear elsewhere in the
garden the nettles can be cut down
and composted or made into liquid
manure (see p. 16), and the ladybirds

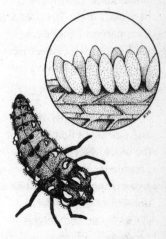

Ladybird larva and eggs

will transfer their attention to the new arrivals.

Ladybirds are beetles, a family of greatly misunderstood and
beneficial creatures. Down on the ground there are other beetles at
work. One of the advantages of adding humus to your soil is that the
organisms which come to feed on it provide a ready food source for
ground beetles and, in particular, rove beetles. The most familiar of
these is the devil's coachhorse beetle but there are hundreds of
others, most of which – in the process of foraging for food in the soil

surface – will clean up dozens of eggs and pupae of soil-living pests, including cabbage rootfly and carrotfly eggs, not to mention fruit pests such as pupating codling moth and sawfly larvae.

The picture is never totally clear-cut. Birds eat insects but include earthworms in their diet. Frogs and toads are not that fussy and regularly snap up beneficial insects as well as pests. Some insects are neither friend nor foe. Earwigs, for example, will chew numerous indentations in ripening fruits but are equally happy with their tenacious jaws sunk into another insect; wasps also damage fruit and dive-bomb the home-brew, but spend most of the season feeding on aphids and small caterpillars as well as pollinating flowers. As a general rule, however, the more diverse your garden is – mixing flowers, fruit and vegetables in a motley patchwork – the more balanced your insect population will be and the less your crops will be damaged.

Prevention is better than cure

The healthy soil conditions created in an organic garden help a great deal in reducing pest and disease problems. A healthy seedling in healthy soil can shrug off pests, which seem instinctively to seek out the weakest plants. A great bonus to the gardener has been the host of new varieties introduced with inbuilt resistance to pest and disease attack. The suggested varieties listed under separate vegetables and fruits include resistant cultivars if these are available.

It is never easy to tell exactly when spring has arrived, even for an experienced gardener, but it is better to restrain your rush of enthusiasm and sow later rather than sooner. These later sowings soon catch up and the earlier sowing prompted by a few warm days could face weeks of cold, sodden ground where seeds will rot. A greenhouse will help to give some plants an earlier start, or a better chance of survival outside by virtue of their size. But even in the greenhouse it is better not to sow too early, otherwise plants may outgrow their space when conditions are not yet right outside.

Hygiene

Plants passed over the fence from a friendly neighbour can save you time and money, but hidden dangers lurk there. You should be aware that skulking in the innocent-looking soil on the roots could be potato eelworm, white rot of onions or clubroot. These problems are impossible to remove once they are established. If you are not certain that your neighbour's garden is free of these conditions, then politely accept the plants and pop them straight into the dustbin. Always buy plants , seeds or seed tubers from a reputable source and, where applicable, look for the guarantee given by a MAFF certificate of plant health (most fruit and seed potatoes).

Seed-bearing plants in the flower borders can be left for the birds but elsewhere crop remains – including apples and pears from the 'June drop' – should be removed to the compost heap.

It is well worth checking round your garden regularly for signs of damage or disease as you can often pinch out a leaf, remove a shoot or squash a problem well before it gets out of hand. Never leave diseased leaves or branches in the hope that they might recover.

Rotation of vegetable crops is a useful way of giving every family of plants the optimum conditions for growth (see p. 38), but it is also a means of reducing the likelihood of soil pests and diseases. Moving a crop makes it harder for pests and diseases to find their host or to become established in a specific plot. Onions grown regularly in the same plot are much more likely to be prey to eelworm or white rot.

Traps and Barriers

If you cannot encourage something to eat your pests for you, you can always keep them out physically – the obvious example of this is a fruit cage. Some modern materials make this much easier and increased understanding of pest life cycles enables us to time and design our protection more accurately.

FLOATING MULCHES AND PROTECTIVE CLOCHES Glass and polythene cloches warm soil and speed germination and growth. These are well-known, but cloches of a fine-mesh polypropylene material are now available which will protect crops from flying insects such as flea-beetles. A similar result is obtained using a spun-bonded opaque fleece as a 'floating mulch' with the edges tucked into the soil. Sufficient material needs to be used to allow the crop to expand to its final size, or the mulch can be removed once the crop is too tall. Early sowings of carrots can be protected from carrotfly, or turnips and cabbage seedlings from flea-beetle. There are many other potential uses for this material in crop protection.

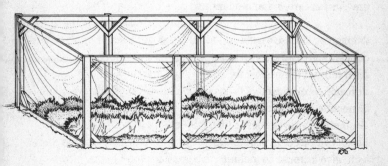

Carrotfly barrier

CARROTFLY BARRIER Carrotfly is usually more severe on maincrop sowings, which are ultimately too tall and bushy to cover easily. Fortunately the carrotfly is small and light and tends to fly close to the ground to avoid being blown away. A structure can be made of separate panels each 1 m (3 ft) long and 0.75 m (2½ ft) tall covered in fine mesh polypropylene or polythene or, more simply, posts with the material stapled tightly to it. Maximum width should be 1.2 m (4 ft), enough for about six rows of carrots or one raised bed. This will considerably reduce damage.

CABBAGE ROOTFLY MATS

The cabbage rootfly lays her eggs on the soil near the stems of host plants. A small square of rubberised carpet underlay or even corrugated cardboard no bigger than 12 cm (5 in) square and slitted to the centre can be fitted round individual seedlings to confound her. This system has regularly proved highly effective. Beetles also tend to congregate under the mats, consuming any eggs or larvae that are laid.

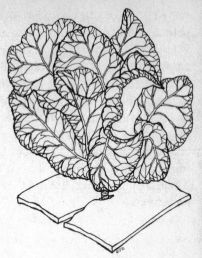

Cabbage rootfly mats

INDIVIDUAL CLOCHES

Slugs, snails and cutworms are hard but not impossible to defeat. Empty plastic lemonade bottles can be put to good effect against these. The bottle can be cut in such a way as to give a cloche to include the neck (without the stopper) about 15 cm (6 in) tall and a ring about 8–10 cm (3–4 in) tall. The cloches can be screwed a few centimetres into the ground to protect individual seedlings such as lettuce, and the rings make collars against cutworms for susceptible crops such as courgettes and pumpkins.

Bottle cloche

TRAPS The remaining base of your plastic lemonade bottle makes a saucer which can be filled with beer or sugary water to trap slugs. Unfortunately such traps tend to drown many beneficial beetles as well. Equally effective is a small pile of outer lettuce leaves or something similar, covered in a flat stone or tile, or a wad of newspaper. A morning inspection will reveal many slugs, which can be despatched with a blade or dumped in hot salty water. Beetles are also likely to inspect these traps for you without harm to themselves.

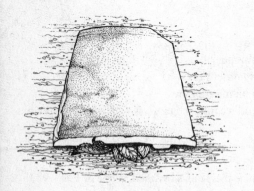

Tile slug trap

One of the most effective traps, provided that it is maintained, is the greaseband used on top fruit. Several flightless female moths need the trunk of the tree (or its stake) to climb up into the egg-laying sites in the branches. Greasebands can be painted on with special tree grease or bought as greased paper for tying on. For very young trees, paper bands are preferable to tree grease. The bands should be in place by late October and kept sticky until late December; renew them in late February to catch the March moth.

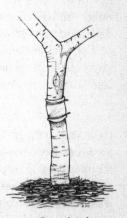

Greasebands

PHEROMONES Scent is a powerful form of communication between insects of the same species. Females of the codling moth, for example, give off an attractant scent (pheromone) which is irresistible to the male. We can make use of this process by setting traps specially made to mimic the pheromone. The traps are kept in place for ten weeks in June, July and August and will at least give an indication of when to spray, as well as greatly reducing the number of male suitors. There are other pest control systems based on pheromones under development, and we may see more available to amateurs in the future.

Pheromone trap

Intercropping

Pests generally recognise their hosts by smell, shape or feel – or all three. By growing non-host plants with a strong smell next to the host or by mixing families of plants which at a certain stage are rather similar in shape, we can hope to baffle the senses of the pest. There are many recommendations offered under the beguiling title of 'Companion Planting', but this is a deep and murky mire of unproven suggestions and vague folklore. Two particular plant combinations, however, have been rigorously tested and are known to work.

CABBAGES AND DWARF FRENCH BEANS Sow cabbages approximately three weeks before dwarf French beans. When ready for transplanting they have a similar shape. Plant them out in alternate rows or a mixed block with 50 cm (20 in) between plants. This confuses the cabbage rootfly, which fails to lay eggs. The eventual dense leaf cover attracts ground beetles, which hunt out any eggs that are laid.

CARROTS AND ONIONS While onions are growing and before they start to bulb, they emit an odour strong enough to mask the smell of carrots from carrotfly. The onions and carrots need to be sown at approximately the same time and you will need four rows of onions to every one of carrots for this to succeed. Maincrop carrots could be sown with spring onions.

The Last Resort – Spraying

All these strategies help to reduce pest and disease troubles a great deal. We can certainly afford to tolerate some damage, and few experienced gardeners expect to come through any year with totally unblemished crops. There are some occasions, however, when spraying is necessary. Early in the season predator populations are often slower to recover from winter than pests. Occasionally a whole crop or a single plant may become infested. Cabbage caterpillars can be hard to control without spraying unless you have only a small crop.

Organic sprays are mostly made from naturally occurring substances such as plants or natural pathogens (biological control), and are acceptable because they are harmless to humans and animals, break down rapidly and cause minimal threat to wildlife. Some of them will kill beneficial insects, including bees, and so should be used with caution. Anthocorid bugs, which are to be found hunting for mites and aphids on many plants, are particularly susceptible to sprays. A list of organic sprays and their uses is set out overleaf:

Organic sprays and their uses

Material	Description	Use
Pesticides		
Derris (sometimes referred to as Rotenone)	Powder or liquid plant extract.	Aphids, fleabeetle, small caterpillars, whiteflies, thrips, sawflies, raspberry beetle. Can kill fish, ladybirds, lacewings and bees.
Pyrethrum (mixed with Derris in some formulations).	Powder or liquid plant extract.	Aphids, whiteflies, thrips, beetles, small caterpillars. Can kill bees and some ladybirds.
Insecticidal soap	Liquid concentrate or dilute solution – more effective and safer than household detergent.	Aphids, whitefly, spider mites, scale insects, thrips and slugworms. Not toxic to bees.
Bacillus thuringiensis	A natural bacterium	Caterpillars of moths and butterflies. Harmless to birds.
Fungicides		
Trichoderma viride	A fungus antagonistic to several other fungi – wettable powder and pellets for insertion into drilled holes.	Preventative and cure for silverleaf. Possibly useful against bacterial canker and other fungal infections. Use wettable powder with water as a pruning paste; use pellets to cure silverleaf on larger trees.
Sulphur	Wettable powder or in solution.	Powdery mildew and some rusts. Can damage some gooseberry and apple varieties.
Bordeaux mixture	Wettable powder. Copper mixed with hydrated lime.	Preventative fungicide. Many plants are harmed by it and copper can build up to toxic levels in soil with regular use.
Bicarbonate of soda	Powder used as raising agent in cooking. Add a squirt of detergent or soft soap to aid sticking.	Surprisingly effective against gooseberry mildew and other powdery mildews. Frequent use is necessary. Dilute 15g in one litre water.

3. Weed Control

The fruit and vegetables that we carefully cultivate all have wild ancestors which, in many instances, we now ruthlessly hound with our hoes as weeds. Their long history gives them an important place in nature, however, amongst other things as food sources for many of the beneficial insects which we want to attract to our gardens. Many of them are fiercely tenacious survivors and some have developed resistance to a few of our cure-all weedkillers. Scrupulous tidiness may work against our best interests; there should always be a place for weeds and wild plants in the organic garden. But weeds cannot be left to grow amongst food crops as they will compete for nutrients and moisture. There are a number of strategies we can adopt, but the most important task is to ensure that we start with relatively clean ground.

New, Neglected and Nightmare Plots

Annual weeds such as groundsel, bittercress and shepherd's purse can easily be removed by hoeing, but a plot that is knee-deep in flowering docks or tangled with couchgrass needs something more drastic. It is best to deal with these problems right from the start, especially before planting fruit or permanent crops, as creeping perennials are difficult to disentangle from growing plants without damaging them.

Many gardeners, when breaking a grass sward to create a new plot, tend to remove the turf before cultivating. It is far better to incorporate this and benefit from the addition of the organic matter in it and the retention of that valuable, very active top few centimetres of soil. The methods described below are suitable for any new or overgrown plot. As a first step to all of them it is advisable to cut down and rake off any tall growth, ideally before seed is set.

Double-digging

If weeds are buried deep enough they will suffocate. In double digging the top 5 cm (2 in) or so of soil and weed roots or turf are sliced off and placed underneath a full depth of topsoil. Docks and dandelions may survive and should be removed as seen when digging, but most other weeds are killed. This method of clearing ground is arduous and not for the faint-hearted. While not suitable for large areas, it is a good way to clear a small plot to grow some food whilst longer methods such as mulching (see opposite) are employed to clear the rest.

Mark out a 60 cm (2 ft) strip across the plot, slice off the surface and take it down to the far end. Dig out all the topsoil and stack it separately at the far end. Loosen the subsoil to the full depth of the tines of a fork, ensuring that topsoil and subsoil do not get mixed. Move the line another 60 cm (2 ft), slice off the surface and drop it

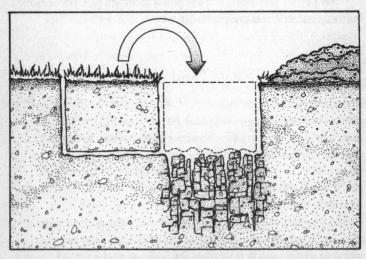

Double digging

into the first trench. Cover it with the topsoil from this second trench, thus exposing the subsoil for loosening. Work back along the plot in this way until you reach the far end where the stacked turf and topsoil are ready to fill the last trench.

Some small pieces of root may regrow and there will undoubtedly be a flush of germinating weed seeds, but these can be easily removed or hoed off.

Rotovating

Marginally less arduous than double-digging is rotovating. Unless you have a powerful rotovator you will need to start by roughly digging the plot with a spade. If the plot is then rotovated at approximately three-week intervals during the growing season and in dry weather, most perennial weeds will be killed. A sowing of a green manure such as grazing rye or tares (see p. 11) to follow this will keep the plot weed-free over winter and it will be ready for use the next season.

Mulching

No plant can survive for ever without access to light. By placing a physical barrier over the top of the plot during the growing season, light can be excluded and the weeds or turf underneath killed. Many materials are suitable for this. Some cost nothing, such as old carpet or opened-up cardboard boxes; others can be bought, such as black polythene, woven strawberry mulch or compressed recycled paper. The lightweight materials need to be secured by burying the edges. Otherwise wire bent into pegs, heavy weights such as bricks or hay and straw can be used to hold the mulch in place. After a whole growing season, the mulch can be removed and the plot cultivated.

Weed Control in Cultivated Land

HOE In various forms, the trusty hoe has been with us for centuries. Gardeners have their preferences and mine is the reciprocating hoe with an oscillating head. Hoeing is most effective in dry weather when weeds are small. If you are persistent during April, May and

June you should find that little weeding is necessary after that. Weeds can be left to wither and decompose on the surface. The secret is never to let weeds drop seed and multiply your problem. Take care not to hoe too deeply where crop roots may get damaged.

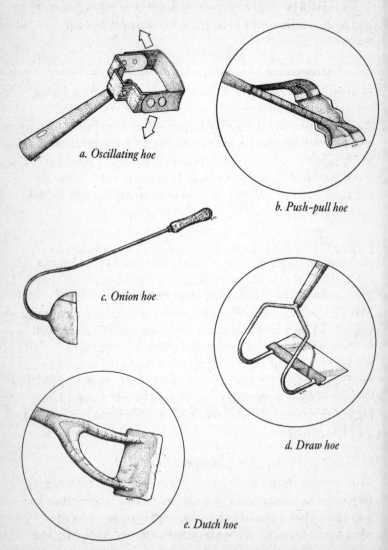

a. Oscillating hoe

b. Push-pull hoe

c. Onion hoe

d. Draw hoe

e. Dutch hoe

HAND-WEEDING Hoeing between closely spaced crops can be difficult and it may be necessary to weed by hand. Once the foliage of the crop has developed, weeds will be shaded out. Deep-rooted or creeping perennials such as dock or buttercup can really only be dealt with by hand-weeding.

MULCHES As well as being useful for clearing ground, many materials are also excellent for weed control in cultivated ground, either between rows or for crops to be planted through. A long-standing crop such as strawberries can be planted through a woven mulch which will allow moisture and air to penetrate but smother weeds. A thick layer of newspaper or cardboard covered in straw or hay alongside rows of raspberries will save hours of work spent hoeing off unwanted spawn as well as conserving valuable water and feeding the soil life.

NO-DIG Digging the soil always brings weed seeds up to the light to germinate, some of them having lain dormant for perhaps forty years. Even in a no-dig garden there is plenty of work to be done, but weeds are less of a problem as weed seeds are left relatively undisturbed in the soil.

FLAME-WEEDER It is now possible to buy relatively cheap flame-weeders fuelled either by gas or paraffin. These kill weeds with a single quick pass, the searing heat bursting plant cell-walls. Flaming between crops is tricky, but paths can be kept weed-free this way and with experience gardeners can learn to flame soil just before a crop emerges – a practice used widely on organic farms on the Continent. A safer use would be to create a clean seed-bed prior to sowing by flaming off the flush of weeds after preparation of the soil.

Some Common Weeds

Name	Annual, Biennial or Perennial	Method of control
ANNUAL MEADOW GRASS	P short-lived	Hand-weed or mulch.
BINDWEED	P very deep-rooted	Mulch. Pull off shoots.
BITTERCRESS	A	Hoe. Do not allow to seed.
BUTTERCUP, ALL TYPES	P	Hand-weed or mulch.
CHICKWEED	A	Hoe.
CLOVER	P	Hand-weed or mulch.
COUCH GRASS	P	Mulch and hand-weed.
DANDELION	P	Mulch, dig out entire roots.
DOCK	P	Mulch, dig out at least first 10cm (4in) of root.
FATHEN	A	Hoe.
GROUND ELDER	P	Mulch, hand-weed.
GROUNDSEL	A	Hoe.
HERB ROBERT	A/B	Hoe.
HORSETAIL	P very deep-rooted	Mulch for possibly 2 years.
LESSER CELANDINE	P spreads by bulbils	Mulch or hand-weed with care. Do not try to hoe.
NETTLE	P	Mulch, hand-weed.
OXALIS	P spreads by bulbils	(See lesser celandine)
ROSEBAY WILLOW-HERB	P	Mulch, hand-weed.
SHEPHERD'S PURSE	A	Hoe.
CREEPING THISTLE	P deep-rooting	Mulch.
ANNUAL THISTLES	A	Hoe.
YARROW	P	Mulch, hand-weed.

4. Vegetables

The vegetable plot is usually a priority for organic gardeners, who know the value of unpolluted crops and appreciate the taste of a harvest from a healthy soil. The ideal site will be open to the sun but closed to the wind. Light shading for part of the day is tolerable, and some food plants such as lettuce, rocket, land cress and even spinach will appreciate a bit of shade in a hot summer. When planning the plot layout have your rows or beds running on a north-south axis so that both sides have access to full sunshine.

Windbreaks

The importance of the effect of the wind should not be underestimated. When an icy blast drives in from the east, we can take refuge in the greenhouse but the vegetables cannot. Exposure to wind can damage crops physically as well as depress yields. The best windbreak is a deciduous hedge because it filters the wind. A solid obstacle, such as a wall, can create turbulence in the lee which sucks plants towards it. Windbreak netting or slatted fencing makes a good alternative, effectively reducing windspeed from a frontal assault up to seven times their height, with the best effect nearest the fence.

Vegetables provide us with good nutrition because they collect large quantities of it from the soil. Much effort will, therefore, be needed to raise and maintain the fertility of the plot – a process which will also improve the water-holding capacity and drainage. Vegetables will grow poorly in waterlogged or arid conditions.

Rotations

Nearly all the vegetables likely to be grown belong to one of eight families. It is best to keep families together because each group has its own nutrient demands and potential enemies. It is good practice to rotate these round identifiable separate plots, not only as an aid to pest and disease control (see p. 19) but also to give you a chance to treat the soil appropriately for that crop and prevent any vegetable from cleaning up the entire local supply of one mineral. A four-year rotation plan is shown, listing the vegetables by families. This is only a suggestion and many variations are possible, provided that families are kept together. In gardens where fewer crops are grown,

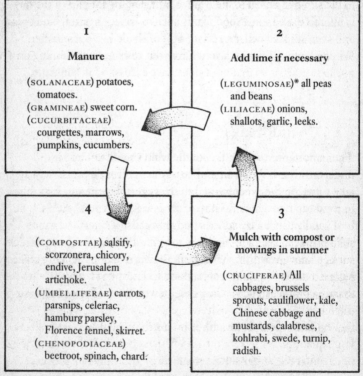

1

Manure

(SOLANACEAE) potatoes, tomatoes.
(GRAMINEAE) sweet corn.
(CUCURBITACEAE) courgettes, marrows, pumpkins, cucumbers.

2

Add lime if necessary

(LEGUMINOSAE)* all peas and beans
(LILIACEAE) onions, shallots, garlic, leeks.

4

(COMPOSITAE) salsify, scorzonera, chicory, endive, Jerusalem artichoke.
(UMBELLIFERAE) carrots, parsnips, celeriac, hamburg parsley, Florence fennel, skirret.
(CHENOPODIACEAE) beetroot, spinach, chard.

3

Mulch with compost or mowings in summer

(CRUCIFERAE) All cabbages, brussels sprouts, cauliflower, kale, Chinese cabbage and mustards, calabrese, kohlrabi, swede, turnip, radish.

*This family fix nitrogen from the air (see p. 11). **Note:** On poorer soils more manuring may be necessary, in which case plots 2 and 3 could also be treated.

a three-year rotation could be used. Appropriate soil treatments are shown on the diagram.

The manure supplied to the potatoes and marrows should still have plenty of steam left for the subsequent peas and beans. These fix their own nitrogen, leaving a legacy for the cabbages if their roots are left in the ground after harvest. Many of the fibrous leek roots will also be left behind to add humus to the soil. A mid-season mulch of compost or mowings to the cabbages will give them a boost and leave enough for the roots that follow. Lime is given to the peas and beans mainly to keep it away from the potatoes, which are more prone to scab in alkaline conditions.

Lettuce is a fast-maturing crop which can be fitted in anywhere. In soils free of clubroot, radish can also be treated in this way.

A small permanent seedbed can be set aside for raising seedlings, or else transplants can be raised in a corner of the appropriate plot (i.e. leeks with the onions, cabbages, etc. with the brassicas).

Digging

Some gardeners enjoy digging, while others submit to it with resignation. Winter digging has become such an established ritual that many gardeners still do not question its value. The action of digging adds air to soil and buries weeds, but it also turns all the active soil life upside down and destroys the network of worm burrows that is so beneficial to drainage and root penetration.

Turning over a clay soil in autumn will certainly allow frost to shatter the clods as a preliminary to cultivating that finely crumbed surface known as 'tilth'. Other soils, however, are more likely to be battered down by rain or compressed by heavy snow to a state worse than the original. Such soils are best protected by a green manure (see p. 11) or a mulch of mature compost or manure, worked in to the soil in spring by rotovator or by spade.

Spade-free zones
It is even possible on well-structured soils to grow vegetables without ever digging. The organic matter is added to the surface to

rot down in its own time. Such soils tend to produce a magnificent natural tilth and apart from a trowel for planting the only tools required are a hoe and a rake.

Double-digging

On the other hand some parts of the garden that are excessively compacted may need digging very deeply. Building sites and old pathways create compacted soil that does not breathe or drain. Rotovators are handy tools but regular use can create a polished, impenetrable soil pan at the depth reached by the blades. Puddles remaining after rain are a reliable sign of the need for treatment; the method is described on p. 32.

Beds

Walking up and down rows of vegetables to harvest or hoe can compact the soil. One way of avoiding this is to grow in narrow beds with permanent paths between them. Beds should be not more than 1.2 m (4 ft) wide, so that the centre of each bed is easily accessible from the sides without treading on the soil. Paths between need be no more than 30–45 cms (12–18 in), with wider paths for the wheelbarrow intersecting the four sections of the rotation.

Beds can be raised by deep digging and the incorporation of

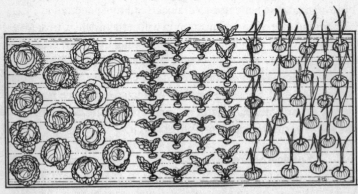

Block planting on beds

organic matter with soil added from the paths to produce a very open, well-drained structure. The growing season tends to be extended with such beds, as they warm up faster and hold their heat longer. Alternatively, beds can be managed on a 'spade-free' system (see p. 39).

Vegetables are sown or planted in close blocks rather than rows at the normal 'in-row' spacing, with a consequent saving of the usual wide gap allowed for walking. Although much space appears to be wasted, beds are actually more productive than conventionally arranged plots.

Making Best Use of Space

The space allowed between plants will determine their ultimate size. Not everyone wants cabbages like footballs, and smaller onions store better. Spacing figures given in this book are intended as a guide; trial and error will tell you what spacing provides you with what you want.

Some vegetables grow to maturity very quickly, which makes them ideal for sowing for a harvest between crops or early in the season before a late-planted vegetable. For example, early turnips can be in and out in plenty of time to plant kale in the same soil. Better use of space can also be made by intercropping transplanted brassica seedlings or courgettes with lettuce or radish, which can be harvested before the main crop shades them out with its canopy.

Extending the Season

The use of cloches or floating mulches can give you an extra few degrees of warmth at the beginning and end of the season. There are many good brands of cloche available, ranging from glass to polythene, with an even wider range of prices. Floating mulches are made either of slitted polythene, which expands with the crop, or of spun-bonded polypropylene fleece, which is re-usable and does not stretch. Whichever you choose to use, it is best to have it in position for a week or two before planting out so that the soil has a chance to warm. Tender plants such as courgettes and tomatoes should be protected with individual cloches to see them through the tricky period after planting, when unexpected late frosts can wither weeks of cosseted growth. Such cloches can be made quite simply with two hoops of wire and a clear polythene bag. Cloches should be removed or opened up on hot sunny days, and can be removed entirely once the soil and air have been warmed by summer weather.

5. Four-Year Crop Rotation Plan

PLOT 1: Potato Family, Cucurbits & Sweetcorn

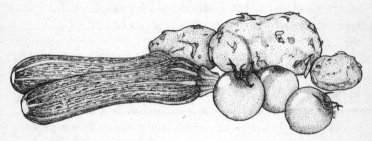

Potatoes

Through extensive breeding, the South American wild potato has now spawned a bewildering selection of varieties. I can give only a sample choice, but trial and error will tell you what is tastiest and most productive in your garden and from your soil.

Varieties are grouped as 'first earlies', maturing in June and July and not suitable for storing; 'second earlies' or 'early maincrops', ready from July; and 'maincrops' generally grown for storage. For the small garden it is only worthwhile to grow early potatoes, finer in flavour than anything available from shops and supermarkets when prices are still high. Even in very small gardens, a crop of an early variety can be successfully grown in large pots or a barrel.

Cultivation

Potatoes thrive on organic matter. Dig in as much manure or compost as you can spare, preferably in autumn – sowing a green manure immediately to cover it (see p. 11) – or early in March. There is never enough organic matter to go round, so if you are short of it save it to line trenches at planting time. Acid conditions reduce the possibility of scab infection, so keep lime applications well away from the potato rotation.

'Seed' potatoes are small tubers from a previous crop. Start to look out for them in February, ensuring that they are certified free from disease. It is now possible to buy organically produced certified seed tubers (see list of suppliers, p. 323).

As soon as possible after buying them, set out the tubers 'rose-end' upwards (the end with the most 'eyes') in a box or egg-tray and leave them in a cool, light, frost-free room but away from direct sunlight. By mid-March they will have produced a fuzz of short sprouts or 'chits' and be ready for planting.

Planting and Aftercare

Earlies are planted out from the middle of March, followed by second earlies and maincrops in late March or early April, either in trenches or, if the soil has been previously manured, in trowel holes 10–15 cm (4–6 in) deep at a spacing of 38 cm (15 in). Allow 38–45 cm (15–18 in) between rows of earlies, 60 cm (2 ft) for second earlies and 75 cm (2½ ft) for maincrops. After planting leave a slight ridge of soil over the row to give added frost protection. As the foliage emerges earth up the crop, repeating this later when the young haulms are well up. If late frosts threaten when the foliage is too tall to earth over, cover with a polythene sheet, old carpet or sacking.

Potatoes can be grown on the flat under black polythene or a thick hay mulch. Splits are made in the polythene to allow the growing shoots to emerge. This method is suitable for 'no dig' plots.

Potatoes grown in beds are not earthed up.

Harvesting

Early potatoes are ready for use when a good show of flowers is visible. Tubers can be lifted as needed. The second earlies and maincrop can be lifted from August if you have already gobbled your way through the earlies, but the tubers for storing should be lifted from the middle of September onwards. Choose a sunny day and leave the potatoes on the surface to dry thoroughly for a few hours before storing them in paper or hessian sacks in a dark, cool frost-free place. Any green potatoes should be discarded and damaged tubers eaten immediately as they will not store.

Suggested varieties

EARLY: Arran Pilot – resistant to blackleg and scab.
Pentland Javelin – resistant to scab, eelworm, mosaic virus.
Vanessa – resistant to drought.
SECOND EARLY: Estima – resistant to blight.
Marfona – resistant to blight, scab.
Wilja – resistant to blight, scab and blackleg.
MAINCROP: Cara – resistant to blight, scab, eelworm, drought, mosaic virus.
Kondor – resistant to blight and scab.
Pentland Squire – partly resistant to blight, scab, less susceptible to slugs.
Romano – resistant to blackleg, blight, mosaic virus.
Pink Fir Apple – resistant to scab and blackleg.
Maris Piper – resistant to blackleg and eelworm.

Buying Guide to Quantity of Seed Potatoes

For each 10 m (33 ft) of row you will need approx 2 kg (4½ lb). For each 4 m (13ft) of bed (1.2 m (4 ft) wide) you will need approx 2½ kg (5½ lb).

Method	5 kg/11 lbs seed is sufficient for	3.2 kg/7 lbs seed is sufficient for
Standard spacing	28 m/93 ft	18 m/60 ft
Bed system 1.2 m (4 ft) wide beds	8 m/26 ft	4 m/14 ft

Pests

Eelworm, slugs, wireworm.

Diseases

Blackleg, blight, scab, leaf-roll virus, mosaic virus.

———

RECIPE IDEAS

Boil both new and old types; bake in their jackets; fry until golden; steam until tender; sauté until crisp; roast alone or around meat; or purée to serve simple or pipe into elaborate shapes and bake. Peel or scrub thoroughly before use. Serve with butter, cream, herbs and other seasonings.

See: **Best-ever Potato Salad,
Layered Vegetable and Cheese Pie,
Leek and Bean Hot Pot.**

———

Tomatoes

Gardeners in the south can usually expect a good crop from outdoor tomatoes. The further north your garden is, the less likely you are to succeed. Plants are grown as bushes or supported and trained on stakes as standards. Bush varieties are usually faster off the mark to fruit.

Cultivation

Sow as for greenhouse tomatoes (see p. 124) in late March or early April. It should be safe to plant them out in late May or early June when the first truss of flowers should be showing, but individual cloches will help them through the first few weeks.

Work some compost or manure into the soil before planting out tall standards at 30–40 cm (12–18 in) apart each way according to variety. Standards will need staking with 1.5 m (5 ft) posts or canes. Bush varieties need no further maintenance other than watering and weeding. Standards, however, must have all side-shoots from the main stem pinched out to ensure that fruits ripen. In late July or early August in the south, stop the plants by pinching out top growth two leaves above the third or fourth truss (southern gardeners may well achieve five trusses).

Suggested varieties

Bush: Red Alert F1 (early), Sleaford Abundance F1, Pixie F1, Alfresco F1. *Standard:* Harbinger, Ronaclave (resistant to cladosporium and verticillium wilt), Golden Sunrise (yellow), Outdoor Girl, Alicante.

Pests

Potato cyst eelworm.

Diseases

Potato blight, mosaic virus.

RECIPE IDEAS

Serve raw or cooked, with or without their skins. Leave whole, slice or chop for salads; cook with butter and herbs if liked as a vegetable accompaniment; stuff and bake as a vegetable gratin; leave chunky or purée smooth as a soup, sauce or drink; bottle as a ketchup, sauce or vegetable; or use as a colourful and attractive garnish for countless recipes.

See: **Sea Bass with Fennel and Tomato Bake,
Mediterranean Salad
Apple and Tomato Chutney,
Ratatouille Pasta and more.**

Courgettes, Marrows, Pumpkins & Squashes

With the exception of some pumpkins, these vegetables are nutritionally not much more than water bottles, although courgettes and summer squashes are not without flavour and versatility for progressive cooks. The best of the pumpkins, on the other hand, deserve a better fate than becoming Hallowe'en lanterns, holding valuable amounts of vitamin A and protein for easy storing well into the winter. Courgettes (or zucchini) are immature marrows, and squashes are summer-fruiting edible gourds that do not store. Cultivation of all these vegetables is similar and none is hardy.

Cultivation

Prepare ground by incorporating plenty of organic matter in spring. Alternatively, early in winter dig out holes – at 90 cm (3 ft) centres for bush types, 120 cm (4 ft) for trailing types – which are a spade's depth and half a metre (2 ft) wide, and fill them similarly to a compost trench (see p. 9). Marrows and pumpkins can be grown in the top of compost and manure heaps with a spadeful of soil inserted into a hollow to start them off.

Sow pairs of seeds in small pots – removing the weakest after germination – in gentle heat in early May or outdoors *in situ* at the end of May under cloches, jam-jars or cut-off lemonade bottles. Plant out seedlings after the last frost after hardening off carefully.

Keep plants well watered during the season. Pick courgettes and summer squashes regularly to ensure a continuous supply. Marrows and pumpkins are best restricted to producing three or four fruits each by pinching out growing points. Trailing types can be kept tidier by training them up wigwams of poles or canes, or by pegging them down in a circular fashion as they grow. When the first frost withers the leaves, harvest marrows and pumpkins and store in nets slung from the roof of a cool, frost-free shed.

Suggested varieties

COURGETTES AND SUMMER SQUASHES All Green Bush, Zucchini F1, Tondo di Nizza (round), Clarella (flask-shaped, pale green), Golden Zucchini (yellow), Crookneck Squash, Little Gem.

MARROWS *Bush type:* Long Green, Custard (flat, like a flying saucer – best eaten young; not for storing). *Trailing type:* Long Green Trailing, Spaghetti (flesh separates into strands when cooked).

PUMPKINS *Trailing type:* Turk's Turban, Buttercup (trailing). *Bush type:* Golden Nugget.

Pests Slugs.

Diseases

Cucumber mosaic virus.

RECIPE IDEAS

Boil courgettes whole, sliced or cubed; fry in butter; sauté in garlic or herb-flavoured oil; grate or slice thinly and use raw for salads; or stuff and bake with savoury mixtures. Stuff young marrows and bake; peel, cube and boil older marrows in water and toss in butter and herbs or serve in a white, flavoured sauce; or use to make a gratin or nutritious soup. Pumpkins make a superb soup and pickle; can be cubed and boiled, then tossed in butter, herbs or a savoury sauce; are delicious baked then puréed for a pie filling; and are tasty stuffed and baked when young. Small varieties of squash should be treated like courgettes, larger like pumpkins or marrow.

See: **Sunny Stir-Fried Liver and Vegetables,
Summer Vegetable Curry,
Piccalilli
Spicy Lamb Kebabs and more.**

Outdoor Cucumbers and Gherkins

Cucumbers don't have to be grown in a greenhouse. There is now quite a good range of outdoor types, all of which will grow that much better in a frame, if you have one. Gherkins are smaller-fruited and used for pickling.

Cultivation

Prepare the site as for marrows, leaving raised mounds 60 cm (2 ft) apart.

Sow seeds two to a small pot in gentle heat indoors during late April. Thin to one good seedling and plant out on the mounds after the last frost. Alternatively, sow directly on to the mounds in mid-May (or late May in the north) and cover with individual cloches or jam-jars.

Cucumbers can be allowed to trail along the ground – in which case a bed of straw will keep fruits clean – or trained on to pea-netting supports. When seven true leaves have formed, pinch out tips to encourage bushy growth. Water well in dry weather,

49

especially when plants begin to flower and fruit. Fruits should be picked as soon as they are ready; this is especially important with gherkins, which can rapidly outgrow a usable size almost overnight. The picking season ends with the first frosts.

Suggested varieties

Burpless Tasty Green F1, Amslic (resistant to mildew), Kyoto, Crystal Apple (round, pale green fruit; pick when small), Gherkin.

Pests Aphids, slugs.

Diseases

Root rot, mosaic virus, powdery mildew.

═══════════

RECIPE IDEAS

Serve cucumbers sliced, grated or chopped raw in salads or as a garnish; cook sliced, chopped or in strips as a vegetable; bake with butter and herbs until tender; use to make pickles, relishes or the base for a cold summer soup. Pickle small gherkins whole or use chopped in relishes and chutneys.

See: **Chinese Leaf Salad Pitta Pockets,**
Salted Cucumbers,
Curly Endive and Citrus Chicken Salad,
Chilled Cucumber Soup.

═══════════

Sweetcorn

Sweetcorn takes up a lot of space, but I can't live without it. Northern gardeners are less likely to grow this successfully without a polytunnel or cloche.

Cultivation

Sweetcorn does not need heavy dressings of manure, but if the previous crop did not receive any it is best to work in some compost or manure before planting.

Outdoor sowings tend to be either too late to ripen cobs or too tempting for mice to resist the seeds. Sow indoors in large-celled modules in April with gentle heat. Pot on into small pots as they grow and harden off thoroughly before planting out after late frosts.

Cobs will only form if plants cross-pollinate. Growing corn in a block formation gives a better chance of this happening. Set out seedlings 37–45 cm (15–18 in) apart – or 30 cms (12 in) for dwarf varieties. A covering of polyester fleece, growing film or clear polythene during the first few weeks will give plants a good start and protect against unexpected late frosts.

Cobs need to be picked when just right and rushed to the pot immediately to get the best flavour. Withered brown tassels at the end of the cob in August (or July in warm southern regions) are the first clue. The best test is a fingernail inserted into a seed: if the juice is milky and not clear, the cob is ready. The colour should be pale yellow.

Suggested varieties

Earliking F1, First of All F1, John Innes Hybrid, Northern Bell F1 (later).

Pests Slugs.

Diseases Rare.

RECIPE IDEAS

Boil or barbecue corn on the cob whole, then serve with melted butter; slice cobs and thread on to skewers with other ingredients; strip the kernels from the cob and boil as a plain vegetable; use in a soup, salad, casserole or vegetable medley; mix the kernels with a batter and deep-fry as fritters; use minature cobs for a colourful stir-fry; and pickle for a tasty relish.

See: **Beanfeast Dumplings,
Hot Pasta and Vegetable Salad,
Gingered Corn Relish,
Crudités with Dips.**

PLOT 2: Peas, Beans & The Onion Family

Broad Beans

The old 1831 variety of Green Windsor provided our predecessors with the once ubiquitous Brown Windsor Soup. The soup is not one of my favourites but the beans are. Some varieties are very hardy and careful planning can give you beans from May to August.

Cultivation

A sowing outside under cloches in late October or November will give you the earliest harvest of beans. Use a reliably hardy variety for this such as Aquadulce Claudia or The Sutton. Overwintered broad beans can rot in cold, wet soils or suffer pest damage, so you should sow several spares next to the rows for gapping up. It is safer to wait until February and sow in trays indoors for planting out, after hardening off, in early April. Set out seeds or plants either in small blocks at 30 cm (12 in) spacing, or in staggered double rows with 23–25 cm (9–10 in) between plants and 60 cm (2 ft) between sets of rows. Seed can be sown outside from February, but cloching is advisable for these sowings. Less hardy types can be sown from May. Sow seed 5 cm (2 in) deep.

Dwarf varieties will not need staking but tall types should be supported with canes and string as they develop. When the beans are about 125 cm (4 ft) high and flowering well, or if the tops become infested with blackfly, pinch out the tips to discourage these aphids and prevent them spreading. Unaffected tips are edible, as are whole pods when young.

When the crop is finished cut off the stems and leave the roots in the soil to retain the extra nitrogen fixed by rhizobia (see p. 39).

Suggested varieties

Aquadulce Claudia (for overwintering), Witkiem Major (for February sowing), The Sutton (dwarf), Bunyard's Exhibition. *For later sowings:* Green Windsor, White Windsor.

Pests

Blackfly, pea and bean weevil.

Diseases

Chocolate spot, rust.

RECIPE IDEAS

Cook immature young broad beans in their pods; otherwise shell and boil until tender, then toss in butter, herbs or a savoury white sauce; use cooked in salads, casseroles, hot-pots and vegetable mixtures; large floury mature beans can be puréed for serving.

French Beans, Climbing and Dwarf

One or two varieties climb, most do not. The beans look much the same either way and taste excellent. After a long, hot summer fully mature dried pods contain haricot beans, suitable for drying and storing.

Cultivation

Seed sown direct is prone to pest attack and rotting in cold soil. It is better to sow indoors in deep trays in April to harden off and plant out in late May. A second sowing three or four weeks later will give

53

a succession of beans. Dwarf beans should be planted 15 cm (6 in) apart each way and supported with twigs. Climbing French beans are grown as runner beans (see below). Keep the crop mulched and well watered. Harvest the pods when young or leave some to mature for drying. Unripe seeds in semi-mature pods can also be cooked fresh.

Suggested varieties

Climbing: Blue Lake, Purple-podded (purple beans). *Dwarf:* Tendergreen, Canadian Wonder, Royalty (purple beans), Mont D'Or Golden Butter (yellow), Loch Ness (for colder regions).

Pests

Slugs, bean seed fly, aphids.

Diseases

Foot and root rot, virus.

RECIPE IDEAS

Boil until tender-crisp and serve as a plain vegetable; add to salads, vegetable mixtures, stir-fried dishes and stews; pickle with other vegetables; or add to a main-course soup such as minestrone.

See: **Summer Vegetable Curry,
Piccalilli,
Kitchen Garden Rice,
Salted Beans,
Mediterranean Salad.**

Runner Beans

Runner beans fully justify their place in the garden, making a brilliant floral wall and giving abundant yields. In small gardens grow them up a fence or wall, or choose a dwarf variety.

Cultivation:

Runner beans like a deep, fertile soil with plenty of organic matter present to hold moisture. Dig two trenches side by side, long enough to take your runner and climbing French beans, 60 cm (2 ft) apart, early in the winter, and fill them with kitchen waste as it becomes available (see Compost trench p. 9). Alternatively load the trenches with compost or manure 10–15 cm (4–6 in) deep, replace the soil and allow it to settle. In the spring build a strong frame of canes or poles 15–20 cm (6–8 in) apart over the trenches, to support the beans through wind and rain when heavily laden in late summer. Where space is at a premium, a 'wigwam' of six to eight canes can be used instead.

Sow the seeds in deep boxes in April to plant out after hardening off when there is no more danger of frost. Keep them well watered, especially when in flower. This will do more to help flowers set than spraying with lime water. When vines reach the top of the support, pinch out the tips to encourage bushier growth below. Beans should be ready from July onwards. The more you pick, the more you get. Dwarf varieties are best supported on pea-sticks or tied to short 60 cm (2 ft) canes to keep pods off the ground.

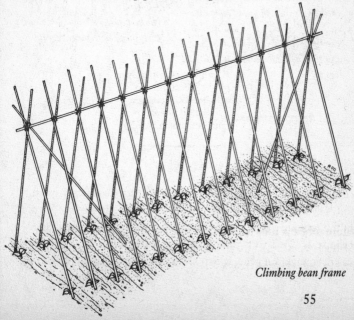

Climbing bean frame

Suggested varieties

Painted Lady (pretty pink and white flowers), Sunset (pink flowers), Scarlet Emperor, Enorma, Kelvedon Marvel (earlier, less tall), Czar (white flowers, dries to butter bean), White Emergo (as Czar), Red Knight (resistant to bean mosaic). *Dwarf:* Hammond's Dwarf Scarlet, Pickwick.

Pests

Aphids, bean seed fly, slugs.

Diseases

Foot and root rot, virus.

RECIPE IDEAS

Top, tail and slice thinly, then boil until tender for the most popular method of serving; then drain and toss in butter, and herbs if liked; also use in salads, soups and casseroles.

See: **Salted Beans.**

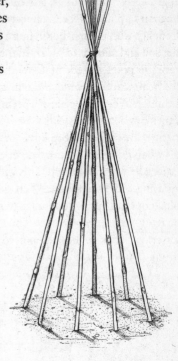

Wigwam for climbing beans

Peas

Summer would not be complete without heaped dishes of sweet, mouth-watering garden peas. The round-seeded types are hardier, but the wrinkle-seeded types have better flavour. Less familiar, perhaps, are Petit Pois, which are very small, sweet peas, and sugar peas or mangetout peas, which are both eaten complete with pods.

Mangetout peas are eaten when the pods are still flat, while with sugar peas, pods are allowed to fill out before picking. Both are extremely expensive in the shops and not particularly difficult to grow, so justify a place in the garden.

Cultivation

In the warmest areas, outdoor sowings of round-seeded peas can be made in October or November under cloches to overwinter. Otherwise it is best to wait until March. These early sowings are prone to fungus diseases and many end up as food for hungry mice. It is possible to avoid such problems by sowing indoors in trays and pricking out when the peas are a few centimetres tall, although this can be a slightly laborious job. A handy trick is to sow in lengths of plastic guttering. When the peas are well-rooted they can be slid straight into the drill.

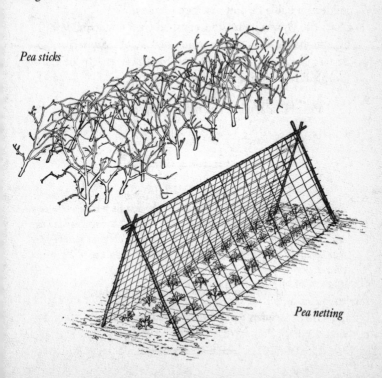

Pea sticks

Pea netting

Peas are sown in flat drills the width of a draw hoe and seed spaced 5 cm (2 in) apart. Birds will help themselves to a snack of germinating peas, so cover drills with wire netting where this is likely. Once tendrils become visible, support will be needed in the form of pea-sticks (ideally twiggy branches of hazel), pea-netting or wire-mesh attached to canes (see illustration p. 57). New leafless varieties do not need support and have edible tendrils.

Successional sowings can be made of maincrop varieties every three or four weeks, and a final sowing in early July of a quick-maturing early variety will give an autumn crop, except in northern or colder areas of the country.

Suggested varieties

EARLY: Pilot, Hurst Beagle, Little Marvel.

EARLY MAINCROP: Early Onward, Kelvedon Wonder (resistant to mildew, suitable for July sowing), Gradus.

MAINCROP: Onward, Hurst Greenshaft (resistant to mildew, exceptional flavour), Bikini (leafless), Lincoln. *Sugar peas:* Sugarsnap. *Mangetout peas:* Dwarf Sweet Green, Roi de Carouby (purple flowers, extra large pods).

Pests Birds, mice, pea moth, thrips.

Diseases Root rot, mildew, virus.

RECIPE IDEAS

Boil and serve with butter and chopped herbs, especially mint; serve in a sauce or with other vegetables like lettuce, carrots or asparagus; add to rice and stir-fry mixtures; use to make a fresh pea soup; or braise Italian-style with tomatoes and smoked meats, then top with a dusting of Parmesan cheese.

See: **Gingered Cauliflower Medley Stir-Fry,**
Kitchen Garden Rice,
Sunny Stir-Fried Liver and Vegetables,
Summer Vegetable Curry.

Asparagus peas

If you have an experimental
streak in you, try these unusual
winged peas. They carry pretty
red pea flowers and are
persistent croppers, starting
early and continuing over a long
period. Pods are eaten whole
and should be picked when no
more than 3 cm (1 in) long.

Asparagus pea

Cultivation

Two sowings are sufficient to give pods from June to October. First
sowings are made indoors in April and transplanted in May 30–
40 cm (12–15 in) apart each way. A second sowing *in situ* in late
May or early June will keep cropping until the first hard frosts.
Growing plants can be left unsupported if grown in a block,
otherwise a few twigs or low strings will help keep trailing stems off
the ground.

Suggested varieties No named varieties.

Pests and diseases None of importance.

RECIPE IDEAS

*Boil the newly picked young pods as soon as possible after picking, then toss
in melted butter and sprinkle with chopped herbs or ground spices like
nutmeg and ginger; use cooked in salads for their visual interest rather
than flavour; or mix with other crisply cooked vegetables in a stir-fry
medley.*

See: **Sunny Stir-Fried Liver and Vegetables,
Sizzling Stir-Fry Scallops.**

Garlic

Garlic is not at all hard to grow and is extremely hardy. It has so many beneficial medicinal qualities and adds such rich flavouring to cooking that the mildly malodorous aftermath is worth tolerating.

Cultivation

Choose the fattest cloves and set them out ideally in October or November but not later than March 10 cm (4 in) apart each way just below the surface.

Save the smaller cloves for planting out 5 cm (2 in) apart from March, for cutting as leaf garlic. Dig up the bulbs in July or August when the leaves start to yellow and dry them thoroughly before storing in ropes or nets in a cool dry, airy atmosphere.

Suggested varieties

For long storage: Marshall's Long-Keeping, Printanor.

Pests Uncommon.

Diseases White rot, Rust.

RECIPE IDEAS

Use as a flavouring whole, chopped or crushed; or rub the inside of salad bowl for a mild hint of the vegetable; add to stews, casseroles, rice mixtures, soups, vegetable assemblies, grills, salads, sauces, marinades, and to spike meat like lamb before roasting. Very mild, young and plump garlic may be cooked whole as a vegetable in its own right, but serving sizes should be small.

See: **Aubergine Pâté,
Spring Cabbage or Pak Choy Salad,
Sizzling Stir-Fry Scallops,
Spicy Lamb Kebabs.**

Leeks

Leeks are one of the great survivors in the winter garden, very hardy and extending in season from early autumn to late spring.

Cultivation

Leeks need a long season to mature and earliest sowings should be made outdoors under a cloche or in a gentle heat indoors in modules during February. They can be multi-sown for three to four seedlings to grow on and be planted out in a clump. Outdoor sowings can be made from March to May for the spring crop. Leeks are planted out in dibber holes 15 cm (6 in) deep or more from May onwards, either singly at 10–15 cm (4–6 in) apart or, if multi-sown, at 23 cm (9 in) apart. Drop the seedlings to the bottom of the hole and water them in well. There is no need to trim roots of seedlings before planting out. For longest white stems, earth up the leeks when they are well-grown.

Suggested varieties

Early: Walton Mammoth, Titan, Jolant. *Late:* Monstruoso di Carentan, Musselburgh, St Victor (blue foliage), Giant Winter.

Pests Onion fly, stem and bulb eelworm.

Diseases White rot, rust.

RECIPE IDEAS

Boil whole or sliced, then serve with melted butter or a savoury sauce such as cheese; use in soups, stews and sauces; use alone or with other vegetables (or wrapped in ham) in a gratin; bake in pastry as a quiche or tart; or use thinly sliced and raw in salads.

See: **Leek and Bean Hot-Pot,
Leave-to-cook Casserole,
Rabbit or Pork with Normandy Sauce.**

Onions, Spring Onions & Shallots

Traditionally the size of a gardener's onions indicated the level of his skill, but actually smaller onions are more useful and store longer.

Cultivation

Onions can be grown from seed or sets, while shallots are always grown from sets and pickling and spring onions always from seed. Onions like a rich, fertile soil but manure or compost should be applied the autumn before planting as they do less well on recently manured land.

GROWING FROM SEED This gives you a greater choice of varieties and less chance of plants bolting. Sow seed in winter – it doesn't have to be Christmas Day, February will do. Onions are well suited to multi-sowing; this will result in a higher total yield, but bulbs will be medium to small in size. Otherwise sow singly in modules indoors in February or outdoors directly where they are to grow in soil raked to a fine, firm tilth. Ideally cover the drills initially with a cloche. Rows should be 30 cm (12 in) apart, and seedlings thinned to a final spacing of 4 cm (1 ½ in) for medium-sized onions or 10 cm (4 in) for larger bulbs. Multi-sown onions are planted out in April or May 25 cm (10 in) apart. Spring onions can be sown broadcast in patches or in drills from March onwards, with a final sowing in July or August to overwinter. There is no need to thin the rows; simply harvest them as you need them.

Onions for pickling are sown broadcast or in 23 cm (9 in) wide drills in March and April, and left unthinned to mature before harvesting and drying in August or September.

An earlier harvest can be gained by using one of the Japanese autumn-sown varieties. These are sown in early August in the extreme north, mid-August in the rest of Britain except south Wales and south-west England, where gardeners can sow at the end of August. These onions will overwinter to mature in June and early July before the maincrop, but are not suitable for storing.

GROWING FROM SETS This is a much simpler way of growing onions, with the advantage of an earlier harvest and less likelihood of onion fly damage. Choose the smaller sets, which are less likely to bolt, and plant them out with 5–10 cm (2–4 in) between bulbs, depending on the size of onion that you require, in rows 25 cm (10 in) apart during March. Plant them in gently scooped-out holes so that only the very tips show. Do not press them in, or the growing roots will push them out again. Check the rows for the first few weeks and replant any tweaked out by birds or exposed by frost. Sets for autumn planting are now available and these should be set out in October.

Shallots are planted out earlier than onion sets, usually in February or early March. Once again, choose the smallest sets (ideal size is about 2 cm (¾ in) diameter), and plant them out 15 cm (6 in) apart in rows 20 cm (8 in) apart. Each set will produce a clump of bulbs for harvesting in July.

Harvesting

Onions and shallots are starting to mature when the neck weakens and top growth topples. There is no need to force the necks over. When leaves begin to yellow, lift bulbs to break the roots and leave them to dry on the surface. In wet seasons, dry bulbs on greenhouse staging or in cold frames.

Suggested varieties

SEED Hygro F1, Hydura F1, Robusta, Oakey (strong flavour), Bedfordshire Champion, Southport Red Globes (red skinned).
FOR PICKLING Paris Silverskin, Aviv.
FOR SPRING ONIONS White Lisbon. Japanese autumn-sown: Express Yellow F1, Senshyu Semi-Globe Yellow.
SETS Stuttgarter Riesen, Sturon, Giant Fen, Rocardo.
AUTUMN-PLANTED SETS Unwin's First Early.
SHALLOTS Giant Yellow, Dutch Red.

Pests

Onion fly, bulb and stem eelworm.

Diseases

Neck rot, white rot, rust.

RECIPE IDEAS

Sliced and chopped onions can be used in countless recipes including soups, stews, hot-pots, gratins, casseroles, salads and quiches; they can also be braised, fried, stewed, boiled and baked as a vegetable in their own right; small varieties can also be pickled or cooked and puréed to make long-lasting bottled sauces. Spring onions are suitable for salads, dips and stir-fries; and shallots are a valuable addition for their flavouring value to stocks, soups, marinades and casseroles.

PLOT 3: Brassicas

For list of pests and diseases of brassicas see p. 74.

Broccoli

Sprouting broccoli is a fine spring vegetable when you can nurse it through our unpredictable winters. It yields abundantly over a long period when grown in fertile soil. Plants will need staking by autumn and protection from pigeons during the winter. The purple cultivars are hardier and crop more heavily than the white. In a small garden early cultivars are more useful, as plants should be over in time to be cleared for the following crop.

Cultivation

Sow mid-April to mid-May outdoors for transplanting in June or July, 60 cm (2 ft) apart.

Suggested varieties

Early Purple, Early White, Improved White Sprouting.

RECIPE IDEAS

Boil and serve plain with butter or a savoury sauce such as Hollandaise or cheese, as a vegetable accompaniment to most meats, fish and game; use in salads, soups and gratins; or cook, then serve cold in salads or chilled appetisers.

See: **Summer Vegetable Curry,
Broccoli and Mushroom Gratin,
Hot Pasta and Vegetable Salad,
Kitchen Garden Rice.**

Brussels Sprouts

The Brussels sprout must be the king of winter greens, and modern hybridisation leading to F1 seeds has greatly improved their quality. Hardy and generous in cropping, sprouts can be available from early autumn until late spring with a succession of varieties. They do, however, take up considerable space and grow sufficiently tall to need firm staking. They are not suited to very small gardens.

Cultivation

Sow early varieties in late February or early March, either indoors or under cloches outdoors. Mid-season and late varieties can be sown from mid-March to mid-April in a seedbed for transplanting when about 10–12 cm (4–5 in) tall. Dwarf types should be planted

65

60–75 cm (2–2½ ft) apart with taller types at 90 cm (3 ft).

Suggested varieties

Early: Peer Gynt F1, Early Half Tall F1. *Maincrop:* Citadel F1, Perfect Line F1, Noisette, Widgeon F1. *Late:* Rampart F1 (resistant to downy mildew), Fortress F1, Achilles F1.

RECIPE IDEAS

Boil, then toss in melted butter or a savoury sauce; mix with cheese and ham or bacon to make tasty gratins; use to make a plain or creamed soup; and cook with crunchy nuts for a vegetable accompaniment.

Cabbage

Cabbages come in a variety of shapes, colours and textures. The most useful crop will be the winter types, but with careful planning cabbage can be available all the year round.

Cultivation

SUMMER CABBAGE Varieties such as Golden Acre, Hispi and Greyhound reach maturity very quickly. Sow these indoors in early March for planting out in April or early May, 30–37 cm (12–15 in) apart. Closer spacing will give smaller heads. The follow-on crop can be sown between March and May outside or from early April under glass.

SUGGESTED SUMMER VARIETIES *Early:* Hispi F1, Greyhound (pointed), Golden Acre, Derby Day (round). *Late Summer:* Primo, Minicole F1 (hard white), Ruby Ball F1 (red).

WINTER CABBAGE This includes smooth-skinned types which generally last until Christmas and the very hardy wrinkled Savoys. The hard white Dutch types can be cut in late autumn for storing. Sow outside in April or May for planting out in July or early August at the latest, 45 cm (18 in) apart.

SUGGESTED WINTER VARIETIES *Early winter:* Christmas
Drumhead, Langedijker Late (hard white), Red Drumhead
(hard red), Winnigstadt (pointed); *Late:* January King, Ormskirk
Late (Savoy), Silva F1 (Savoy), Celtic F1.

SPRING CABBAGE These are grown either for spring greens
(collards) or as hearted cabbages. In a closely spaced row,
thinnings can be removed early as collards to allow the rest to
heart up. Sow in early August (or July in the north) in a seedbed
and plant out in September or October at 10 cm (4 in) spacings,
thinning finally in spring to 30 cm (12 in).

SUGGESTED SPRING VARIETIES Pixie, Durham Early, Offenham
Flower of Spring.

RECIPE IDEAS

*Boil whole, in wedges or shredded as a plain vegetable accompaniment; toss
in a savoury sauce or with soured cream with herbs or spices for a more
exotic dish; use in soups, casseroles and gratins for flavour and texture; use
cooked or raw in salads; stuff the hollowed-out head or large leaves with a
rice, vegetable or meat mixture, then bake; or use to make pickled sauerkraut or pickled red cabbage.*

See: **Sparerib of Pork Braised with Cabbage and Prunes,
Pink Winter Salad,
Pickled Red Cabbage and Onion,
Spring Cabbage or Pak Choy Salad.**

Chinese Cabbage

This is altogether a different vegetable from the other cabbages,
looking much more like a cos lettuce. The leaves are juicy and crisp
and can be eaten raw or cooked. Chinese cabbage matures very
quickly but grows best during shorter days, when it is less prone to
bolt. The open-hearted Serrated Leaved Santo is the only hardy
type.

Cultivation

Sow in July or early August in modular trays indoors, or directly outside in rows 45 cm (18 in) apart. Direct sowings should be thinned progressively to 60 cm (12 in). Transplants can be set out at this spacing when large enough. A few varieties are resistant to bolting and are suitable for earlier sowing in April and May. Ensure that the crop receives plenty of water if conditions are dry. Beware of slugs.

Suggested varieties

Sampan F1, Michihili Pe-Tsai F1, Tip-Top F1 (suitable for earlier sowing), Serrated Leaved Santo (non-hearting, very hardy).

RECIPE IDEAS

Boil the whole head for a vegetable accompaniment; cook the whole leaves or shredded pieces in stock for a braise; steam with fish Chinese style; use in soups and stir-frys; or raw in crisp salads.

See: **Chinese Leaf Salad Pitta Pockets.**

Calabrese

Those who mourn the passing of the sprouting broccoli season need look no further than calabrese. This delicious summer vegetable is rapidly growing in popularity.

Cultivation

Sow in modules indoors in April and plant out 30 cm (12 in) apart or sow direct, three seeds per station at 30 cm (12 in) intervals, thinning seedlings to one. Cut the cauliflower-like green head when it forms and side-shoots will then be produced. Keep the crop watered as it dislikes any check to growth.

Suggested varieties

Corvet F1, Green Comet F1, Romanesco (sow in May), Mercedes F1. RECIPE IDEAS as for broccoli, page 65.

Cauliflower

Cauliflowers can be produced for all seasons, but it is doubtful if even allotment-holders can find space in the rotation for a full selection. Since the summer garden overwhelms us with its generous and varied bounty, perhaps the autumn, winter or early spring cauliflowers are the best value. For those with very restricted space mini-cauliflowers can be produced by close spacing as detailed below.

Cultivation

Cauliflowers definitely need fertile but not freshly manured soil and will fail if they suffer any major check or setback such as shortage of water or restricted roots.

SUMMER Sow in October in an unheated greenhouse for earliest crops using soil blocks or modules. Pot on if necessary and grow on in a cold frame or unheated greenhouse, planting out in March, 50 cm (20 in) apart. These will be ready in June and July. A March sowing indoors or April outdoors will provide curds to follow until September, planted out at the same spacing.

SUGGESTED SUMMER VARIETIES All The Year Round, Nevada, Mechelse Delta, Dok Elgon, Dominant.

Mini-cauliflowers are produced using early summer varieties (Dominant, Garant, Snow Queen F1) at 15 cm (6 in) square spacing or at 10 cm (4 in) by 30 cm (12 in).

AUTUMN Sow outdoors after mid-May for planting out in July 60 cm (2 ft) apart each way.

SUGGESTED AUTUMN VARIETIES All The Year Round, Veitch's Self-Protecting, Wallaby, Barrier Reef.

WINTER In the warmer areas of the south and west, winter-heading varieties can be produced from an early May sowing, transplanted to 75 cm (2½ ft) apart in July.

SUGGESTED WINTER VARIETIES Angers No. 1, Snow White.

SPRING These are not suitable for warmer areas (they can't have all the advantages). Sow in late May, transplanting to 75 cm (2½ ft) apart in July to over-winter. In early winter heel the plants over to

face north and avoid damage to the curd from rapidly thawing
frost.

SUGGESTED SPRING VARIETIES Angers No 2, Purple Cape
(purple curd), St George, Late Queen.

RECIPE IDEAS

*Boil whole or in florets, then serve with butter, cream, a savoury sauce or
sprinkling of buttered breadcrumbs as a vegetable accompaniment; use it to
make a tasty soup, soufflé, raw salad or dip ingredient; or toss in batter and
fry until crisp.*

See: **Piccalilli,
Gingered Cauliflower Medley Stir Fry,
Crudités with Dips,
Cauliflower Fritters.**

Kale

Kales are great survivors, hardy in even a severe winter. The most
commonly grown kales are the borecoles, curly-leaved varieties that
provide large dark green leaves in the autumn and fresh young
shoots in the very early spring. The broad-leaved kales are
sometimes referred to as rape kale, and these are grown purely for
the prolific young spring growth.

Cultivation

Sow from late April to May for transplanting in July and August.
Space dwarf varieties 45 cm (1½ ft) and tall varieties 75 cm
(2–2½ ft) apart each way.

Suggested varieties

Rape Kales: Pentland Brig (tall), Cottager's (tall), Ragged Jack (half-
tall). *Borecoles:* Dwarf Green Curled, Frosty F1 (dwarf), Fribor F1
(dwarf), Tall Green Curled. N.B. Both Green Curled varieties have
some resistance to clubroot.

Kohlrabi

This 'aerial turnip' is rapidly growing in popularity. The plant takes up less space than other members of this family and is a fast finisher. Kohlrabi is best eaten when no bigger than a tennis ball. It also has some resistance to clubroot.

Cultivation

Sow *in situ* in drills 30 cm (12 in) apart from March onwards. Sow green varieties early and save the purple types for a summer sowing. Thin seedlings to 27 cm (9 in) when small.

Suggested varieties

White or Green Vienna, Purple Vienna, Fekara (white).

Pak Choy (Chinese Mustard Greens)

This group of oriental vegetables deserves greater popularity. They are fast-growing and high-yielding. One or two have a very hot flavour, especially when mature, but most are mild and palatable. All of them can be used as closely spaced repeat-cutting crops for salads, and since they are generally winter crops needing only light cloche protection, they make a nutritious alternative to flabby lettuce for winter salads. Celery mustards are neat rosetted plants with broad midribs, ultimately producing edible flower-shoots as well. The leafy group of Pak Choy are larger, bulkier, non-hearting bushy greens with a stronger flavour.

Cultivation

Sow for an outdoor crop from late June to August either *in situ*, thinning when large enough, or in modules to transplant at 23 cm (9 in) for celery mustard, 30 cm (12 in) for leafy types. For protected crops, sow in September in modules and plant out in October.

Suggested varieties

CELERY MUSTARDS: Chinese Pak Choy, Purple Pak Choy (for flowering shoots), Japanese White.

LEAFY MUSTARDS Mizuna (decorative, finely divided leaf), Tendergreen, Green in the Snow (very hardy, hot flavour).

Use the leaves and stems raw in salads; sauté or stir-fry; or use in soups for a flavouring.

See: **Spring Cabbage,
Pak Choy Salad.**

Swede

Swedes are a good winter staple, being completely frost hardy. They can be left in the ground right through the winter, but are best lifted and stored after Christmas as they may become welded to the ground by a hard frost after this, and tend to woodiness eventually anyway.

Cultivation

Sow *in situ* in late April or early May in northern gardens, in late May to early June in the south, in drills 40–45 cm (15–18 in) apart. Thin eventually to 25–30 cm (9–12 in) apart. Keep an eye out for root rots and remove any affected immediately.

Suggested varieties

Marian (resistant to mildew and clubroot), Acme.

RECIPE IDEAS

Peel, quarter, slice or cube and boil to serve as a plain vegetable; boil, then mash with butter, cream and seasonings for a richer offering; grate coarsely and use raw for salads, especially with dried fruits; roast alongside a meat joint rather like potatoes; or add to casseroles, stews and hot-pots.

See: **Beanfeast Dumplings**

Turnip

Turnips mature faster than swedes but are not all hardy.

Cultivation

The earliest sowings can be made under cloches in February or unprotected in March in rows 22 cm (9 in) apart, thinning to 10 cm (4 in) between plants. These plants will be ready for harvest in May and June and will not stand long before deteriorating. Early varieties are useful as catch crops or intercropped, especially since they tolerate light shading. Main sowings are carried out in July and August at similar spacing to early turnips. Any of the crop still remaining at Christmas should be lifted and stored.

For turnip greens, broadcast in March or under a cloche in February and start cutting when leaves are about 15 cm (6 in) tall.

Suggested varieties

Early: Snowball, Tokyo Cross F1.
Maincrop and for storing: Golden Ball, Green Top Stone (very hardy), Veitch's Red Globe, Purple Top Milan.

RECIPE IDEAS

Boil for a plain vegetable; toss in butter and herbs or coat with a creamy white sauce; cook then mash with butter and spices, especially mace, for a vegetable dish or savoury pie topping; coarsely grated or thin strips of raw turnip make a welcome crunchy addition to a winter salad.

See: **Beanfeast Dumplings.**

Pests

Aphid, mealy cabbage aphid, birds, cabbage rootfly, whitefly, caterpillars, flea beetle, leatherjackets, slugs and snails.

Diseases

Botrytis, clubroot, leaf spots, mildew, virus.

PLOT 4: The Roots

COMPOSITAE

Artichokes (Jerusalem)

Up to ten feet of stem and foliage make these an unwise choice for a small plot. The tubers are nutritious and very hardy: they are still quite edible when chiselled out of a frosted soil. Always plant them on the north side to avoid shading other crops.

Cultivation

Set out tubers in March and April, 10–15 cm deep (4–6 in) and about 30 cm (12 in) apart. Stake the crop in summer and keep the head cut back to 1½–2 m (5–6 ft). After leaf fall, cut stems right down to leave a few centimetres showing.

Suggested varieties

Use tubers from the greengrocers and save your own. Occasionally available: Boston, Fuseau.

Pests and diseases

None of importance.

For Chicory and Endive see 'Salads' (p. 89).

Salsify and Scorzonera

Cultivation of these two less familiar vegetables is similar. They are well worth growing for their unusual, subtle flavour and relative freedom from pests or diseases. Salsify is a white-rooted biennial, while scorzonera is a perennial with black roots.

Cultivation

As with parsnip, seed of these two is unreliable if more than twelve months old. Sow in March and April in rows 15 cm (6 in) apart, thinning seedlings to 10 cm (4 in) apart. You can start harvesting from October onwards, but the young spring growth from unused roots of salsify is edible and can be blanched by earthing up in March. Flowerheads are also edible. Scorzonera can be left to grow for a second year, when roots will be thicker without becoming tough. You can expect the scorzonera to flower in the second season, but this will not impair yield or flavour. Both plants will overwinter in the soil, but some can be lifted and stored as for parsnips.

Suggested varieties

SALSIFY: Sandwich Island.
SCORZONERA: Giant Rooted.

Pests and diseases

None of importance.

═══════════

RECIPE IDEAS

Rinse and boil in water with a little lemon juice until tender. (Scorzonera is easier to peel after it has been boiled; salsify is easier scraped before cooking.) Then toss in a little butter or serve in a sauce as a vegetable accompaniment; alternatively bake as a gratin; or use to make creamy soups. The young leaves also make a delicious salad ingredient; the fresh roots, if grated and tossed in lemon juice, can also be added to winter salad mixtures.

See: **Salsify au Gratin,
Scorzonera au Gratin.**

═══════════

UMBELLIFERAE

Carrots

Carrots prefer light sandy soils, but the stump-rooted types can be grown on less friendly clays.

Cultivation

First outdoor sowings are made in late March or early April in drills 15 cm (6 in) apart. Thin to 2.5–5 cm (1–2 in) early. Maincrop carrots for autumn and winter use are sown in June and early July.

Suggested varieties

SHORT Early Nantes, Kundulus, Paris Rondo, Amsterdam Forcing.

INTERMEDIATE & LONG Chantenay Red Cored, St Valery, Autumn King, James Scarlet Intermediate, Berlicum Berjo.

Pests Carrotfly, aphids.

Diseases

Violet root rot, bacterial soft rot, virus.

RECIPE IDEAS

Boil whole, sliced, quartered or in thin julienne strips for a plain vegetable; toss in butter, herbs, spices, cream or a sauce for something more elaborate; use thinly sliced or grated for a raw salad, crudité vegetable or dip accompaniment; use for substance, flavouring and colour in stews, hot-pots, casseroles, soups, stocks and gratin dishes; grated, it also makes a valuable sweet cake ingredient.

See: **Carrot and Lentil Revival Soup,**
Savoury Carrot Bake,
Cheese and Carrot Oaties,
Honey and Carrot Cake.

Celeriac

Growing good celery can be difficult. Celeriac makes an excellent – if not preferable – alternative, producing a swollen stem similar in size to a turnip.

Cultivation

Sow indoors in a propagator or on a heated bench in late February or early March. If you have no heat in your greenhouse, use a warm windowsill in the house. Either sow in large-celled modules or a seed tray for pricking out into boxes when large enough to handle safely, spaced 5–6 cm (2–3 in) apart. Harden off outside before planting out in late May or early June after the last frost, 30 cm (12 in) apart, with rows 35 cm (15 in) apart. Keep the plants well watered. From about September remove lower leaves to expose the swollen stem and rub off any side shoots. Celeriac is not fully hardy, so should be lifted and stored before really hard frosts set in.

Suggested varieties

Tellus, Globus, Marble Ball.

Pests

Celery leaf-miner.

RECIPE IDEAS

Use the upper leafy tops to make soups, sauces, salads and garnishes; peel the root end, then slice or chop and toss in lemon juice to prevent discolouration and boil for a plain vegetable; for something special, toss in a sauce, cream like potatoes, or toss in butter with herbs; use it raw, rather like celery, in salads, appetisers and for dips; also consider it for a gratin, soup or vegetable stir-fry dish.

See: **Celeriac and Apple Rémoulade.**

Celery

Celery may not be high in nutritional value but adds crisp, fresh flavour to winter salads. Old-fashioned blanched celery is hard work to grow and takes up a great deal of space, but is undoubtedly better flavoured and hardier. Modern self-blanching types are simple and need no trenches.

Cultivation

Celery does best on well-manured ground. In spring fork in a generous amount of manure or compost. For traditional blanched celery, dig out trenches 120 cm (4 ft) apart and 45 cm (18 in) wide, and put a 10 cm (4 in) layer of manure in the bottom. Replace the soil to within 10–15 cm (4–6 in) of the top of the trench, leaving the remainder in a flat-topped ridge between rows. This soil can be used to inter-crop lettuces and radishes until it is needed for earthing up in August.

Sow seed in large-celled modules in late March or early April in gentle heat. Seed is fine and should be sown on the surface without covering, as light is essential for germination. Unless you have a propagator or heated bench that will guarantee a steady temperature, it is better to buy in plants – fluctuating temperatures or any check to growth may mean premature bolting after transplanting. Thin seedlings to one per cell and harden off carefully before planting out after the last frost.

Trench celery is planted out in a staggered double row with 23 cm (10 in) between plants. Self-blanching types are planted in a block with 23 cm (9 in) between plants. Keep well watered, mulching self-blanching celery to retain as much moisture as possible.

In August level the soil into celery trenches, and earth them up again in September after trimming off lower leaves and any suckers. A cardboard collar will keep soil out of the crowns. Earthed-up ridges should be patted firmly with a spade to give a smooth surface for rain to run off. Plants will be ready to harvest after the first frosts. Straw tucked round outer rows of self-blanching celery will aid blanching. Start harvesting earliest varieties of self-blanching types in July, aiming to lift the last of the crop before frosty weather kills it. Trench celery is not harvested until after the first frosts, red varieties lasting well into early spring.

RECIPE IDEAS

Leave whole, cut into pieces or simply use the heart and boil, braise or steam in water or stock for a plain vegetable; serve raw with cheese, in salads and for crudités with a dip; stuff and bake to serve hot, or fill along the length of the stems for cocktail nibbles.

See: **Carrot and Lentil Revival Soup,**
Pear Waldorf Salad,
Piccalilli,
Crudités with Dips.

Suggested varieties

Trench celery: Giant White, Clayworth Prize Pink. *Self-blanching:* Avonpearl (resistant to bolting), Golden Spartan, Lathom Self-Blanching (resistant to bolting). *American green types* (non-blanching): Greensnap, American Green.

Pests

Celery leaf-miner, slugs.

Florence Fennel

This is a tricky and unreliable crop in our climate that tends to bolt at the slightest provocation. The reward for success is the highly prized and highly priced bulbous-rooted fennel with a fine delicate flavour. The leaves can be used too.

Cultivation

Sow from May to early July in modules or *in situ* for a final spacing of 30 cm (12 in) between plants and between rows. One more sowing is possible in late July in southern gardens, for finishing under cloches in October.

Suggested varieties

Zefa Fino (resistant to bolting), Perfection.

Pests Aphids

———

RECIPE IDEAS

Use the chopped, sliced, quartered or grated bulb in salads; use the feathery tops as an attractive garnish; boil, bake or use to make a gratin vegetable accompaniment with complementary vegetables, especially tomatoes; or sprinkle with lemon juice and serve raw with dips, appetisers and nibbles.

See: **Sea Bass with Fennel and Tomato Bake,
Crudités with Dips.**

———

Hamburg Parsley

By the end of winter, when your mouth no longer waters at the thought of roast parsnips or leeks, you might wish that you had grown some Hamburg parsley as an unusual alternative. As hardy as parsnip, it can overwinter in the ground or be stored in sand or peat. Above ground it looks like plain-leaved French parsley, while below ground it hides a fat, white-fleshed parsley-flavoured root.

Cultivation

Sow in April or May in drills 25 cm (10 in) apart, thinning seedlings to 15 cm (6 in) apart. As with parsnips, germination is slow and radishes can be used as a catch crop to mark the row between station-sown seeds.

Suggested varieties Sold as Hamburg parsley.

Pests Carrotfly.

Diseases Canker, violet root rot, bacterial soft rot.

RECIPE IDEAS
As for parsnips, page 83.

Parsnips

Once considered a poor man's vegetable, this is now a winter favourite. Parsnips are quite reliably hardy and their flavour actually improves with frosting.

Cultivation

Early sowings can be made in February but sowing in April and early May will give a more reliable germination and good-sized roots. Buy fresh seed every year as old seed rarely germinates. Station sow three to five seeds every 8 cm (3 in) in rows between 20–30 cm (8–12 in) apart depending on the size of root required. Reduce seedlings to one per station and again to 15 cm (6 in) spacing if you plan to harvest large roots. Sowing radishes between the stations helps to mark the row for hoeing as parsnips germinate much more slowly than weeds. Roots can be left in the ground over winter, but store a few in a box of peat or sand for rock-solid frosty days when harvesting is impossible.

Suggested varieties

Short-rooted: Avonresister (resistant to canker), White Gem (resistant to canker).
Long-rooted: Tender and True, The Student (very long).

Pests

Carrotfly, celery leaf-miner.

Diseases

Canker, bacterial soft rot, violet root rot.

RECIPE IDEAS

Slice or quarter lengthways, then boil in water or stock for a plain vegetable; toss in herbs, butter or soured cream if liked; roast like potatoes around a meat joint; fry after par-boiling for a side dish; use for a thick nourishing soup; add to casseroles, stews and hot-pots; or mash with other root vegetables such as carrots and turnips for an interesting pie topping.

See: **Beanfeast Dumplings.**

Skirret

This very unusual vegetable was so highly prized by the Emperor Tiberius that he had it specially shipped from Germany every year. The Victorians knew it well, but it has since become rare in cultivation. Seed is not easy to obtain but some herb specialists sell plants.

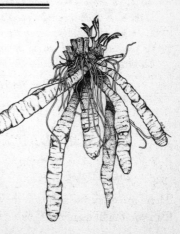

Cultivation

Skirret is an herbaceous perennial, producing a slowly spreading crown of shoots. These crowns can be divided in autumn or spring and replanted. Seed should be sown in March or April in modules or short drills in a seedbed, thinning seedlings to 7–10 cm (3–4 in) apart. After leaf-fall, cut back stems to leave just a few centimetres showing. Plants can be reused year after year, replanting in fresh soil annually, allowing greater space between them as they develop. Ultimately large plants can be divided. Plants grow about 1.2 m (4 ft) tall and can be expected to flower.

Harvesting

Part of the root system develops into swollen storage organs. These can be snapped off as required and the plant heeled in again to await replanting.

Pests and diseases

None of importance.

———

RECIPE IDEAS

Use the edible swollen roots only – scrub the roots well and dip into water with a few drops of lemon juice added, removing any brown fibrous strands in the roots. Boil, then rub or peel away the skins if liked, and serve plain as a vegetable accompaniment; top with a little béchamel or mornay sauce for something special; cream or mash to a purée with a spice or herb flavouring; use to make fritters; or with potatoes and herbs to make a soup.

See: **Skirret au Gratin.**

———

CHENOPODIACEAE

Beetroot

There are more variations to the standard deep red round beetroot than you might imagine. Golden beetroot looks most impressive on a plate, or try the Italian striped variety. Beetroot stores well.

Cultivation

For most economic use of space beetroot can be multi-sown, with three to four seeds to a station. Some modern varieties are single-seeded, but otherwise each 'seed' is actually a capsule of seeds, so produces several seedlings. Earliest sowings should be multi-sown in modules in early March, using a bolt-resistant variety. Washing or soaking seed prior to sowing will improve germination by removing natural growth inhibitors. Allow four or five seedlings to grow in each clump and plant out in April, 20–23 cm (8–9 in) apart. They will happily shoulder each other out of the way without losing their shape. A follow-on crop can be sown outside using a bolt-resistant variety in April, and maincrop sowings of other types are made in May and June. These can either be station-sown at 7.5 cm (3 in) spacings in rows 20–22 cm (8–10 in) apart or drilled, thinning eventually to 7.5 cm (3 in). Thinnings can be used as baby beet or pickled. Beetroot is not hardy and should be harvested and stored before the first hard frosts.

RECIPE IDEAS

Boil in their skins, peel or rub off the skins, then slice, cube or cut into julienne strips for serving; serve plain or with a creamy sauce as a vegetable accompaniment; pickle with apple, onion, vinegar and spices as a relish or side dish; make into a hot or cold soup, which can be topped with soured cream; or slice, chop, cube or grate for a tasty salad ingredient.

See: **Pink Winter Salad.**

Suggested varieties

Early bolt-resistant: Boltardy, Detroit Regala.
Maincrop round: Crimson Globe, Detroit Little Ball, Burpee's Golden (yellow), Barbietola di Chioggia (concentric red and white rings).
Tall, cylindrical types: Cylindra, Forono.

Pests
Sparrows

Diseases
Mildew, root rot.

Chard

Chard is a large, dark green leafy vegetable similar to spinach but with a broad, edible midrib and none of the oxalic acid of spinach, which can lock up calcium and iron in the body (proving that Popeye was no nutritionist).

Cultivation
Sow from March to July in drills 30 cm (12 in) apart and thin seedlings to 30 cm (12 in) spacing in the row. Thinnings can be eaten. Later sowings may survive the winter but chard is not fully hardy. Ruby Chard is very attractive with red midribs and reddish purple leaves, but rapidly runs to seed, so has a limited season.

RECIPE IDEAS
Use the leaves like spinach for cooking or tossing in a vinaigrette for a salad mixture; treat the mid ribs more like sea kale and cook rather like thin asparagus by tying in bundles and boiling or steaming in water or stock; when cooked the mid ribs can be served with melted butter or hollandaise sauce; if liked the bundles can be parboiled, then placed in a baking dish and covered with a cheese sauce to bake as a gratin in the oven.

Suggested varieties
Swiss Chard, Lucullus, Ruby Chard (red).

Pests Sparrows.

Spinach and Perpetual Spinach (leaf beet)

Round-seeded spinach is a fast-growing summer crop, while the prickly-seeded types are hardy and will over-winter for a spring crop. Leaf beet is longer-lived and so slower to bolt, surviving through the winter to give a very long cropping season. Also used as spinach is New Zealand spinach, a fleshy-leaved tender plant that often self-seeds freely.

RECIPE IDEAS

Cook with just the water clinging to the leaves for a plain vegetable accompaniment, either chopped or puréed as liked; make into a soup, soufflé or stuffing for pancakes, pasta dishes and layered vegetable terrines; or at its freshest use for a salad – it goes especially well with bacon, mushrooms, pine nuts, anchovies and cheese.

See: **Spinach and Mushroom Salad,**
Layered Vegetable and Cheese Pie,
Spring Spinach and Rice Salad,
Eggs Florentine.

Cultivation

SUMMER SPINACH: Make successional sowings from March to May in drills 30 cm (12 in) apart. Thin plants to 15 cm (6 in) apart.

WINTER SPINACH Sow in August or September in drills 30 cm (12 in) apart and thin seedlings to 22 cm (9 in) apart. This should then crop from November onwards. A sowing in the greenhouse border or under a cloche will give higher yields. Both summer and winter spinach can be broadcast as a cut-and-come-again crop.

NEW ZEALAND SPINACH Sow indoors in April to plant out at the end of May – or later where late frosts are expected – 45 cm (18 in) apart each way. This is a spreading, straggly plant that might threaten to take over the garden if it were not so tender.

LEAF BEET Sow in March or April in rows 40 cm (15 in) apart, thinning seedlings to 30 cm (12 in). A second sowing can be made in July or August, but the early crop can be expected to last well into the following season.

Suggested varieties

Summer round-seeded: Victoria, Bloomsdale.
Winter, prickly-seeded: Norvak, Broad-leaved Prickly, Sigmaleaf.
New Zealand spinach and leaf beet: No named varieties.

Pests

Sparrows.

Diseases

Downy mildew, mosaic virus.

6. Salads

Anything eaten raw could be classified as a salad – our salads at home are often supplemented by an assortment of hedgerow delicacies such as young hazel and dandelion leaves. I am restricting this section to radishes and leafy vegetables grown specifically for use in salads. Some are grown in unthinned, broadcast blocks for repeated cutting from the seedling stage onwards; these are covered under a separate heading of 'cutting salads'. Salad crops can be intercropped (see p. 96) or fitted into gaps in the rotation beds, wherever space allows. (See p. 268 for salad recipes.)

Chicory

With the exception of the Witloof types, which are grown for forcing, chicories are grown either as cutting salads or to produce loose or hearted heads. Leaves add a slightly bitter taste to salads.

Cultivation

WITLOOF TYPES Sow seed outside in drills 30 cm (12 in) apart during May or early June. As the seedlings grow, thin to 23 cm (9 in) apart. In November lift the complete plant and cut off the leaves 2–3 cm (1 in) above the crown; this part is discarded on the compost heap or can be fed to livestock. Trim the roots to about 20 cm (8 in) and place them in boxes of sand or peat in a cold shed until they are required for forcing.

The stout white shoots known as chicons are produced by

bringing the roots into the warm and growing them in the absence of light. This can be done very simply using two clay flowerpots, one upturned on top of the other with a piece of black plastic or cardboard covering the exposed drainage hole. An old 23 cm (9 in) pot will hold three tightly packed roots. Alternatively, a tea chest half filled with sand or peat can take very many more roots. Light can be excluded by draping the box in old carpets or heavy curtains. In spring the space under greenhouse staging will be warm enough for the boxes.

Forcing chicons

Suggested varieties

Brussels Witloof, Normato.

Sugarloaf Chicory

This type produces a tight, semi-conical head of self-blanched leaves used principally as a late autumn or winter salad ingredient. Modern varieties are hardy enough to survive the winter.

Cultivation

Sow in June outdoors in rows 30 cm (12 in) apart, thinning eventually to 25 cm (10 in) between plants. Cut whole heads and leave the stump to resprout in early spring. Heads can be stored in the shed in crates or nets. Sugarloaf types can also be broadcast as cutting salads from spring.

Suggested varieties

Pan di Zucchero, Bianca di Milano.

Other Red, Green and Variegated Chicories

These are generally grown either as seedlings for cutting salads or as full-sized plants. Red and variegated types start their lives with green foliage, but with the onset of colder autumn weather they put on rich-coloured winter plumage. Pick single leaves or allow them to head (not all varieties make heads).

Cultivation

As for Sugarloaf types. An August sowing in modules will give plants in October to fill greenhouse borders as cucumbers and tomatoes finish. Plant them 15 cm (6 in) apart each way. Red Verona cultivars can also be treated like Witloof chicory to produce attractive pale pink-streaked chicons.

RECIPE IDEAS

Use in any number of mixed or green salads, especially those with citrus fruits, or as a tasty dip ingredient. Cook as a vegetable in stock or water or braise with butter over a low heat. Cooked chicory is good served with melted butter or a béchamel, mornay or hollandaise sauce.

Suggested varieties

Red, suitable for forcing: Rossa di Verona, Rossa di Treviso; *variegated:* Variegata di Chioggia, Castelfranco; *green:* Grumolo Verde (non-hearting), Biondissima di Trieste (good for cutting salads).

Cutting Salads

Many plants are suitable for growing broadcast for a seedling crop or for resprouting from repeated cutting. Many of the following are ideal for sowing in greenhouse borders for winter salads:

CORN SALAD (LAMB'S LETTUCE) Sow in March or April outside *in situ* for summer use. For winter salads, sow in late July or early August or in a greenhouse in September. Rows should be 15 cm (6 in) apart with 10 cm (4 in) between plants. Pick leaves as required.

CELERY LEAF These celery-flavoured leaves make a useful alternative to celery for flavouring salads. Sow in late May or early June in drills or modules for planting out. Final spacing is 13 cm (5 in) between plants. If left to flower, plants may self-sow in the second year.

CORIANDER This is grown for its spicy leaves as well as its seeds. Make successional sowings from March to June, broadcast or in 10 cm (4 in) wide bands. Sowings made in summer tend to bolt unless well shaded and watered. A final sowing can be made in a greenhouse border in October.

LAND CRESS (AMERICAN CRESS) You do not need a supply of clear running water to grow hot-flavoured cress. Land cress has the same flavour and needs only light moist shade to grow well. Sowings in July and August are productive over a long period and last through the winter. A spring sowing will give leaves for summer use. Thin seedlings to 15 cm (6 in) apart. Pick leaves as needed.

MUSTARD AND CRESS, SALAD RAPE Every child should know how to grow mustard and cress on blotting-paper. Salad rape is just as easy. Seed of all three can be mixed or sown separately, broadcast outdoors from March to September, or indoors in trays or greenhouse borders in October. For a succession of cropping during the growing season, sow every ten days. Mustard germinates faster than the others, so should be sown three days later where a mixture is to grow. Salad rape has a milder flavour than mustard. Mustard is susceptible to clubroot.

CHOP SUEY GREENS (GARLAND CRYSANTHEMUM OR SHUN-GIKU) Another oriental import with a tangy flavour to add a touch of the unfamiliar to salads and stir-fries. The flowers can also be cooked fresh or dried. Sow from March until June either broadcast or in unthinned rows. Pick shoots when young, as the flavour of older shoots is strong and unpalatable.

FENUGREEK Fenugreek leaves have a lemony taste. Sow from March to June outdoors in broadcast blocks, with a final sowing in the greenhouse border in October. Cut regularly with scissors or a sharp knife once plants are 10 cm (4 in) tall or more, and leave to resprout.

SUMMER PURSLANE The fleshy leaves of this tender plant have a mild tangy flavour. Sow seeds indoors in modules in May and plant out in June 15 cm (6 in) apart each way in full sun. This plant needs plenty of warmth and a well-drained soil to grow well. Pick leaves and stems, but always leave two to three leaves at the base to allow regrowth.

WINTER PURSLANE (MINER'S LETTUCE OR CLAYTONIA) This is not related to summer purslane and is quite hardy. It thoroughly justifies its place as a winter salad by providing eight times more Vitamin C than a winter lettuce. Leaves, stem and flowers are all edible. Sow seed outdoors in July/August to cut through the winter. It will continue to resprout well into spring before running to seed. Best results come from an indoor border sowing in September. Sow in rows about 23 cm (9 in) apart. Thinning plants to 15 cm (6 in) apart may lengthen the life of a crop but is not essential.

ROCKET Rocket has an unusual sharp flavour, not unlike mustard. It can be sown broadcast as a seedling crop or in rows 20 cm (8 in) apart with 15 cm (6 in) between plants. Sow from March to June for summer use, in August for an autumn crop, or in early October to over-winter. Rocket is relatively hardy but rapidly runs to seed during the summer.

CHINESE MUSTARDS Mizuna, Green in the Snow and others are extremely useful as winter salads grown in frames or cold greenhouse borders (see Chapter 9).

Salad Mixtures

Mixtures of lettuces, endives, chicories, and herbs are sometimes sold in packets for broadcasting as cutting salads. A single sweep of a knife provides a bowlful of mixed salad. You can make up your own mixture, but restrict chicories and endives to one-third or less of the seed, unless you enjoy more than a touch of bitterness. You can add rocket, salad rape, coriander or any of the others that you fancy for extra variety.

Endive

Endives are such close relations of chicories that Continental gardeners do not distinguish between them. Just as chicories, they are bitter but can be blanched to make them sweeter. They fall into two categories, curled (frisée), or plain-leaved. The curled types are particularly attractive, and are also most suitable for broadcasting as a cutting salad. Neither type is fully hardy, and late sowings are best given the protection of a cloche, frame or greenhouse. They are relatively disease-free.

Cultivation

Earliest sowings can be made in March using modules. Main sowings are made in April or May for the summer and June or July for the autumn, sowing *in situ* in drills 25 cm (10 in) apart for curled types, and 38 cm (15 in) for broad-leaved types, with the same distances between seedlings. An August sowing in modules for transplanting under cover will give a winter crop. Use only hardy varieties and halve the spacing, as this crop is best used unblanched with leaves picked as needed.

Blanch plants when fully grown, three or four at a time by pulling the leaves together and tying them with raffia. Place a large flowerpot over them, covering drainage holes to ensure darkness and weighting them with a brick if necessary. Ensure plants are absolutely dry before blanching.

Endives can be lifted in autumn to be blanched in a frame under a thick covering of straw, but slugs can be a problem with this technique. After cutting, roots will resprout.

Suggested varieties

Curled: Fine Maraichere (not hardy), Frisée de Namur (hardy).
Plain: Batavian Green, Cornet de Bordeaux (very hardy).

Pests Slugs.

═══════════

RECIPE IDEAS

Separate the head into leaves, leave whole or cut into shreds and then toss in a flavoursome dressing for a salad; to cook, boil whole – cut into quarters or torn into large sprigs in water and lemon juice – then serve plain or with melted butter or a savoury sauce; alternatively cook the endive then wrap in ham and cover with a cheese sauce to make a tasty gratin.

See: **Curly Endive and Citrus Chicken Salad.**

═══════════

Lettuce

It is possible even for the amateur (with a greenhouse) to have a crop of lettuces maturing almost all the year round. What often happens is that half the summer crop spends its glory in a blaze of yellow flowers, while in early spring there is never enough. Winter lettuces readily succumb to disease and are best grown with a supporting cast of other winter salads for variety and as a 'fail-safe' back-up. Lettuces fall into several categories: soft-leaved butterheads, crisp icebergs, conical cos types and loose-leaved non-hearting varieties.

Cultivation

It is worth remembering that lettuce does not germinate well at temperatures over 25°C (77°F). First sowings for the new season are made in modules indoors in early March (southern gardeners can sow a little earlier); they should be planted out under cloches when they are large enough. Main sowings can start from the end of March and continue until early July; these sowings can be made indoors in modules or in short drills in an outdoor seedbed until

May for transplanting. Lettuces are wanted in succession, so should be sown at intervals of approximately a fortnight – longer for earlier sowings – a mere pinch of seed at a time. After the end of April, it is better to make outdoor sowings *in situ* and thin the rows later. Spacing between plants varies according to the variety and it is best to check the seed packet for exact details. As a rough guide, dwarf varieties such as Tom Thumb or Little Gem are planted 23 cm (9 in) apart each way, with larger varieties anything from 25–38 cm (10–15 in) according to type.

Winter supplies are provided by sowings from late August through September of suitable 'cool structure' varieties, either in modules or in an outdoor seedbed for transplanting into a greenhouse border or cold frame. They can be followed by the hardy overwintering types which will heart up by May if grown under cloches; these are sown indoors *in situ* at the end of August and thinned initially to 8 cm (3 in) apart for the winter. Thin them again in spring to 30 cm (12 in) apart each way, planting out the thinnings to mature two weeks later.

Lettuce is best rotated. It can be used to fill gaps as other crops are harvested, or early sowings can be intercropped with young brassicas or sweetcorn and between rows of peas and broad beans.

Suggested varieties

For early spring sowing: Tom Thumb (dwarf), Little Gem, Salad Bowl (loose leaf).
Main sowings: Butterhead – Avondefiance (resistant to root aphid and downy mildew), Musette (resistant to virus), Dolly (resistant to mildew), Continuity (red); Iceberg – Avoncrisp (resistant to root aphid, downy mildew), Lakeland (resistant to root aphid, downy mildew), Regina dei Ghiaccia; Cos – Little Gem, Vaux's Self Folding; Loose Leaf – Lollo Red, Lollo Green (both very frilly and decorative), Salad Bowl.
For overwintering – with protection: Kwiek, Rougette du Midi (red), Bruna di Germania;
Outdoors: Winter Density (Cos), Valdor (Butterhead).

RECIPE IDEAS

Most popularly served raw either as the whole leaf, torn into pieces or shredded finely with other ingredients for a green or mixed salad mixture; also used for lining a dish for a savoury mixture, or as the base for a fish cocktail; the leaves can be used to wrap around fish, meat and stuffings for braising or steaming; it can be prepared as a braised vegetable in its own right by the addition of a little stock and seasonings; used to make delicious light creamy soup when combined with potatoes and cream; layered with meats, fish, poultry or eggs and other salad vegetables in sandwiches; or mixed with vegetables and a sauce to make a vegetable gratin.

See: **Greek Summer Salad,
Curly Endive and Citrus Chicken Salad,
Pear Waldorf Salad,
Cut and Come Again Stilton and Peach Salad.**

Pests

Root aphid, slugs, sparrows, cutworm.

Diseases

Botrytis, downy mildew, mosaic virus.

Nasturtiums

A scattering of nasturtium flowers turns an ordinary bowl of salad into a dazzling spectacle. The leaves are hot and peppery. Surprisingly, they flower abundantly on poor soils.

Cultivation

Sow seeds indoors in April in modules to plant out after last frosts in late May or early June, 15 cm (6 in) apart. Plants will set a lot of seed, much of it will germinate the following spring. Nasturtiums are tender and the first frosts will kill them. Some varieties are climbing.

RECIPE IDEAS

Use as a decorative flower garnish for salads, fruit salads, water ices, ice creams and other desserts. Fill the flower heads with savoury cream cheese mixtures or other uncooked stuffings for a light lunch or starter dish.

Suggested varieties

Tom Thumb (very dwarf), Whirlybird (flowers face upwards), Alaska (variegated).

Pests

Black bean aphid, slugs.

Radishes

Summer radishes are amongst the fastest maturing crops, but the hardier winter types are slower and generally larger. A greenhouse will help you crop radishes all year round. Let some bolt and try the crisp, green seedpods – they are delicious.

Cultivation

Summer radishes are sown *in situ* outdoors or in a greenhouse border in shallow drills. Sow thinly and leave rows unthinned, harvesting them as you need them. Their speed makes them ideal for intercropping and catch cropping between plantings of other vegetables. They are also useful as row markers for slower roots such as parsnips or Hamburg parsley. Early and protected sowings will escape cabbage rootfly, but from May onwards it is advisable to cover sowings with spun polypropylene fleece or fine mesh polythene net.

Winter radishes are sown in July and August in rows 20–25 cm (8–10 in) apart, and thinned to 10–15 cm (4–6 in) between seedlings. Most winter radishes are hardy enough to stand over winter, but it is better to lift and store some, especially if slugs are a menace in your garden.

RECIPE IDEAS

Radishes are popular sprinkled with salt and served with cheese but also use as a colourful salad or dip ingredient, sandwich filling or attractive garnish.

Suggested varieties

Summer: French Breakfast, Robino, Flamenco (resistant to mildew), Sparkler, Cherry Belle, Icicle (long white), Munchen Bier (for podding);
Winter: China Rose, Round Black Spanish, Violet de Gournay (purple skin).

Pests

Flea beetle, slugs, cabbage rootfly.

Diseases

Mildew, clubroot (winter types).

7. Permanent Plantings

I f you have space, it is worth putting aside part of your plot outside the rotations to accommodate the perennial herbaceous crops, of which rhubarb is probably the most familiar. These will all benefit by an annual dressing of compost, possibly alternated with leaf-mould, after foliage has died down. All the following are available as seed but can also be bought as plants.

Asparagus

You have to be very keen on this vegetable to give it the space that it needs for its short season. Some of the established religious ritual of asparagus growing has been discarded now as unfounded. It can be grown on flat beds rather than ridges without annual doses of salt (thought to remind it of its seaside origins).

Cultivation

For quickest results, buy one-year-old crowns in March and keep them moist at all times until planted. Nowadays varieties are available as all male with larger spears; older varieties are mixed male and female, and some fronds will carry berries by the end of the season. Make sure the plot is completely free of perennial weeds and work in plenty of manure or compost the previous autumn. Take out trenches about 20 cm (8 in) deep, leaving a ridge of soil 10 cm (4 in) high in the centre, and spread the brittle roots of the crown carefully over this ridge. Cover them with 5–7 cm (2–3 in) of soil to leave a few centimetres of trench for filling in as the plants grow during the season. Acid soils should be limed. Plants should be spaced 45 cm (18 in) apart, with 45–60 cm (18–24 in) between rows. Asparagus can be grown from seed either sown outside in March in drills 5 cm (2 in) deep or in modules indoors, potted on when large enough. Crowns are planted the following March or April.

You will not reap a harvest from your crop until its second year after planting. Spears will start to push through the soil in April. Cut the thickest spears when about 15 cm (6 in) tall, just below the soil surface, and continue cutting for up to six weeks. In following years the harvest can continue for up to eight weeks. The life of a bed is generally between ten and twenty years.

After cutting is over, allow the ferny fronds to grow and resist the temptation to cut them for floral arrangements. By the middle of summer they will need supporting with canes or posts and string. In autumn the foliage yellows and dies. Cut it down and dress the bed with compost or leaf-mould.

―――――

RECIPE IDEAS

Tie asparagus in bundles and boil, tips uppermost, for a starter or vegetable accompaniment – serve with melted butter or a hollandaise sauce; use as a salad ingredient with an aromatic dressing; use to make soups, aspic dishes or gratins; consider too as a cooked filling for omelettes, soufflés and other egg-based dishes.

―――――

Suggested varieties
Connover's Colossal; all males – Limbras F1, Lucullus F1, Cito.

Pests
Asparagus beetle.

Diseases
Violet root rot.

Globe Artichokes

The immature flower-heads of this handsome silvery plant are edible. Artichokes need full sun, protection from the wind and a rich, friable soil. The plant does not look out of place in a flower border.

Cultivation

Plants can be raised from seed, sown indoors in February, but are best bought as sturdy offsets from named varieties. Plant them out 75 cm (2½ ft) apart in March or April, having worked in a generous quantity of manure or compost. During the growing season mulch with straw, hay or lawn-mowings. In autumn, cut off dead foliage and dress with compost or leaf-mould.

In the first season a single head will be produced, but in the second year full cropping will start. After three years you will need to replace the plants with new offsets. Scrape the soil away from the roots and cut off the best shoots with as much root as possible. Most varieties will be hardy in the south except in cold, heavy soils. Further north, a covering of bracken or straw will protect crowns until they start to grow in April.

The heads are harvested while still tightly folded, cutting with 2–3 cm (1 in) of stalk attached. Secondary heads from the main stems can be removed early on to ensure larger primary heads, but this is not essential.

━━━━━━━━

RECIPE IDEAS

The most popular use is boiled as a starter with a piquant dressing; also consider boiling and then stuffing for a main course or boiling, stuffing and baking; very young or immature artichokes can also be fried or cooked in a casserole; use the bottoms for starters and salads; or the hearts for appetisers and salads.

━━━━━━━━

Suggested varieties

Green Globe, Vert de Laon, Violetta di Chioggia (purple heads – rogue out green-budded plants).

Pests and Diseases

None of importance.

Rhubarb

Rhubarb is generally served sweet and thought of as fruit, but is really a vegetable. The leaves are poisonous and can be boiled up to produce a free aphid killer, but the stalks are edible and especially tender and sweet if blanched. It is quite unfussy about soil type or pH.

Cultivation

Rhubarb is generally bought as a crown with one or two fat buds visible. It is also possible to grow it from seed sown in drills in March or April and thinned to 15 cm (6 in) apart. Thoroughly weed the planting site and work in as much manure as you can spare. Plant crowns in late autumn or winter with 90 cm (3 ft) between them. Wait until the second year after planting before harvesting. The harvesting season lasts from March until about early-to mid-June, after which plants should be left alone to gather energy for the following season. Remove any flower stems that develop. When foliage has died down, cover the crowns with a good layer of manure.

After five years or so the crowns will be getting large and the shoots spindly. Lift them in autumn and split off single-budded sections to replant with the bud just showing above the soil.

Forcing

An earlier harvest can be obtained by lifting a crown in winter and leaving it exposed to hard frosts for a week or two before planting it in a large pot or box and bringing it indoors.

Forced rhubarb is usually blanched by excluding light. A simple method is to use a black plastic sack propped open with canes inserted into the pot. Outdoor crops can also be blanched, using anything from an old upturned dustbin to a smart clay forcing-pot. This cover should be removed to allow the crop to grow freely by the end of May.

RECIPE IDEAS

Use as a filling for pastries and pies; as a base for fools, custards and other cream-based desserts; as a piquant and acidic sauce for oily fish like mackerel; with other fruits for jams, jellies and conserves; and as a sharp contrasting fruit to serve with ice cream, mousse or creamy parfait.

See: **Rhubarb and Apple Ice Cream,
Rhubarb Conserve.**

Suggested varieties

Timperley Early, Victoria (late), Glaskin's Perpetual (low oxalic acid – see spinach).

Pests Slugs.

Diseases Crown rot.

Seakale

This popular Victorian vegetable is rarely seen nowadays. Seakale is sold as root cuttings, but can be grown from seed with varying success. If your soil is an acid clay you can forget seakale, which grows best on sandy soils with high organic matter and a fairly neutral pH.

Cultivation

Prepare the site by working in manure, compost or seaweed. If you are growing from seed, sow in spring in drills 37 cm (15 in) apart,

thinning to 30 cm (12 in) between seedlings, and leave them to grow
on till the autumn of the following year. To save on space, seedlings
can be raised and grown on in pots until ready to plant. Otherwise
plant out root cuttings about 5 cm (2 in)
deep, 30 cm (12 in) apart, and leave them
to establish for the first year. If your soil
is acid, apply ground limestone or
dolomite in the spring.

In the autumn of the second year
remove all dead foliage and cover the
crown with a forcing-pot or bucket to
exclude light. In spring, cut the young
shoots when they are 18–25 cm (7–10 in)
long and allow the plants to grow on
uncovered for the rest of the season.
Plants can be lifted and blanched indoors
in the same manner as chicory, severing
the main root just above the point where
it branches. New root cuttings should be
taken from these and the forced plants
discarded after harvest. After the fourth
or fifth year of harvest plants should be

Forcing seakale

lifted anyway, new cuttings taken and planted in a different site.
Cuttings are taken from the smaller roots and should be about
7–8 cm (2–3 in) long. A permanent bed can be used for seakale, but
should be kept heavily limed to keep clubroot at bay.

RECIPE IDEAS

*Cook as a plain vegetable accompaniment by shredding and boiling in
salted water for serving with bacon, fatty meats and spicy sausages; shred
coarsely and toss in a spicy dressing for a salad; or serve cooked, hot and
fancy with a sophisticated cream sauce.*

Suggested varieties

Lilywhite.

Pests

Slugs.

Diseases

Clubroot, violet root rot.

8. Herbs

Herb growing need not be a specialised activity. Most of the common culinary herbs are easy to grow and need little fuss. Out of the 150 or so herbs which are grown in this country, I have restricted myself to a handful of those regularly used which will enhance your cooking, feed your bees and butterflies, brighten your borders and scent the air.

Many of the popular herbs such as thyme, rosemary and sage have Mediterranean origins where they are used to dry, well-drained soil and are not likely to encounter the icy blasts of our early spring weather. They are therefore best grown in a well-sheltered site in full sun. Other herbs such as mint, sorrel and chives will tolerate light shading for part of the day, while yet others do much better in the warmth and protection of the greenhouse. Growing information on basil and sweet marjoram, which fall into this last category, will be found under Chapter 9, In the Greenhouse (p. 116). Many herbs grow well without heavy applications of manure.

Bay

Bay leaves grow on trees – quite large trees in their country of origin. In southern counties they will happily grow outside once established, provided they are reasonably sheltered, and in time may reach up to 6 metres (18 ft). In a harsh winter they may be cut to the ground by frost, but should shoot again from the base of the trunk. Annual pruning to create a dome-shaped bush will restrain the habit of the tree and keep plenty of fresh leaves well within reach. In other parts of the country it is advisable to grow bay in a large terracotta pot, moving it into the greenhouse for the winter. Eventually the tree will outgrow its pot and you will have to start again with a new one. Buying a new plant is simple, but ambitious gardeners may like to try rooting cuttings. Peel off short shoots of the current season's growth with a heel in September and insert them in a mixture of half peat, half sharp sand or vermiculite in a propagator. Success is not guaranteed and it may take up to a year for shoots to root.

Pests

Scale insects (on indoor plants).

Basil

(*see* In the Greenhouse, p. 116).

Chives

The onion-flavoured leaves of chives appear early in the year and crop for a very long period. Chives are readily bought as small clumps, but can be raised from seed sown in a pot in March and planted out in small clumps 30 cm (12 in) apart in a sunny position. Established clumps can be divided if they become too large. To prevent unwanted seeding in the garden, cut down the clumps as flowers fade; this will hasten the flush of new leaves for the kitchen. Chives will benefit from the addition of a little compost to the soil before planting.

Fennel

Fennel is a deep-rooting, tall perennial growing to 1½ metres (5 ft), with soft feathery foliage smelling and tasting of aniseed. The common form is green, but there is a bronze form that is particularly handsome. Fennel germinates readily from seed sown in spring in a pot, or even outdoors. One plant will probably be all you need and this must be 60 cm (2 ft) from other plants. Established clumps can be lifted and divided for replanting. Leaves, seeds and stalks are used in cooking.

Pests Aphids.

Lovage

The celery-like leaves of lovage have a strong almost curry-like flavour that defies description. It is a deep-rooting perennial with a tall habit, pushing its flower heads 2 metres (6 ft) into the air. It needs a lot of room (about 1 metre, or 3ft) to prevent other nearby plants from being smothered, although occasional clipping will restrain its height and also provide more of the preferred young shoots for salads. One plant is ample for a family garden. Find it a space at the back of a well-fed border and chop round the edges of the clump in autumn to keep it in bounds. These cut portions of root will make new plants; otherwise it can be sown from seed in spring. Seeds also make useful flavouring.

Pests
Celery leaf-miner.

Pot Marjoram and Oregano

(for Sweet Marjoram *see* In the Greenhouse, p. 116).
Unlike their tender relative sweet marjoram, these two very similar shrubby perennials are hardy and compact, growing to 38 cm (15 in) in height and spread. There is an attractive golden form with less flavour. Sow seed in April to produce seedlings for planting out in autumn or the following spring. Established plants can be

divided. Marjoram needs a sunny site in light well-drained soil. Leaf-mould will help to lighten heavier soils; compost is generally unnecessary except for very poor soil.

Mint

There are many kinds of mint, of which the most commonly used are spearmint, apple mint and peppermint. All these will spread rapidly unless restrained. Plants are grown from small clumps of roots or root cuttings as small as a single piece from which shoots develop. The simplest method of restraint is an old potting compost bag cut down to be about 25–30 cm (10–12 in) deep when filled. Prick holes in the base of the bag and put a layer of manure in the bottom. Bury the bag so as to leave a very short lip showing, fill it with the excavated soil, and set the mint division just below the surface in the centre, choosing for preference a slightly shaded site. By the end of the season the mint will have filled the bag. Cut down the foliage, tip out the mint and repeat the process, using new soil and manure. Mint is always best lifted, divided and replanted annually in clean, enriched soil. Established, neglected clumps can become infested with rust as well as taking over the garden. For early supplies set some roots shallowly in a seed-tray and bring it into the warm.

Diseases Rust.

Parsley

The most well-known form of parsley is the mossy 'curled' type, but there are plain-leaved French and Italian parsleys, which are taller, as well as Hamburg parsley (see p. 81), which has edible roots as well as leaves.

Parsley needs a rich, moist soil for best results and it most definitely pays to keep moving the site with successive sowings, as far away as is practicable from the previous row or patch in order to avoid the build-up of virus. Sow seed in drills from March onwards until late summer. The best value comes from July sowings which will overwinter and give several weeks of spring cropping before running to seed. Germination is very slow. Sowing the seed in modules on a heated bench will speed the process. Final spacing for plants is 15–20 cm (6–8 in). A sowing in the greenhouse border in August will give fresh parsley through the winter, or use a cloche over outdoor sowings.

Pests Carrotfly, aphids.

Diseases Virus.

Rosemary

Rosemary

The scent of rosemary in summer carries me away on a balmy Mediterranean daydream – and the bees like it too. If choosing named varieties, be careful to pick a hardy one, unless you have a warm, sheltered site. 'Miss Jessop's Variety', hardiest of the hybrids, is reliable in most counties and common rosemary survives most winters. Rosemary succeeds well in a pot to be carried into the greenhouse for the winter, but will eventually need replacing.

Outside it prefers a light soil that drains well. Rosemary is propagated from softwood cuttings taken in early spring or, rather easier, by layering. Growing from seed is unreliable. Common rosemary will grow to 1 metre (3 ft) in height and spread under favourable conditions.

Sage

Common sage is a hardy shrub which, like other Mediterranean herbs, prefers light, well-drained soils and sunshine and does not need heavy feeding. Bushes tend to get very straggly if not hard pruned every year after flowering. Its 1 metre (3 ft) spread is rather greater than its height. After three years take heeled cuttings in late spring or early autumn, which root readily, to replace your bushes the following year.

Salad burnet

Salad Burnet

The mild, slightly nutty flavour of salad burnet makes an interesting addition to salads, especially since leaves can be picked all through the winter. It grows readily from seed sown in spring or summer and will ultimately reach to 30 cm (1 ft) in height and spread. It will not succeed on very acid soils, but is otherwise unfussy as to soil or site. Remove seed-heads and older leaves after flowering.

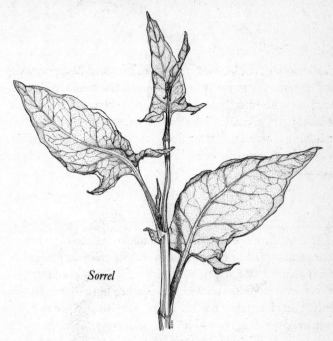

Sorrel

Sorrel

Sorrel is a hardy perennial with a sharp, tangy flavour. Its thick taproot prefers rich, moist soil and it benefits from some light shading. Sorrel grows readily from seed sown outdoors in March or April. You will not need to sow much, as each plant will grow to 75 cm (2½ ft) with an ample supply of leaves. Space them at least 30 cm (1 ft) from other plants. There is a more compact narrow-leaved type, referred to as 'French' or 'buckler' sorrel. Cut off any flowering shoots as they develop and when clumps get large, divide them with a spade in the autumn. Slugs can be a problem and sparrows may peck at leaves.

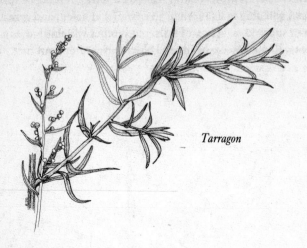

Tarragon

Tarragon

For cooking purposes French tarragon is the more palatable and, in the garden, the more restrained, keeping to a height of 50 cm (20 in) and spreading less vigorously with its creeping perennial root system than the vigorous Russian type. It may need some protection in cold sites until well established but will then be quite hardy. French tarragon prefers a light, well-drained soil in full sun. It will need dividing every four years, selecting younger growth from the outside of the clump for replanting.

Thyme

One of the strongly aromatic scents of 'bouquet garni' comes from the common garden thyme in its ingredients. There are many forms of thyme – extremely decorative, delicately variegated types as well as the more commonly-grown upright thyme, wild creeping thyme and lemon thyme. All of them are hardy evergreens needing full sun, a light, free-draining soil and some lime. Common thyme is easy from seed, to be planted out 30 cm (1 ft) apart in its final position. It can also be propagated from layered shoots or softwood cuttings taken in late spring. Creeping thyme is propagated from seed or by division in autumn or spring and will quickly make a ground-covering mat if planted out 15 cm (6 in) apart or slightly more. Trim back bushes by about a third after flowering so as to keep a neat shape.

9. In the Greenhouse

A greenhouse is a valuable asset to the gardener, giving space to grow more tender crops which would not reach maturity in our short, cool season, and winter cropping possibilities to provide food when outdoor-growing has ended. After a busy summer it is tempting to clear the garden in autumn and then sit back and relax until spring. Timely sowings in the greenhouse, however, can give you much earlier crops of carrots and spinach or a Christmas harvest of pot-grown early potatoes. Starting seeds and growing on seedlings in comparative warmth can also give you several weeks' extra growing time for some outdoor crops and avoid losses to birds, mice and slugs, or from cold, inhospitable soil.

Greenhouse Management

In the closed, confined atmosphere of a greenhouse, pests and fungal diseases can rapidly get out of control. Hygiene is therefore of paramount importance. Once tomatoes and cucumbers have been cleared away in October, it is wise to give the inside of the structure a really good clean. Hot soapy water is as good as anything for this, but you may feel more confident adding a disinfectant such as Jeyes Fluid. Make sure you include the bench in the clean-up and change any sand, gravel or other medium that you may be using for water retention, drainage or propagation. Ventilate the greenhouse and allow the glass to dry thoroughly before putting up any insulation. Check over plants regularly for pests, signs of disease or dead leaves, which should not be allowed to stay on plants or litter the bench or floor.

These regular inspections should help you to spot trouble before it gets out of hand. The most common pests of greenhouses are aphids, whitefly and red spider mites (see p. 118 for details of biological pest control). Removing a single infested or sick pot-plant in time can save all plants in the greenhouse from becoming affected.

Fungal diseases generally thrive in damp, still conditions, so it is important to think about ventilation. Automatic vents will help to prevent temperatures becoming excessive in summer, but are not always enough to ensure a good flow of air. In spring and summer the door should be opened as the temperature starts to rise, and if the nights are warm can be left open. Even in winter ventilation is necessary, and a window at least should be open by day except in frosty or wet conditions. Unfortunately some plants, such as cucumbers, prefer humid air and it is impossible to arrange suitable conditions for everything in a small mixed greenhouse.

Border soil in the greenhouse needs as much attention as other garden plots and will benefit from annual dressings of well-rotted manure or compost. To reduce the chances of root infections taking hold, it is good practice to change the border soil every three or four years and to alternate tomatoes and cucumbers if they are grown regularly in the greenhouse. Check the pH every few years and lime the soil with ground limestone or dolomite if it dips below 6.0.

Shading

The sun can be surprisingly powerful during the summer and greenhouse plants can be scorched. Various forms of shading are available to protect plants, either as a wettable white powder for painting on to the glass or as physical screens. Melons, however, prefer maximum light and do not need shading.

Heating and insulation

For the purposes of growing the fruit and vegetables covered in this book, or for raising seedlings, a sophisticated heating system is not essential. The most valuable investment is some form of bench heating, either a soil-warming cable or polyester heating blanket.

For the smaller greenhouse a propagator, bought or home-made, is adequate.

Insulating your greenhouse with bubble polythene will save a great deal of heat loss. This can be simply stapled or pinned to the inside of wooden structures, while for aluminium greenhouses special clips are available. Ensure a gap of at least 2½ cm (1 in) between the glass and the insulation.

Potting mixtures

Nowadays it is possible to buy quite a range of excellent organic potting mixes based either on manure or worm-worked compost. However, this can be an expensive way to grow plants for cropping in large pots, such as peppers or aubergines. A good standard mixture for these can be made up as follows:

  4 buckets good garden soil (preferably steam-pasteurised)
  2 buckets peat
  1 spadeful of chopped well-rotted manure or compost
  250 gm (8 oz) seaweed meal
  125 gm (4 oz) bonemeal
  60 gm (2 oz) calcified seaweed

Biological pest control

Good control of the two major greenhouse pests can be effected by introducing their natural enemies. *Encarsia formosa* is a tiny fly that parasitises glasshouse whitefly scales, turning them black in the process, whereas the red spider mite predator, *Phytoseiulus persimilis*, hunts and eats its prey. Timing is important, as these insects will not survive long in cold temperatures nor without a host. Suppliers of these biological controls will advise on optimum timing.

Constant cropping

It is possible to keep even an unheated greenhouse working for you all the year round. Raising seedlings will mostly be over by the end of May, giving room on the bench for pot-grown basils, sweet marjoram and perhaps chilli peppers. Meanwhile the soil borders offer space for tomatoes and cucumbers or melons from spring until early autumn, after which time there is room for parsley, winter salads and early sowings of spring onions or spinach.

Aubergine

Even at the height of the season aubergines are not cheap. Plants are relatively compact and can even be grown successfully in large pots.

Sow two seeds to an 8 cm (3 in) pot in early March, and thin to the best seedling after emergence. Place pots on a heated bench or in a propagator to ensure faster germination. If you don't have a propagator, delay sowing until early May. Pot plants on as they require it, and either plant out in a well-manured border or into large pots in the standard potting mixture (see above). Pot-grown plants will need regular feeding with a liquid manure (see p. 15) once they are in flower.

Plants are unlikely to crop very heavily but, in any case, should not carry more than four fruits per bush. Nip out the tips of any bushes that fail to branch and any side shoots once four fruits have set. Harvest fruits with a knife when the skin is taut and glossy.

=====

RECIPE IDEAS

Slice and degorge to remove the bitter juices, then steam, fry, braise, bake or sauté as a vegetable dish; cook with complementary vegetables like tomatoes, courgettes and peppers for a classic stewed ratatouille dish; stuff and bake with a savoury mixture; or layer with a savoury mixture, potatoes and a sauce for baking as in the classic dish moussaka.

See: **Aubergine Pâté,
Ratatouille Pasta.**

=====

Suggested varieties

Black Prince, Short Tom F1, Dusky F1 (resistant to tobacco mosaic virus).

Pests

Whitefly, aphids.

Diseases

Mildew, botrytis, virus.

Cape Gooseberries

The curious lantern-shaped flowers of this plant do not open until the dried brown calyx splits to reveal a small, round bright orange ripe fruit inside. The fruit is sweet and sharp to taste.

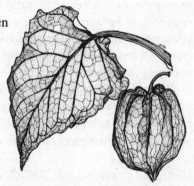

For sowing details, see Aubergines. Cape goose-berries should not be grown in border soil as under these conditions they tend to produce massive foliage and little fruit (usually too late to ripen). Feed plants twice weekly with a liquid feed once flowering starts.

RECIPE IDEAS

Remove the fruits from their calyx leaf surround and use in an exotic fruit salad; stew for a dessert; dip in fondant, icing sugar or caramel as a sweetmeat; or use to make jam.

Suggested varieties

Golden Berry.

Pests

Aphids, whitefly, red spider mite.

Diseases

Virus.

Cucumbers

Although varieties of outdoor ridge cucumbers have greatly improved recently, greenhouse cucumbers are still finer in appearance and thinner-skinned.

Sow two seeds to a small pot at the end of April or in early May in a minimum temperature of 21°C (70°F) and thin to leave the strongest seedling. Place pots on a hot bench or in a propagator, as cucumbers need plenty of heat to keep them growing. By the middle to end of May they should be ready for planting out 45–60 cm (1½–2 ft) apart in a well-manured border. Do not grow cucumbers in the same soil for successive years. Either alternate them with another crop in the opposite border, or change the soil.

Train the plants up strings or nets, winding the growing top round the string or tying it in (cucumbers are self-clinging but need a little help). Remove all side shoots up to the first 30 cm (12 in) of growth, and thereafter pinch them out at one or two leaves from the stem to restrict foliage growth and number of fruits. Feed the plants if necessary and keep them well-watered. Nowadays a good selection of all-female flowered varieties is available. Male flowers on other varieties must be removed to prevent fruits from becoming bitter.

Suggested varieties

Telegraph Improved, Femspot F1 (all-female), Diana F1 (all-female), Petita F1 (all-female, small fruits).

Pests

Aphids, whitefly, red spider mite.

Diseases

Mildew, mosaic virus, foot and root rot, botrytis.

Herbs

Most herbs grow well outside without protection, but sweet marjoram and basil (green and purple) greatly benefit from being grown in the greenhouse. Sow seed in mid-March and grow in pots on the bench through the summer. Pinch out all flowers to prolong the cropping period and keep tips pinched back initially to form a bushy shape.

An August sowing of parsley in modules can be planted out in October after border crops have been removed. This will provide winter and early spring supplies.

Melon

Some modern varieties of melon perform well outdoors in the south, but all do even better in a greenhouse. They are rampant growers in the right conditions, so do not expect to grow too many other plants if your greenhouse is small. Pot-grown plants will be much more restrained but need regular feeding and watering.

For sowing details, see Cucumbers. Plant them out in May, 30–40 cm (12–15 in) apart.

After planting out, prune back plants to leave two true leaves. From these two shoots will be produced, which can be allowed to trail or be trained up wires. Stop these again after eight to ten leaves or, in the case of pot-grown melons, pinch them out after three or four leaves. Fruits develop on side-shoots from these stems. The female flowers on embryo fruits may need pollinating by hand with a soft paintbrush unless pollinating insects are seen to be busy.

Allow only five fruits to develop on each plant, fewer on pot-grown specimens. As fruitlets appear, pinch out any growth from two leaves beyond the fruit. Keep plants well-watered in a humid atmosphere and feed pot-grown melons twice weekly until the fruit is ripening, after which a dry, airy atmosphere is necessary. Fruits on wire-trained plants will need supporting in individual nets slung from the roof. Fruits are ripe when the ends feel soft.

Suggested varieties

Hero of Lockinge, Sweetheart F1, Romeo F1, Ogen.

Pests and diseases

See Cucumbers.

RECIPE IDEAS

Use across the menu for a starter, main course or dessert: chill, cube and serve plain as a starter or dessert; serve with smoked meats as an appetiser; toss with other fruits for a fruit salad dessert; mix with a multitude of vegetables, meat, fish and poultry in main-course salads; use to make a refreshing sorbet for an in-between course palate cleanser or meal finale; preserve in much the same way as gherkins as a pickle; simply season with salt and ginger for an appetiser, or with sugar and nutmeg as the simplest of desserts; or mix with other chilled ingredients for an iced summer soup.

See: **Melon and Orange Caprice.**

Peppers

Hot chillis to take your breath away grow as well in an English greenhouse as the more commonly grown sweet peppers. Where space is limited they can be grown in 20 cm (8 in) pots on the bench.

Sow seed from early March in individual 8 cm (3 in) pots or modules at a temperature between 18 and 21°C (65–70°F). Pot them on until they are ready to plant out in pots or a border in May, 45–60 cm (18–24 in) apart. Feed pot-grown peppers twice weekly once flowering commences. Harvest chillis when green for immediate use or when red for drying. Sweet peppers can be picked green or left to mature when they become red or yellow.

RECIPE IDEAS

Use raw in salads, sandwiches, as a crudité vegetable and in marinades; cook by stewing, braising or sautéing alone or with other vegetables such as tomatoes, aubergines and courgettes; alternatively, hollow out the centre by removing the core and seeds and stuff with a savoury mixture all the better for baking; or thread cubes on to kebab skewers where their colour and flavour is much appreciated with meat, fish, poultry and other vegetables.

See: **Noodles with Creole Sauce,
Apple and Red Pepper Chutney,
Gingered Cauliflower Medley Stir-Fry.**

Suggested varieties

Sweet peppers: Luteus F1 (yellow, resistant to tobacco mosaic virus), New Ace F1, Redskin F1, Reubens F1, Hungarian Hot Wax (slightly hot). *Chillis:* Serrano (very hot), Antler F1.

Pests

Aphids, red spider mite.

Diseases

Tobacco virus, botrytis.

Tomatoes

Given a few feet of spare space, the majority of gardeners will grow tomatoes in their greenhouses. Northerners will not be able to ripen a crop outside, but can expect a good harvest under glass.

Sow seed earlier than for the outdoor crop – in late February for southern gardeners, early March for the Midlands and the north. Sow as for peppers. By the time the first truss of flowers has formed, they are ready to plant out 30 cm (12 in) apart.

Train the plants up strings, pinching off any side-shoots, and keep the plants well watered. Feeding plants in fertile soil is generally unnecessary, but if plants are not growing well feed weekly with a liquid fertiliser (see p. 15). Defoliation of plants is unnecessary and may even cause the condition 'greenback', where part of the fruit remains green and hard. When plants reach the roof of the greenhouse, or in early September, stop them growing by pinching out the top. Reduce watering late in the season. The crop will be over by early October and remaining fruits can be ripened in trays in a warm room.

RECIPE IDEAS

Serve raw or cooked, with or without their skins. Leave whole, slice or chop for salads; cook with butter and herbs if liked as a vegetable accompaniment; stuff and bake as a vegetable gratin; leave chunky or purée smooth as a soup, sauce or drink; bottle as a ketchup, sauce or vegetable; or use as a colourful and attractive garnish for countless recipes.

See: **Greek Summer Salad,
Layered Vegetable and Cheese Pie,
Home-made Tomato Sauce.**

Suggested varieties

Alicante (resistant to greenback), Ida (resistant to tobacco mosaic virus and wilts), Estrella (resistant to greenback, tobacco mosaic virus and wilts), Herald. *Cherry Tomatoes*: Gardener's Delight, Sweet 100. *Beefsteak Types*: Dona (resistant to mosaic virus).

Pests

Aphids, whitefly, red spider mite.

Diseases

Blight, blossom end rot, virus, wilts, eelworm*.

Crops suitable for cold greenhouse borders in winter include the following:

Chicory	Fenugreek	Rocket
Coriander	Green-in-the-Snow	Salad rape
Corn salad	Land cress	Spinach (summer)
Endive	Lettuce (hardy types)	Spring onions
	Mizuna	Winter purslane
	Radish (summer types)	

If you have space for a small polytunnel you could include:

Chard	Early peas	Tarragon
Calabrese	Mint	Chives
Early carrots		

*Note: It is possible to graft tomatoes on to a rootstock (available as seed) that is resistant to the major soil-borne diseases of tomatoes. Full instructions come with the packet.

10. *Common Pests and Diseases of Vegetables*

For general information on pest and disease control see Chapter 2.

CROP	Pests
Most crops, greenhouse crops	**Aphids** Dense clusters of sap-suckers on leaves and young shoots. Very common pest. May be black, green, white or pink. Lettuce root aphid attacks below ground. CONTROL: Encourage predatory and parasitic insects. Choose resistant varieties of lettuce. Pinch out affected shoots, especially top of broad beans. Earliest sowings of broad beans escape. *Spray*: Insecticidal soap.
All brassicas except kohlrabi and Chinese cabbage	**Mealy cabbage aphid** Species of aphid forming grey powdery-coated colonies on brassicas. Sometimes work deep into heart of plants. CONTROL: Inspect crop regularly and squash embryo colonies. *Spray*: Insecticidal soap.
Asparagus	**Asparagus beetle** Black and yellow adult beetles. Larvae dull-coloured – ravage foliage and stems from May. CONTROL: Hand-pick or use derris as dust or spray.

Peas, beans	**Bean seed fly** Tunnel into germinating seeds and seedlings mainly early in season. Destroy complete sowings in cold spring. CONTROL: Raise seedlings indoors for transplanting or wait for warmer weather for outdoor sowings.
Peas, seedlings, young lettuce, brassicas	**Birds** Pigeons, magpies, jays and sparrows can all be troublesome. Peas are taken when germinating or from pods. Leaf crops can be stripped. CONTROL: Net susceptible crops. Black cotton thread will keep sparrows off lettuce seedlings.
All brassicas, including radish	**Cabbage rootfly** Small white grubs tunnel into roots, causing plants to wilt and flag. Affected leaf crops pull up easily. Main attack April to July, but damage possible later. Brussels sprout buttons may be tunnelled. CONTROL: Earth up and mulch plants if you suspect damage. Use carpet squares or barriers (see p. 26). Interplant with beans (p. 28).
All brassicas	**Cabbage whitefly** Dart-shaped white winged insects. Fly up in clouds from disturbed foliage. Sooty mould may grow on excreted honeydew. Active even in winter. CONTROL: Ensure a break between brassica crops in spring if possible. Stumps of affected plants should be shredded or smashed and buried in compost trenches or compost heaps. *Spray*: Insecticidal soap regularly on underside of leaves.
Carrots Hamburg parsley Parsley Parsnips	**Carrotfly** White grubs tunnel in roots causing foliage to redden. Early sowings less affected. Damage to carrots can be severe. Infection by canker usually follows damage to parsley, parsnips.

CONTROL: Sow early fast-maturing carrot variety in late May to miss early hatch. Lift maincrop carrots and store rather than leave them in the soil. Use carrotfly barrier (p. 25) or interplant with onions (p. 29).

Brassicas
Nasturtiums

Caterpillars Cabbage moth, large and small white butterfly caterpillars feed extensively on brassicas, April and May and especially July and August.
CONTROL: Inspect plants regularly, looking especially in hearts and under leaves. Crush eggs, which may be yellow or white, in clusters or singly, and pick off caterpillars. *Spray*: *Bacillus thuringiensis* fortnightly or less as necessary or use derris or pyrethrum.

Most crops

Cutworms Bite through young stems after dark, leaving toppled plants.
CONTROL: Winter digging exposes larvae for birds and frost. Searches in soil near affected plants can reveal the fat grubs. Use cutworm collars (p. 26).

Onion family,
Parsnips

Eelworm (stem and bulb) Microscopic pest. Onions develop swollen and distorted leaves and split, rotting bulbs or plant bases. Parsnip crowns rot and leaf bases swell and crack. Plants eventually die. Similar symptoms to white rot and onion fly.
CONTROL: Avoid introducing contaminated soil (p. 24). Try to spot damage early and remove plant and surrounding soil to dustbin.

Potatoes

Eelworm (potato cyst) Patches of stunted yellow or dying plants in rows. Yields very low. Cysts containing eggs on lifted tubers only visible with

129

magnifying glass.

CONTROL: See stem and bulb eelworm. Use certified seed tubers. Where soil already contaminated, try growing potatoes in barrels of compost.

All brassicas

Flea beetle Tiny black jumping beetles make pinholes in leaves of all brassicas. Young seedlings can be crippled severely. Worse in dry weather.
CONTROL: Moderate damage to seedlings can be tolerated. Cover seedlings with floating cloche or other barrier. Spray or dust with derris.

Beets
Celeriac
Celery
Cucumber
Lovage
Parsley
Parsnips
Peas
Spinach

Leaf-miner Maggots tunnel in leaves causing pale, twisting trails between surfaces.
CONTROL: Older plants can happily sustain their damage. Squash maggots or pick off affected leaves. Winter digging exposes pupae. Start seeds in modules to give a good start where possible.

Brassicas
Lettuces

Leatherjackets Fat dun-coloured larvae of the crane-fly. Mainly a problem on newly-turned pasture or lawn. Feed on roots in spring causing yellowing, wilting, even death.
CONTROL: Problem usually wanes with time as pest prefers grassland. Regular cultivation will expose pupae and larvae to birds.

Broad beans
Peas

Mice Fond of germinating peas and broad beans, especially early and late in season when food is scarce.
CONTROL: Sow early varieties indoors to transplant. Set traps, but cover well to exclude birds.

Leeks Onions Shallots	**Onion fly** Small white grubs feed round base of bulb from May onwards. Plants yellow and die. Similar symptoms to eelworm and white rot (q.v.) CONTROL: Sets less likely to be affected than seed-grown seedlings. Remove and destroy affected plants and check soil nearby for grubs. Avoid need to thin onions by raising seedlings in modules.
Peas	**Pea moth** Adults lay eggs from early June on flowers and pods. Caterpillars tunnel into pods and feed on growing peas, leaving a trail of frass. March and April sowings most susceptible. CONTROL: Raise early sowings indoors in trays or guttering to advance flowering. Later sowings should be safe. Damage is generally tolerable. Fine mesh netting could be used from early June to late July if practicable.
Broad beans Peas	**Pea thrips** Cause misshapen pods and distorted growth often covered in silvery sheen. Worst in June and July if hot and dry. CONTROL: Very difficult but damage not usually severe. *Spray*: Derris or pyrethrum.
Most crops	**Slugs and snails** Seedlings most at risk. Keeled slugs can hollow out potato tubers. CONTROL: Protect susceptible seedlings with individual cloches. Use traps (see p. 27). Keep drooping plants off ground with pea-sticks or string. Aluminium sulphate preparations have some effect, but may harm seedlings.
Carrots Potatoes	**Wireworm** Long, yellowish larvae bore into potato tubers and carrots (less frequent). Mainly a problem of newly-turned turf or weedy plots.

CONTROL: Keep down weeds and cultivate thoroughly while damage persists. Lift maincrop potatoes early.

Broad beans
Peas

Pea and bean weevil Feeds at night, notching leaves like train tickets. Worst damage to spring plantings when growth is slow.
CONTROL: Damage generally tolerable except in cold, late springs. Dust plants with derris.

CROP

Greenhouse Pests

Glasshouse red spider mite Not visible to naked eye. Causes light-coloured mottling of leaves and progressive discolouration. Fine silvery webbing eventually visible under leaves. Dislike moisture.
CONTROL: Keep greenhouse atmosphere moist by regular misting or damping down paths in hot, dry weather. Remove infested plants. Introduce red spider mite predator (see p. 118).

Glasshouse whitefly Similar in appearance and damage to cabbage whitefly, but will not survive outside greenhouse. Main host is tomato. Translucent scales visible on underside of lower leaves.
CONTROL: Best control is whitefly parasite (see p. 118). Sticky yellow traps attract adults – or suck off with small hand-held vacuum cleaner. *Spray*: Insecticidal soap.

CROP	# Diseases
Potatoes Tomatoes	**Blight** Leaves and tomato fruits develop brownish-black patches. Spores washed into soil affect potato tubers which become soft and rotten. Spread rapidly in long spells of damp or humid weather. Rare before mid-July. CONTROL: Grow resistant varieties. If blight takes hold, remove haulms immediately to soil level and wait three weeks before lifting tubers. Remove affected tomato leaves and fruit immediately. Inspect stored tubers regularly. *Spray*: Bordeaux mixture from mid-July fortnightly to prevent if weather favours blight.
Potatoes	**Blackleg** Haulms blacken and soften at soil level. Foliage dies. Spread from mother to daughter tuber. CONTROL: Choose less susceptible varieties. Remove all tubers of affected plants and eat or destroy them.
Beans Brassicas Greenhouse crops Lettuces Potatoes	**Botrytis** Causes brown rotting leaves, covered eventually in grey fluffy mould. Severe on lettuces. CONTROL: Keep greenhouses well ventilated for susceptible crops. Avoid overcrowding. Remove affected parts to compost heap and keep garden clear of rotting debris.
Broad beans	**Chocolate spot** Brown, rounded rings on leaves spreading to other parts. Reduces yields. Late crops most adversely affected. CONTROL: Avoid damp, shaded sites and close spacing. Potash shortage exacerbates the problem, therefore attend to soil management, using seaweed meal or comfrey mulches where potash is known to be low.

Parsley Parsnips	**Canker** Rusty red canker affects shoulders of root, spreading down and invading carrotfly or hoe damage. Purple canker possible on peaty or highly organic soils. CONTROL: Choose resistant varieties.
Rhubarb	**Crown rot** Main bud rots. Secondary growth will occur but may also rot. CONTROL: Remove crown and replace.
All brassicas, especially Chinese mustards	**Clubroot** Serious, persistent disease, especially of acid soils. Roots of brassicas clump into fat, distorted galls. Growth is stunted and possibly discoloured. Leaves wilt by day and recover at night. May last in soil many years without a host. CONTROL: This disease cannot be cured and is virtually impossible to eradicate. Do not bring contaminated soil into your garden on plants, tools or boots. Heavy liming of affected soil will reduce the effect. In gardens with clubroot, raise seedlings in isolation and grow on in pots of clean potting compost. Planted out into trenches, where soil has been replaced by compost, these plants stand a good chance of reaching maturity. Swede 'Marian' is resistant, and resistant varieties of Chinese cabbage may become available eventually.
Asparagus Beans Greenhouse cucumbers Peas Tomatoes	**Foot and root rots** Various fungi attack plant roots. Leaves yellow and wilt, plants quickly die. CONTROL: Attention to drainage and soil management will reduce likelihood of attack. Remove affected plants. Rotate crops.
Asparagus Beetroot Carrot ...	**Other root rots** *Bacterial soft rot* turns turnips into foul-smelling slime. Also affects other root crops. *Violet root rot* can be serious on long-term crops

. . .Celery Parsnip Seakale	(asparagus, seakale). Rare in north. CONTROL: Burn affected roots. Adhere to strict rotations. For affected long-term crops a new clean bed will be necessary.
Brassicas	**Leaf spots** Various types. Look nasty but mainly a cosmetic problem. Cauliflower curds may be spoiled by dark patches. CONTROL: Keep calm. Clear away dead brassica leaves regularly and remove plants after harvest.
Courgettes Cucumbers Marrows Melons Peas Swede Turnips	**Powdery mildews** Powdery white coating on leaves. Mainly a problem late in the season, especially with late sowings of peas. CONTROL: Choose resistant varieties where available. *Spray*: Bicarbonate of soda or sulphur may help to reduce spread. Sulphur can scorch some plants. Peas inside affected pods are still edible.
Broad beans Garlic Leeks Onions Marjoram Mint	**Rusts** Reminiscent of metallic rust, often starting as spots or streaks and then spreading. Broad beans mainly affected towards end of crop or later in season. Leeks quite susceptible, but problem tends to subside in autumn. On mint and marjoram symptoms differ: pale, distorted leaves early in season, followed by dirty orange cups on stems and backs of leaves. CONTROL: Rotate crops; lift, divide and replant mint annually. Remove and burn diseased material. Mint rust can be cured by burning off leaves and scorching soil with flame-weeder. Harvested leeks, onions and garlic are still edible.
Potatoes	**Scab** Worse on alkaline soils. Potatoes develop brown scabs on skin – no internal damage.

CONTROL: Keep lime to furthest rotation from potatoes. On alkaline soils lower pH by putting manure, comfrey or mowings in potato trenches. Affected potatoes still edible.

Garlic
Onions
Shallots

Storage rots Most common is neck rot, particularly of shallots. Neck becomes soft, sunken and discoloured. Whole bulb will rot.
CONTROL: Medium-sized onions store better than large ones. Ensure crop is fully dried before storing. Peel off any loose, flaking and soil-marked skin. Store in cool, dry, ventilated conditions and check crop regularly for rot.

All crops

Virus Stunted and disfigured growth, spotted or discoloured foliage, poor yields. Spread on soil, by insects or by contact. Commonest garden viruses: *Cucumber mosaic* affects all cucurbits (see p. 43) and spinach; *tobacco mosaic* affects potatoes and tomatoes; *leaf-roll virus* affects potatoes; *carrot motley dwarf* reddens and stunts carrots and parsley (but note symptoms of carrotfly).
CONTROL: Inspect crops regularly and remove and burn affected plants at first signs. Adhere to strict rotations. Always buy certified seed potato tubers and use resistant varieties if available.

Onion family

White rot Persistent, ineradicable soil-borne disease. Leaves suddenly yellow and wilt, plants topple. Bulb rots and fluffy white fungal growth envelops base. Spreads rapidly.
CONTROL: Do not bring contaminated soil into your garden on plants, tools or boots. Remove affected plants and a generous proportion of surrounding soil as soon as possible. Do not compost affected plants.

CROP

Greenhouse Diseases

The following diseases may affect outdoor crops but are more common in greenhouses:

Tomatoes only

Blossom end rot Fruits develop a sunken dark brown or black circle of hard tissue. Immediate cause is deficiency of calcium, usually induced by shortage of water. More prevalent with growbags.
CONTROL: Does not spread. Remedy by regular watering. If this fails, soil or growbag may be calcium deficient.

Cucumbers
Tomatoes

Verticillium and fusarium wilts Plants suddenly wilt despite being well watered. Dark staining of internal tissue in stem well above soil level. Identification difficult. Soils can become contaminated.
CONTROL: No cure available. Remove plant and burn. Delay plantings until soil is warm. Choose resistant varieties. KNVF rootstock gives tomatoes resistance. Change infected soil or cover with polythene and use growbags.

Seedlings

Damping-off Seedlings in drills or seed-trays suddenly collapse in patches and die.
CONTROL: Ensure adequate ventilation but do not let seedlings get too cold. Do not overwater or leave puddles on floors in cold, wet weather. Sow thinly and prick out early on. Use only good quality fresh compost.

II. *Fruit*

Fruit growing has changed dramatically during the course of this century and some of the changes are greatly to the benefit of amateur gardeners. The development of new varieties and dwarfing rootstocks have meant that even small gardens can provide space for a few apple trees, which are much more likely to crop well than the delicious but unreliable Cox's Orange Pippin. Organic gardeners too can benefit from varieties developed with inbuilt resistance or less susceptibility to disease such as the mildew-resistant Invicta gooseberry or virus-tolerant raspberry Malling Jewel.

Fruit is usually referred to as either 'top' or 'soft'. Top fruits are the tree fruits such as apples, pears and plums, while soft fruit refers to strawberries and the bush and cane fruits. There are other important terms used which cannot easily be avoided in describing the plantings and growing of fruit. A short glossary of pruning and training terminology is given below.

The creation of a diverse habitat and other general principles of organic pest and disease control are as relevant to fruit growing as they are to vegetable cropping (see p. 20).

The site and soil

You cannot choose your soil, but you can choose your fruit to suit it. Fruit grows best when protected from wind and late frosts, which can damage fruits, branches and blossom and prevent pollination. Windbreak netting and hedges can alleviate this, but frost pockets of low-lying land at the bottom of slopes will restrict the selection of top fruit to late-flowering varieties of apple and cannot be remedied.

The ideal soil for fruit growing is a free-draining, slightly acid, deep loam, but any soil with good organic cultivation can support a reasonable fruit crop. It is a good idea to have your soil analysed before planting to ensure that conditions are suitable (see p. 3). The best position should be reserved for pears, plums and dessert apples amongst top fruit, for strawberries and raspberries amongst soft fruit.

Choosing plants

With a very few exceptions it is now possible to buy any type of fruit stock with a guarantee that it has been raised from virus-free material. This does not mean to say that *all* stock offered for sale carries such a guarantee, and you should look for a specific statement in catalogues.

The widest choice of varieties will only be available from specialist suppliers at their nurseries or by mail order. When choosing you should take account of your growing conditions: a warm protected site in the south will suit earlier varieties and a wide selection of pears and gages, while a cold, frosty site will severely limit the choice. Fruit prefers full sunshine but blackcurrants, gooseberries, blackberries and redcurrants will tolerate some shading for part of the day.

Top fruit is always grafted on to a rootstock. This controls the vigour, eventual height and the speed with which the tree comes into full fruiting. Nurseries will usually offer a choice of rootstocks for any variety. Details of the rootstocks are given in the relevant sections for individual fruits, but you will need to take account of your soil type before you decide.

Although some top fruit varieties will self-pollinate, most need at least one other variety nearby and some apples (known as 'triploids) require two others to set fruit. Varieties are classified into flowering groups, and you should ensure that the varieties you choose will be compatible by belonging to the same group or the one before or after. Numbers in brackets after varieties listed in the relevant sections indicate the flowering group.

Finally you should look for any varieties with inbred resistance to pest or disease. This is always sound organic practice, and will help you grow healthy fruit without, for example, the twenty sprays that a commercial grower may use before harvesting his apples.

Preparation and planting

Planting holes dug straight into uncultivated land are likely to act as water sumps, especially on poorly drained soils. It is much better to mark out the area to be occupied by the bushes, canes or trees, and to cultivate it all before planting. Turf provides a great deal of valuable humus and should be dug or rotovated into the soil, combined with manure at the rate of one barrowload for every 2–3 sq m (approx. 3 sq yds). Rock minerals being used to correct deficiencies should be applied at this time, but dolomite or ground limestone can wait for a few months. This treatment should keep your fruit happy for several years, with the exception of the blackcurrants which may need extra hoof and horn at the rate of 125 gm per sq m (4 oz per sq yd) to encourage plenty of vigorous young growth and compensate for heavy pruning. At planting time a handful of bonemeal mixed into the soil round the roots will give additional slowly-released phosphate to stimulate healthy root formation during the life of the plant. The best time for planting is November and December, but any time during winter before well-rested buds begin to burst into life will do, provided that the weather is not frosty.

In May the soil is warm and it is time to mulch the fruit. To suppress weed growth a thick layer of newspapers or cardboard can be laid, covered with old hay, straw, strawy manure or lawn mowings. In further years you should only need to top up the mulch, although raspberries – with their tendency to wander energetically from their appointed row – can be kept in order with a renewed thick layer of newspaper.

The renewal of the mulch may well be all the feeding that your fruit needs. If you plants are hungry they will tell you by the way that they grow and you should respond with the appropriate organic fertiliser (see p. 17).

Pruning and Training

Pruning is not a cosmetic exercise for skilled experts but an essential part of fruit production, ensuring sound, healthy plants, maximum cropping, balanced growth and an open, airy framework for the sun to ripen fruit. Fruit trees and bushes are fairly flexible and by pruning and training it is possible to produce a variety of shapes, each of which has its advantages to suit certain situations. A short glossary of pruning and training terms follows.

BASAL CLUSTER The cluster of leaves at the base of this season's new growth.

BUSH A goblet-shaped, usually dwarf, tree with a short trunk and open framework of branches. This form is the easiest to manage for top fruit. Larger versions of this shape are called *half-standards* and *standards*.

CANE The stem of a raspberry or blackberry.

CORDON A single straight stem, carrying fruiting spurs along its length. This is used for apples, pears, gooseberries and redcurrants. It is also possible to create double and triple cordons from one tree or bush.

ESPALIER Pairs of horizontal branches trained at right-angles to the trunk on wires in a flat plane, often against a wall. Espaliers can have as many tiers of branches as you wish, ranging from one upwards, but usually confined to three or four. Suitable for apples and pears.

FAMILY TREE A tree formed from three varieties grafted on to one rootstock. Normally grown as an open bush.

FAN A number of leaders trained to canes, often against a wall, in a fan shape. Suitable for all top fruit, gooseberries and redcurrants.

LATERAL Shoot growing from leader (see p. 164).

LEADER Selected main leading shoots that make up the branch framework (see p. 164).

MAIDEN A one-year-old tree. Maidens that are branched are called 'feathered'. This is a good size to buy your trees as it allows you to carry out formative pruning yourself.

PYRAMID Another shape with a central leader suitable for apples, pears and plums. Branches are longer at the base to create a pyramid shape. Pruning is more complex, but this is a highly productive shape.

SPINDLE A practical and productive training form without much charm used extensively in commercial orchards for apples and pears. A central stem supports a framework of four or more main branches which are replaced by new ones every four years. Pruning is mainly light and simple.

SPUR A short, pruned shoot or complex of shoots carrying one or more fruit buds (see p. 164). Fruit buds are recognised by being fatter and rounder than wood buds.

STOOL The root system and crown of a raspberry, blackberry or blackcurrant.

TOP FRUIT

Apples

Rootstocks

M27 – a very dwarfing rootstock, giving a bush only 1.6 m (4–5 ft) high. Allows you to grow a tree in a large pot or tub or a single-tiered espalier, known as a 'step-over'. Needs rich soil and a

permanent stake but can be allowed to crop in its second year from planting. Plant bushes 1.5–2 m (4–6 ft) apart.

M9 – will make a dwarf bush on fertile soil. It will need permanent staking and crops early in its life. Plant bushes 2.5–3 m (8–10 ft) apart. Remove blossom in the first year after planting.

M26 – is less dwarfing but the best choice for dwarf forms on poor soils. It will need a stake for the first few years of its life. Plant at 3–4.5 m (10–15 ft) apart. It can be allowed to crop after two years.

MM106 – is more vigorous than M26, but dwarfing on poor soils. It has the advantage of producing a tree resistant to woolly aphid. Do not allow it to crop until it has had three or four years to establish. Plant trees 3.5–5.5 m (12–18 ft) apart.

Training and pruning

SPUR TRAINING With certain important exceptions, pruning aims at creating short fruiting spurs along the length of leaders. The spindle form is not spur-pruned; details of pruning for this tree are given below. Varieties fall into three categories for pruning purposes: those which fruit on short lateral spurs, those which fruit on medium-length spurs and those which tend to fruit at the tips of one-year-old shoots. The latter type are pruned by cutting back strong growing laterals to five or six buds and leaving a selection of less vigorous well-spaced shoots of 23 cm (9 in) length or less to carry fruit at the tips. With spur-fruiting varieties laterals that arise directly from the leader are cut back to three or four buds with 'short spur' trees, five or six buds with 'medium spur' trees.

SUMMER PRUNING A healthy tree pruned in winter will tend to grow away vigorously, whereas a tree pruned in early August will be considerably more restrained. Summer pruning is normally only carried out on restricted forms such as cordons, pyramids or espaliers, but can be used to control excessive growth on bush forms if necessary. Wait until laterals are about 12 cm (9 in) long before cutting back to three or six leaves according to variety (see above). Central leaders are not summer pruned. A second session

Pruning of apple trees

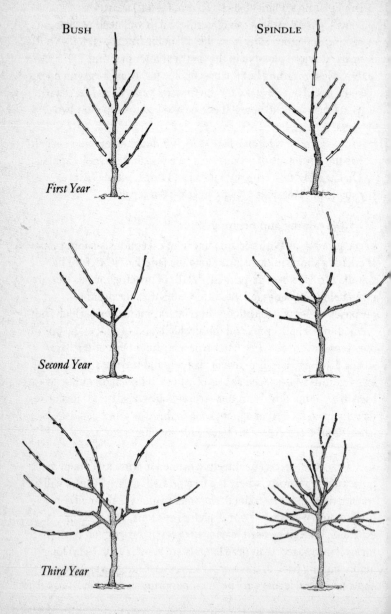

BUSH

SPINDLE

First Year

Second Year

Third Year

PYRAMID   CORDON

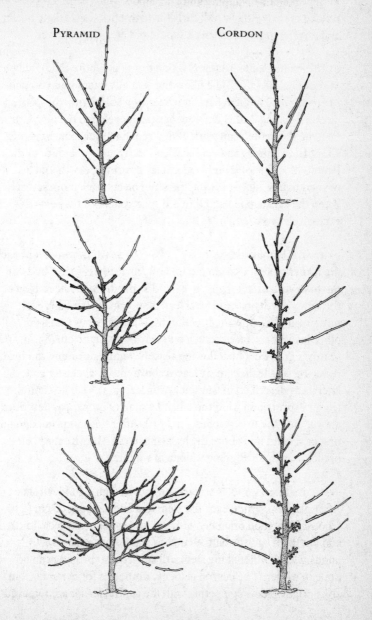

in September will allow pruning of shoots which were too short to reduce in early August. All early formative pruning is done in winter and any tree not growing well should not be cut in summer.

BUSH Prune maidens after planting to a point above four good buds at about 60 cm (2 ft). The following year allow four main branches to grow, pruning them back in winter by a half to two-thirds to an outward-facing bud. The branches that develop in the next year will become the main framework of the tree. Each subsequent winter, spur prune laterals and cut back leaders by up to one third of their length. As a rule of thumb, vigorously growing trees should be pruned lightly, slow-growing trees can be cut back more severely. Keep the centre open and thin out spur systems if they get excessively crowded.

PYRAMID Plant maidens 1.8–2 m (5–6 ft) apart. In winter, cut back the leader to about 50 cm (20 in) and any feathers to five buds. In the following winter measure a hand's span from the beginning of the new growth on the central leader and cut to a suitable bud pointing in the opposite direction from the previous year's cut. All other leaders are reduced to a bud leaving about 20 cm (8 in) of the season's growth. The following season, summer pruning can begin, reducing side leaders to six leaves above the basal cluster and laterals as described in 'summer pruning' (p. 143). The central leader is pruned in winter to a hand's span of growth, as described above, until the tree reaches 2 m (7 ft). After this it is pruned to the first or second bud above the basal cluster in May. Removal of branches or spur thinning is done in winter.

SPINDLE Plant spindles 2 m (6–7 ft) apart, with a good tall stake. After planting, prune back the stem to a bud at about 90 cm (3 ft). Choose four good branches with the lowest at about 60 cm (2 ft) and cut them back by half. Branches should not arise directly opposite each other at the stem. All subsequent pruning can be done in winter. The central leader is pruned as for pyramids, but any upright shoots competing with the central leader are removed entirely. Each winter, simply cut out any strong upright-growing laterals. After four years or if leaders become excessively long, prune back to a weak lateral or fruit bud, or prune out the branch entirely, leaving a short stub.

CORDONS Cordons are best bought as maidens on a dwarfing rootstock. You will need a permanent framework of horizontal wires 45 cm (18 in) apart for these, either free-standing or against a wall. Plant trees 75 cm (2½ ft) apart at an angle of 45° and tie the stems to canes fixed firmly on to the wires. Spur pruning is carried out each summer as detailed above (summer pruning and spur pruning). The central stem is left as an unpruned leader until it has reached the desired height. It can then be pruned back to one or two buds of the current season's growth in May.

ESPALIER It takes several years to complete the formative training of espaliers, but the final result is productive and attractive. Again a permanent framework of posts and wires is needed with one wire for each tier to whatever number is required. The first wire should be 45 cm (18 in) from the ground and subsequent wires 30 cm (1 ft) apart.

For a larger espalier use rootstock MM106 at a planting distance of 4–4.5 m (12–15 ft). Smaller trees will be produced on M26, planted 3.2–3.5 metres (10–12 ft) apart. A single-tiered low espalier can be grown on M27 at a spacing of 2.5–3 m (7–9 ft). After planting, cut back the maiden to a bud just above the first wire, ensuring that there are two buds just below it facing in opposite directions roughly along the line of the wires. During the summer, allow the growth from the top bud to extend directly upwards by tying it firmly to a cane as it grows. The side shoots from the lower buds should be trained to canes set at an angle of 45°. At the end of the season, lower these shoots to the horizontal and tie them to the wire. The central stem should by then have passed the second wire and is pruned during the winter in exactly the same way. The extending arms of the espalier are pruned as cordons (see above) and any additional growth from the central stem is spur-pruned in summer or removed entirely if awkwardly placed. Where the arms have reached the required length, prune them back each May to one or two buds of the previous season's growth. When the top wire is reached, prune to two buds instead of three and train in as described above.

Maintenance

FRUIT THINNING In a good year, trees will set a great deal more fruit than they can reasonably ripen. Their natural response to this is to discard fruit in late June and early July, a process referred to as the 'June drop'. This may still leave too many fruits on the tree and judicious thinning is advisable, as too heavy a crop one year will discourage a tree from cropping in the next and may cause physical damage through weight alone.

In mid-July work round the trees, removing any damaged or misshapen fruits first. The central apple in each cluster is usually removed and remaining fruitlets thinned to a maximum of two per cluster (one per cluster for large-fruited and cooking varieties), with about 15 cm (6 in) between trusses.

Harvesting and Storing

Not all apples are suitable for storing. Fruits of early varieties should not be left too long on the tree once they are ready for picking. Fruit is ready to pick when it comes away from the spur easily with a slight twist. You will find that not all the apples on one tree are ready for picking at once, which is useful with early varieties but not so convenient with apples going into store. It is only the late varieties that are suitable for storing. All of these should have been picked by the end of October, but can be left into November if they are not quite ripe, provided that there is no threat of severe frost or gales.

Apples for storing should be dry and sound. Any bruised or damaged fruit should be used immediately and badly scabbed fruit used next, as these will not store successfully. Smaller apples keep longer than large ones but, generally speaking, all stored late varieties need to be kept for a few weeks before they develop their

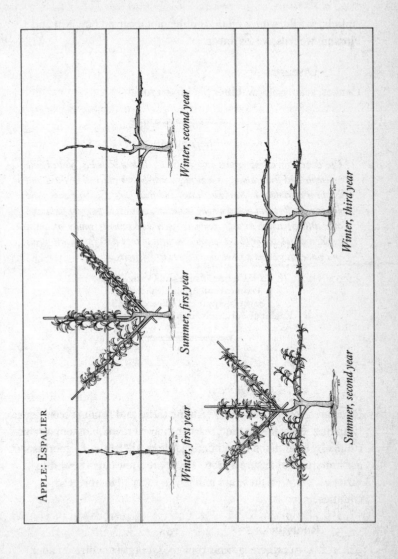

APPLE: ESPALIER

Winter, first year

Summer, first year

Winter, second year

Summer, second year

Winter, third year

full flavour. For hints on storage methods, see Chapter 16, p. 217.

Pests

Aphids, sawfly, winter moth, codling moth, capsid bug, leaf and blossom weevils, wasps, birds.

Diseases

Canker, scab, mildew, bitter pit, brown rot.

RECIPE IDEAS

Use dessert or eating apples raw in fruit salads and jellies; grated into vegetable and fruit salads; as a picnic, lunch-box or snack-time fruit; and use firm specimens in fruit pies, cakes and fruit fools. Cooking apples are delicious stuffed and baked whole; made into a purée or pulp for flans and cake fillings; make a tasty compote, sweet and savoury sauce; or are a wonderful 'roasted or baked' accompaniment to cook with fatty roast meats and game; as well as a whole host of prepared desserts.

See: **Country Apple and Orange Pie,
Oatmeal and Apple Crunch Bars,
Savoury Apple and Cheese Quiche,
Rabbit or Pork with Normandy Sauce** and more.

Pears *(and Quinces)*

Pears are grown with similar training forms and pruning techniques to apples. They flower much earlier, however, and blossom can be ruined by frost. Even in southern gardens, shelter and a good aspect are important to ensure a crop. There are a few later-flowering varieties, but even these are unlikely to succeed in northern counties.

Rootstocks

QUINCE A – a rather vigorous rootstock, but best choice on poor soils. Plant bushes 3.5–4.5 m (12–15 ft) apart.

Suggested varieties

Dessert apples

Variety	Pollination	Pruning	Pick	Eat	Scab Resistant	Mildew Resistant	Notes
DISCOVERY	3	3	Aug	Aug/Sep	Yes		
FORTUNE	3	1	Sep	Sep/Oct	Yes		
LORD LAMBOURNE	2	3	Sep/Oct	Oct/Nov	Yes		Canker prone
MOTHER	5	2	Sep/Oct	Oct/Nov	Yes		
EGREMONT RUSSET	2	2	Sep/Oct	Oct/Dec	Yes		
SUNSET	3	1	Sep/Oct	Oct/Dec	Yes	Yes	
ASHMEAD'S KERNEL	4	1	Oct	Dec/Feb	Yes		
D'ARCY SPICE	3	3	end Oct	Dec/Apr	Yes		Poor looks, good taste

Cooking apples

Variety	Pollination	Pruning	Pick	Eat	Scab Resistant	Mildew Resistant	Notes
GRENADIER	3	1	Aug	Aug/Oct	Yes		
ARTHUR TURNER	3	1	Aug	Aug/Oct	Yes		
BLENHEIM ORANGE (T)	3	2	Oct	Nov/Jan		Yes	Dual purpose. Erratic cropping
NEWTON WONDER	5	2	Oct	Nov/Mar	Yes		Some resistance to canker
BRAMLEY'S SEEDLING (T)	3	3	Oct	Nov/Mar	Yes		Some resistance to canker
EDWARD VII	6	1	Oct	Dec/Apr	Yes		

Key
(T) = Triploid; needs two other pollinators.
Pollination groups: apples will generally cross-pollinate with other varieties in the same group or one either side.
Pruning guide:
1 = short spurs;
2 = long spurs;
3 = tip-fruiting (see p. 143).

QUINCE C – more dwarfing and best choice for vigorous varieties. Not suitable for poor soils.

Trees on both rootstocks should be deblossomed in the first year after planting to allow them to become established.

RECIPE IDEAS

Dessert or eating pears are ideal raw in fruit salads, as a cheeseboard fruit or simply served as a snack fruit; cooked in a syrup, they may be served with a complementary sauce such as chocolate, cream or honey. Cooking pears are perhaps best poached in a syrup, after peeling and brushing with lemon juice to prevent discoloration, but may be baked with a sweet filling; alternatively use as a pie filling, tart ingredient or store-cupboard bottled fruit for emergency occasions.

See: **Pear Waldorf Salad,**
Pear and Orange Custard Tart,
Autumn Fruit Layer Pudding,
Strawberry and Kiwi Pavlova.

Training and Pruning

Follow general advice given for apples. Summer pruning starts slightly earlier than for apples, and pruning early in the life of the trees can afford to be lighter.

Maintenance

Fruit thinning is necessary for pears and should be done when the fruitlets bend downwards. Thin fruitlets to one or two per cluster. Support heavily laden branches later in the season.

Harvesting and Storing

The general rules on the fruit picking of apples apply also to pears, but timing is critical. Early varieties are best picked just before they ripen, when fully formed but still hard and green. Left in a warm room for a few days, they will ripen for eating. Late varieties can be stored; these should be left on the tree until they come away easily with a slight twist. Store only perfect fruit. Storing pears is not easy, and you may prefer to bottle them or dry them in rings.

Pests

Aphids, pear midge, leaf blister mites, blossom and leaf weevils, winter moth, birds, wasps.

Diseases

Scab, fireblight, canker, brown rot.

Suggested varieties

Except where indicated, most varieties quoted are relatively hardy.

Variety	Pollin-ation	Pick	Eat	Notes
JARGONELLE (T)	3	early Aug	Aug	Tip-bearer. Scab resistant.
GORHAM	4	Sep	Sep	
DR JULES GUYOT	3	Sep	Sep	Some resistance to scab.
BEURRE HARDY	3	Sep	Oct	
HESSLE	4	Sep	Oct	Some resistance to scab.
LOUISE BONNE OF JERSEY	2	Sep	Oct	
CONFERENCE	3	end Sep	Oct/Nov	
SECKLE	2	end Sep	Oct/Nov	Needs warmth. Not pollinated by Louise Bonne.
JOSEPHINE DE MALINES	3	Oct	Dec/Jan	Tip-bearer. Needs warmth.
WINTER NELIS	4	Oct	Dec/Jan	Pick before fruit turns red.
CATILLAC (T)	4	Oct	Feb/Apr	For culinary use.

Plums (including damsons and gages)

Plums flower early and may lose blossom to the frost, especially in low-lying frost pockets. Fruiting varies enormously from year to year, but in a good season very heavy crops can result. Plums are usually grown as bushes, fans or pyramids, and do not suit restrictive forms as readily as apples or pears.

Rootstocks

PIXY The most dwarfing rootstock suitable for all forms, and giving owners of small gardens a chance to grow plums that do not shade out everything else. Plant bushes 2–2.5 m (6–8 ft) apart.

ST JULIEN A The standard semi-dwarfing variety, giving a larger tree than Pixy, which will take five years to come into bearing but ultimately produce heavier crops. Trees should be deblossomed during these early years. Plant bushes 3.5–4.5 m (12–15 ft) apart.

BROMPTON The rootstock for full-sized trees. You will eventually need a ladder to pick the fruit. Trees should be 6 m (20 ft) apart or more.

Training and Pruning

Pruning plums or cherries in winter can give unwelcome access to the deadly silverleaf disease (see p. 30), so pruning is generally done while trees are actively growing, when wounds heal quickly, and all pruning cuts are treated with Trichoderma paste (see p. 30). Bush forms need relatively little pruning after the initial shape has been created.

BUSH Trees are often only available as two- or three-year-olds, in which case no pruning should be done in the first year. Maidens are pruned back in the April after planting to a point about 1 m (3 ft) from the ground just above a point where three buds or feathers point in roughly opposite directions. Any feathers lower down are shortened to four or five leaves during the summer of the next year, before final removal in the second summer.

In the second year, choose four good branches to make the main framework of the tree and cut them back by half in April, removing any others. That year's growth may need similar treatment in the next spring.

Pruning of bush trees, once formed, is light and consists of cutting out any dead, diseased or damaged branches and any growth that is rubbing or badly placed. This is best done in summer.

PYRAMID For best results with this shape, you will need to buy a maiden on Pixy. In April, prune back the central leader to leave the tree about 1.5 m (5 ft) tall, just above a bud. Any branches less than 45 cm (18 in) from the ground should be completely removed, and any other feathers cut back by half. During the first summer, towards the end of July, prune all the side branches back to a downward facing bud to leave about 20 cm (8 in) of new growth. Laterals are shortened to 15 cm (6 in).

The central leader is not pruned until the following April, when it is shortened to leave about a hand's span of new growth, cutting at a bud pointing in the opposite direction from the previous year's pruning. This process is repeated every year until the tree reaches 2 metres (6 or 7 feet). After this, prune back to 2–3 cm (1 in) of new growth every May.

Every summer, in late July, prune back side branches to 20 cm (8 in), laterals to 15 cm (6 in) and sub-laterals to 8 cm (3 in), and completely remove any branch near the top that tries to grow upwards and compete with the central leader. Any very congested growth is also pruned out at this time.

FAN If you are keen to have one of the ambrosial-flavoured but rather reluctant gages, then grow it as a fan against a south-facing wall. Pixy and St Julien A are both suitable rootstocks for this shape. Trees are often available with preliminary training complete, but you may like to try starting with a maiden. Plant trees on Pixy 3 to 3.6 m (10–12 ft) apart, on St Julien A 4.5–5.5 m (15–18 ft) apart. Keep the roots at least 15–30 cm (10–12 in) from the base of the wall where it tends to be rather dry and angle the trunk backwards.

You will need a permanent framework of wires starting 35–40 cm (about 15 in) from the ground and continuing to about 2 m (6–7 ft) at 30 cm (12 in) intervals.

In the April after planting, prune back the maiden to a bud at 60 cm (2 ft), with two good buds or feathers just below it pointing in

Pruning of plum trees

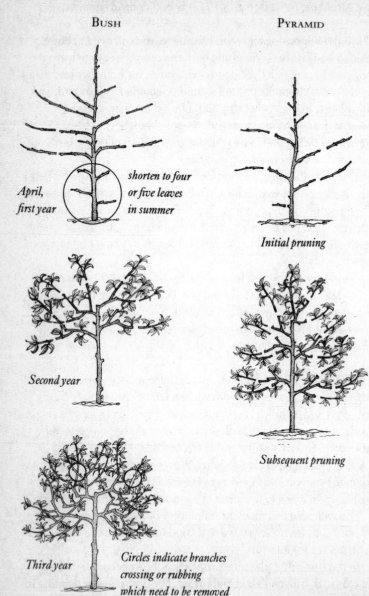

BUSH

PYRAMID

April, first year

shorten to four or five leaves in summer

Initial pruning

Second year

Subsequent pruning

Third year

Circles indicate branches crossing or rubbing which need to be removed

156

FAN

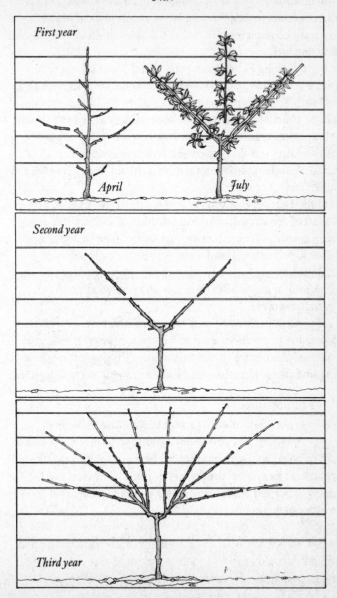

First year

April   *July*

Second year

Third year

opposite directions along the line of the wall. Cut back the feathers by two-thirds to an upward-pointing bud. As these arms grow, tie them in to canes set at 45° on the wires and in July cut out the centre leader completely. Any other side growth should be pinched back to one leaf.

In the following February or early March, cut back these two arms to a bud at 30–45 cm (12–18 in) from the stem and paint the wound with Trichoderma paste immediately. In the summer you should be able to find enough extension growth to tie in the leader and three other branches on each arm, two above and one below, spaced about 15 cm (6 in) apart or a little less, in the shape of an open fan. All others shoots not required should be pinched back to one leaf.

Cutting these ribs back in April of the third year to 60–75 cm (2–2½ ft) of growth will provide a selection of shoots to fill in gaps between existing ribs in summer. Any shoots growing towards the wall should be removed, and those growing directly outwards pruned back to one leaf. Any other shoots not wanted for ribs are pinched back at this time to six leaves and pruned again to three leaves in September.

This process is repeated until the wall is well covered with ribs spaced about 15 cm (6 in) apart at their tips. Every July pinch back laterals to six leaves. In September, or after fruiting, prune these back again to three leaves and thin laterals to about 10 cm (4 in) apart.

Maintenance

FROST It is not practicable to protect large bushes from frost damage to blossom, but wall-trained trees can be protected with a curtain of polythene, spun polypropylene, hessian or even old net curtains, held away from the flowers by canes. The skirt needs to be weighted or pegged down to prevent the wind blowing it off and the covers should be removed during the day.

FEEDING AND WATERING A heavy mulch of hay or straw topped up annually should keep tree roots moist, weed-free and well-fed. Young trees may need watering in a dry year and trees planted against walls can exhaust supplies of water in this potentially dry area. Plums do not need much lime.

DEBLOSSOMING AND FRUIT THINNING Remove all blossom from trees until early formative pruning in the first two years is over. Trees bought as two- or three-year-olds should be given a year to recover after planting before being allowed to crop.

Once trees start to crop, the fruit will need to be thinned if there is a good set. Aim at leaving 5–8 cm (2–3 in) between fruits, or a little more for large-fruited varieties like Victoria. Do this in two stages, starting in early June and completing it at the end of the month, by which time some fruitlets may have dropped naturally. Branches on bushes may need supporting with props if the crop is heavy.

RECIPE IDEAS

Fresh ripe fruits in peak condition make wonderful fruit salad ingredients or fresh dessert fruits; more acid specimens are best cooked, where they are ideal in tarts, puddings, pie-fillings and sauces for fatty meats; both can be used in a whole host of jams and preserves.

See: **Plum Conserve,
Damson and Plum Butter,
Autumn Fruit Layer Pudding,
Tudor Damson Jam,
Greengages in Honey Syrup.**

Harvesting
Plums cannot be stored except by preserving and freezing and are best eaten soon after picking when they are fully ripe.

Pests
Aphids, plum fruit moth, codling moth, wasps, birds.

Diseases
Silver leaf, brown rot, bacterial canker.

Suggested varieties

Most plums are self-fertile and do not need another pollinator.
These are marked 's/f' in the Notes column below.

Variety	Pollination	Pick	Notes
Dessert			
OULLIN'S GAGE	4	Aug	s/f
OPAL	3	Aug	s/f
DENNISTON'S SUPERB	2	late Aug	s/f
VICTORIA	3	Aug/Sep	s/f Dual-purpose.
JEFFERSON	1	Aug/Sep	
KIRKE'S BLUE	4	Aug/Sep	
Culinary			
EARLY RIVERS	3	Jul/Aug	
CZAR	3	Aug	s/f
BELLE DE LOUVAIN	5	Aug	s/f Less susceptible to bacterial canker
EDWARDS	3	Sep	s/f
WARWICKSHIRE DROOPER	2	Sep	s/f
MARJORIE'S SEEDLING	5	Sep/Oct	s/f Less susceptible to bacterial canker.
Damson (all varieties are hardy)			
MERRYWEATHER	3	Sep	s/f
KING OF THE DAMSONS (BRADLEY'S KING)	4	Sep	s/f
PRUNE DAMSON	4	Sep/Oct	s/f

Cherries

Cherries are classified as sweet, duke or acid. There is a significant
difference in growth and pruning methods between the only
commonly grown acid cherry, Morello, and the other types. Acid

cherries are less vigorous and less attractive to birds, making them more suitable for small gardens. The new dwarfing rootstock Inmil, however, makes the growing of sweet cherries a much more viable proposition for warm, sheltered gardens, but space is needed for more than one tree to allow cross-pollination, with the exception of Stella, which is self-fertile. Other dwarfing rootstocks are currently being trialled and should become fairly generally available within a few years.

SWEET (AND DUKE) TYPES

Rootstocks

INMIL Dwarfing. Plant bushes 3–3.5 m (10–12 ft) apart and fans 3.5–4.5 m (12–15 ft) apart. Not available for all varieties.
COLT Semi-dwarfing. Plant bushes 6–7 m (20–25 ft) apart and fans 4.5–5.5 m (15–18 ft) apart.

Training and Pruning

Cherries are as susceptible as plums to infection by silver leaf and bacterial canker and should, therefore, only be pruned during the growing season. Formative pruning is generally done at bud-burst. The best shape for a garden is the fan, ideally trained against a south or west wall for ease of netting, although the development of Inmil should allow bush-sized trees to be grown inside a fruit cage.

Fans and bushes are formed and pruned similarly to plums (see p. 156). Cherries on Colt may be rather exuberant in growth and need more drastic pruning, as fruiting spurs become too long or jostle each other for space and the top shoots outgrow the wall. Prune these back in spring by up to two-thirds to a suitable weak lateral or bud. Paint all wounds with Trichoderma paste (see p. 154).

Maintenance and Harvesting

No fruit thinning is needed with cherries, but attention to water is essential to avoid split fruits. A heavy mulch of hay or strawy manure should retain sufficient moisture. Protect ripening fruit from birds with netting and pick the cherries with stalk attached as soon as they are ripe. Few cherries will make it further than the back door, but those that are left can be successfully frozen.

Suggested varieties

Not all cherries happily cross-pollinate and only Stella is self-fertile. In general, two trees of the same variety will not cross-pollinate either. Combinations are suggested by simplified pollination groups shown below, but advice should be sought from an expert before selecting varieties not mentioned here.

Variety	Pollination Group	Pick	Notes
EARLY RIVERS	A	June	
MERMAT	A and B	June	Partially resistant to bacterial canker.
ROUNDEL	B	early July	
MERCHANT	A and B	early July	Partially resistant to bacterial canker.
NAPOLEON BIGARREAU	B	late July	
STELLA	B	late July	Self-fertile.

Promising new variety: CHEROKEE – heavy cropping with fruit less susceptible to splitting.
Pollination groups: Pairs of trees in the same group will successfully cross-pollinate.

ACID TYPES

Rootstocks

INMIL: very dwarfing. Plant bushes and fans 3–3.5 m (10–12 ft) apart and stake bushes firmly.

COLT: Bushes and fans on this stock should be planted 3.5–4.5 m (12–15 ft) apart. Support bushes with a stake.

Training and Pruning

Any aspect will suit acid cherries, which tolerate shade sufficiently to grow well even against a north wall. As with sweet cherries, these are best grown as fans against walls for ease of netting, but the fruits are less often taken by birds and so bushes can be worth growing.

BUSH Choose a well-feathered maiden and plant it during the dormant season, not later than February but ideally in November. Prune out any feathers below 0.75 m (2 ft), and select four or five well-spread laterals above this to form the framework. Cut out the stem above these and prune back the chosen laterals by two-thirds to an upward-facing bud. A tree bought as a two-year-old should have had this early pruning completed. The growth from this should be pruned back in the same way to a suitable bud in the spring of the following two years.

After this the tree can be allowed to fruit. Fruit is formed on one-year-old wood so that routine pruning consists in pruning out about a quarter of the fruited branches to a suitable new lateral in September. If the tree is getting congested or straggly in habit, cut out some of the three- and four-year-old branches. It is important to treat all wounds with Trichoderma paste.

PRUNING OF ACID CHERRIES: BUSH

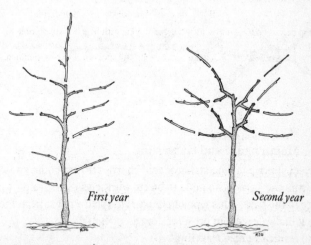

First year

Second year

FAN You will need a wall or fence at least 2 m tall for this shape, particularly if you have a tree on a Colt rootstock, with wires fixed horizontally at 15 cm (6 in) apart, starting at about 45 cm (18 in) from the ground. Keep the roots away from the very dry soil at the base of the wall and incline the stem back.

It is usually possible to buy partly trained fans, but if you decide to start with a maiden follow the formative pruning method for plums (see p. 156) until the main framework of ribs has been completed. It is better to pinch out any flowers in these first few years in order to allow the tree to fill the wall space rapidly.

Once the fan shape is completed, you can allow fruiting laterals to develop. In early summer thin these out to be about 5–8 cm (2–3 in) apart along the ribs and tie them in as they grow. The next summer these laterals will fruit and further shoots will develop. Allow one of these to grow from near the base of each fruiting lateral and, in the spring, prune back to these. In time these laterals will become too long and should be pruned back to a young lateral nearer the rib.

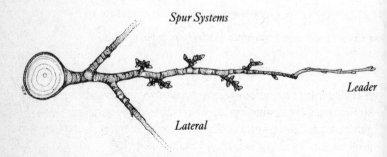

Spur Systems

Leader

Lateral

Maintenance and Harvesting

(*See* sweet cherries.) The stalks of acid cherries do not come away easily from the branch, so need to be cut with scissors to avoid damage to the fruit. This type of cherry is too sharp to eat from the tree, but makes excellent preserves or can be bottled.

Suggested variety

Morello – self-fertile; fruiting in August or September but later on a north wall.

Pests

Birds, aphids, slugworm.

Diseases

Bacterial canker, silver leaf, brown rot.

RECIPE IDEAS

Sweet cherries are best served as a dessert fruit, in fruit salads or drinks; acid cherries are better cooked and served in compotes, pies and tarts; can be used to flavour ice creams and water ices; or for making preserves.

See: **Bottled Fruit Salad,
Cherry Brandy,
Crunchy Cheese with Cherry Sauce.**

SOFT FRUIT
(Also see general introduction to fruit growing pp. 138–42.)

Strawberries

Not all gardens can offer space to a fruit tree, but irresistible strawberries can be fitted in anywhere. Even in the smallest gardens, a tub or 'tower' can support a crop, although strawberries grown in beds will last longer and require less skill.

Strawberries are sun-lovers but not at all greedy. Most soils have sufficient phosphate and potash to feed a crop of strawberries during their stay, provided that adequate organic matter is incorporated before planting. They thrive in well-drained acid soils with a good supply of humus in the top few centimetres, but with good management will tolerate less hospitable soils.

Preparation and Planting

It is best to rotate strawberries, since after three years (or four in the case of Cambridge Favourite) they will have formed dense woody crowns, lost their young vigour and become prone to pests, root rots and virus. A simple way of doing this is to incorporate strawberries into the vegetable rotation with a row in each plot of varying age, ensuring continuity of supply. Alternatively they can be given a separate bed, which could grow flowers or salads before the strawberries return after a rest of at least three years.

Prepare the ground by working in one barrowload of manure or compost to every 2 square metres, taking care not to bury the organic matter too deeply. If you are breaking new ground, dig in the turf early in the spring, adding rock minerals if necessary and a small amount of manure, before covering the whole plot in black polythene, woven strawberry mulch or old carpet until the crowns arrive in August or September. Lime is only necessary on soils with a pH of 5.5 or less.

It is always advisable to buy crowns that are certified virus-free. Now it is even possible to buy organically raised certified strawberry crowns of excellent quality. The crowns should be planted by mid-September to ensure a good start before winter and a crop in the first year. Crowns planted later should have their blossom removed in the first spring. Where black polythene or woven polypropylene is used, the crowns could be planted through it to eliminate any need for weeding during their life. The woven mulch has the added advantage of allowing water to penetrate. Beds under black polythene should be slightly domed to allow water to drain.

Crowns should be planted 40–45 cm (15–18 in) apart in the row, with 75 cm (2½ ft) between rows, or in staggered rows with 60 cm (2 ft) between plants. The more fertile your soil, the wider the spacing. Trim off any dead or dying leaves and keep the plants watered in dry weather until growth stops in autumn.

Maintenance

Strawberries are heavy with juice and droop to the ground as they ripen; a mulch of straw at this stage will keep the fruit clean. You will also need to net your crop, as blackbirds will have their beady eyes on those fruits and are no more patient than children – pecking at the fruit even before it is fully ripe.

After cropping, trim all foliage to 10 cm (4 in) or so of stalk, and remove runners, unless you are planning to propagate your own crowns. Clear away the straw mulch and compost the lot, mixing in some lawn mowings to ensure a hot heap.

Perpetual-cropping or remontant strawberries

The strawberry season is usually over by August, but can be extended by growing remontant varieties. These will, if left to their own devices, crop heavily in summer and sporadically through till the autumn. To make best use of them, however, it is best to deblossom the summer flush; this will improve the size of the late crop, which will ripen over a long period from August or earlier onwards, although you will never be able to pick a great many at a time. A cloche covering from mid-September will extend the season.

RECIPE IDEAS

Use when ripe and at their best raw in fruit salads, tarts, pastries and cakes, or better still just on their own with a sprinkling of sugar or freshly ground black pepper; surplus or slightly imperfect fruit can be used to flavour drinks, sauces, fools, ice creams and mousses; alternatively, use alone or with other fruits to make a good selection of preserves.

See: **Bottled Fruit Salad,
Strawberry and Kiwi Pavlova.**

Suggested varieties

Pantagruella (early; best for indoor cropping). Tamella (early/mid), Cambridge Vigour (early/mid), Redgauntlet (will produce a second crop in the south, resistant to mildew), Hapil (good on dry, light soils), Cambridge Favourite (less susceptible to mildew and botrytis), Saladin (resistant to red core, mildew and botrytis), Troubadour (resistant to red core, wilt and leaf mildew).
Remontants: Aromel (good flavour, susceptible to botrytis), Selva.

Pests

Birds, slugs, aphids, red spider mite.

Diseases

Botrytis, mildew, virus.

Raspberries

As your gorged palate is tiring of summer-sweet strawberries, the raspberries come to the rescue with a succession of fruiting from July until the frosts wither the autumn-fruiting crop. Raspberries will not grow well on thin chalk soils or heavy clays, and may suffer iron deficiency on alkaline soils with young leaves yellowing between veins and branches dying back. Under good conditions, however, raspberries will keep cropping for up to twelve years before they need replacing, so attention to good soil preparation is essential (for general information on soil preparation for fruit see p. 140).

Planting

The canes will need the protection of a fruit cage and the support of permanent posts and wires. The simplest system is a line of uprights with 1.5 m (5 ft) above ground and 45 cm (18 in) below. End posts are braced with posts set at 45° and butted against a brick under the surface. Taut wires are stretched between the posts at 60 cm, 105 cm and 150 cm (2 ft, 3½ ft and 5 ft respectively).

Buy canes of certified stock and plant them out 40 cm (15 in) apart and 1.8–2 m (6–7 ft) between rows, with the

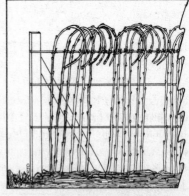

Raspberry training

root system just below the soil surface. This is best done in November, but should not be left later than the end of March. After planting, trim back the cane to a bud at about 23 cm (9 in) if this has not already been done by the nursery.

In spring, as soon as any new growth is apparent, cut back the old cane to soil level. As new canes grow, tie them into the wires. By May the soil is warm and it is time to mulch it with a layer of whole newspapers opened out flat and overlapping, leaving a gap of 15 cm (6 in) either side of the canes for new growth to develop. Cover the newspaper with straw or hay and you will then only need to weed the central strip. Raspberries are particularly vulnerable to drought in their first season, so ensure that adequate water is supplied in dry weather.

Maintenance

In the second season the few first-year canes will fruit and a new full crop of vigorous canes will start to push upwards. These should be thinned in June to allow six to eight to each stool. During April and early May, hoe off or pull out any young shoots (spawn) that develop away from the established row, then replace the mulch to keep spawn and weeds in check for the rest of the season. Any spawn that breaks through the mulch or is surplus to the selected canes should be removed at soil level.

After fruiting cut out the fruited canes, leaving no stub, and tie in the new. In September or October arch over any very long tips and tie them in to the top wire to reduce wind damage. These can be cut back to a bud 10–15 cm (4–6 in) above the top wire in late February or early March.

Autumn-fruiting raspberries

Some varieties of raspberry will fruit on current season's growth late in the season. Generally these fruit too late to ripen in the colder areas of the country, but one or two varieties are suitable for the north provided that they are well sheltered. Canes do not need tying in, but may need the support of lengths of twine down the sides of the row to prevent wind damage.

Initial training in the first year is the same as for summer-fruiting types, but in February each year all canes are cut out to ground level. As new canes develop, restrict them to a band 30–45 cm (12–18 in) wide, thinning canes to about 5 cm (2 in) apart, removing the weakest first.

RECIPE IDEAS

Serve very much like strawberries, raw as a dessert fruit with a sprinkling of sugar if liked and cream; and in drinks like Sauternes and champagne. Cooked, they are popular in jams and jellies; to flavour cordials and liqueurs; to make sauces for fruit; purées for ice cream, water ices and parfaits; or layered into tarts and other pastries.

See: **Raspberry Vinegar,
Piquant Raspberry Jam,
Gooseberry and Raspberry Jam with Sherry.**

Pests

Aphids, raspberry beetle, cane midge.

Diseases

Cane spot, cane blight, spur blight, virus, botrytis.

Suggested varieties

EARLY Glen Moy (resistant to aphids), Malling Promise (tolerant of virus).

MID-SEASON Malling Jewel (tolerant of virus), Glen Prosen (resistant to aphids), Malling Admiral (resistant to spur blight and cane botrytis, but susceptible to cane spot and aphids).

LATE Malling Joy (resistant to aphids), Leo (resistant to aphids).

Autumn-fruiting: Zeva, Autumn Bliss (resistant to aphids; early enough for northern gardens).

Blackberries and Hybrid Berries

If you don't mind your blackberries being polluted by car exhaust or chemical spraydrift, then you will be content to pick a free harvest from the hedgerows. The wide range of cultivated blackberries and hybrid berries now available, however, allows you to grow your own organically and choose the season when you want them ready. Cultivated blackberries are excellent value for space as they crop heavily, but most need too much room for very small gardens. There is now a certification scheme for blackberries, guaranteeing stock free from virus.

Planting

Follow the general directions for soil preparation given on p. 140. Blackberries and hybrid berries have similar requirements to raspberries and are not happy on poor shallow soils, particularly if they are very alkaline. Blackberries will tolerate light shading for part of the day but ideally you should choose a sheltered sunny spot, giving hybrid berries all the sunshine they can get. Northern gardeners should avoid late-ripening varieties such as Oregon Thornless unless they can provide a warm south-facing wall.

The canes will need strong support for their bumper crops either against a wall or on a free-standing structure similar to that described for raspberries but taller. Wires should be spaced 30 cm (12 in) apart, starting 90 cm (3 ft) from the ground and finishing at 1.8 m (6 ft). Allow space for canes to be trained in opposite directions in alternate years (see overleaf).

Plant out the crowns during the dormant season, ideally in November, with the fat new buds just below the soil surface, adding a little bonemeal to the planting soil. The chart below shows spacing requirements for different varieties. Cut back any canes – if not already done by the nursery – to a bud about 20–25 cm (8–10 in) from the ground. As soon as growth starts in spring these canes should be removed completely to soil level. In May mulch the crowns with a thick layer of hay, straw or strawy manure, using cardboard or newspaper underneath if weeds are troublesome.

Training blackberries & hybrid berries

FAN

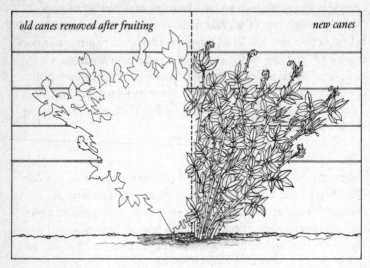

old canes removed after fruiting

new canes

ROPING

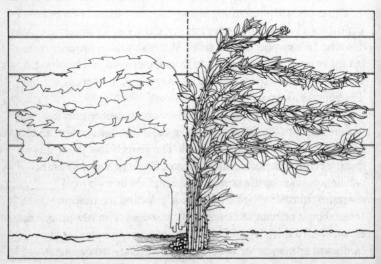

WEAVING

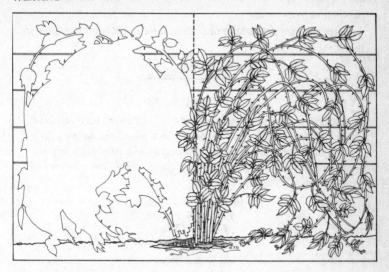

Maintenance

The canes will be growing very rapidly by midsummer, up to 30 cm (12 in) every week, and will need tying in frequently. Arrange your planting so that all the new canes can be trained into one direction or 'bay'. Next year's canes will then be trained into the alternate bay, so preventing old canes from cross-infecting new ones with any disease (see diagram). Very stiff-caned varieties such as Oregon Thornless, Boysenberry or King's Acre Berry are best trained into a fan shape – or, with care, into 'ropes' or bundles of canes. 'Roping' suits most varieties, but the most vigorous, such as Marionberry and Ashton Cross, will need to be bent and tied in up and down the wires in a method known as 'weaving' (see diagram). This makes best use of space but is time-consuming. Where space is limited fruiting canes can be trained either side each year with new canes bundled together and tied in vertically until old canes have been removed.

Each year in May, top up the mulch. No other feeding should be necessary if the soil was well-prepared but if deficiency symptoms were apparent in the previous season, remedy them with the appropriate organic fertiliser before mulching. Ripe fruits will need protection from birds.

After fruiting cut out the old canes, shred them and put them in the compost heap.

RECIPE IDEAS

Use plump, ripe fruit as a dessert fruit or in fruit salads and drinks. Tart fruit needs cooking for summer-style puddings, pie-fillings, compotes, fools, tarts and other fruit desserts. Used alone or with other fruits they also make wonderful jams, jellies and fruit cheeses; wines, fruit vinegars and punch ingredients.

See: **Blackberry and Apple Curd,**
Bottled Fruit Salad,
Bramble Cheese,
Piquant Raspberry Jam.

Suggested varieties

Variety	Pick	Spacing	Weave, Rope or Fan	Description
Blackberries				
BEDFORD GIANT	July	4.5 m (15 ft)	Weave	Vigorous, very large berry.
HIMALAYAN GIANT	July/Aug	4.5 m (15 ft)	Weave	Very thorny, heavy cropping.
MERTON THORNLESS	July/Aug	2 m (6½ ft)	Rope/ Fan	Best for smaller gardens.
ASHTON CROSS	Aug	3.5 m (11½ ft)	Weave/ Rope	Virus resistant.
MARIONBERRY	Aug/Sep	3.5 m (11½ ft)	Weave/ Rope	Heavy cropping, good flavour.
OREGON THORNLESS	Sep/Nov	2 m (6½ ft)	Rope/ Fan	Acid flavour. Ornamental foliage. Not for cold gardens.

Hybrid Berries

KING'S ACRE BERRY	July/Aug	3.5 m (11½ ft)	Rope	Dark red fruit. Blackberry flavour.
LOGANBERRY LY59	July/Aug	2.5 m (8 ft)	Rope	For preserving. Pick when dark red.
LOGANBERRY L654	July/Aug	2.5 m (8 ft)	Rope	Thornless variant of above.
SUNBERRY	July/Aug	4.5 m (15 ft)	Weave	Vigorous and spiny. Dark red fruit of good flavour.
TAYBERRY	July/Aug	2.5 m (8 ft)	Fan/ Rope	Large sweet fruit for preserves and jams.
TUMMELBERRY	late July/ Aug	2.5 m (8 ft)	Fan/ Rope	More acid and hardier than Tayberry.
BOYSENBERRY	July/Aug	2.5 m (8 ft)	Fan/ Rope	Thornless form available. Tolerates drought. Fruits large, purple.

Pests

Aphids, raspberry beetle, birds.

Diseases

Cane spot, spur blight, purple blotch.

Gooseberies *(Jostaberries and Worcesterberries)*

Gooseberries can sometimes be the cinderellas of the garden,
ignored for most of the year and undervalued as a fruit.
Picked before they are fully ripe, the fruits do not yield up their
true, surprisingly sweet flavour. Gooseberries make excellent jams
and preserves and are usually the first fruits of the garden to reach
the kitchen, but it is well worth leaving a good proportion of the
crop to ripen fully if you are growing a dessert variety.

Planting

Gooseberries do not have a high nitrogen requirement and should
receive less manure than that recommended for general soil

preparation before fruit (see p. 140). Excess nitrogen will encourage over-exuberant growth, leaving bushes prone to wind damage and mildew.

Try to buy plants with a 'leg', 15 cm (6 in) of clear stem before branches develop. Plant bushes up to the original soil mark, removing any suckers or buds developing from below this point. Gooseberries can be grown as bushes, cordons, fans or even espaliers and spacing will vary according to the shape. Bushes should be 1.3–1.5 m (4–5 ft) apart, fans and espaliers 1.8 m (6 ft) and cordons 30 cm (1 ft) apart. Birds are not fussy about the shape of the bush but enjoy the fruit, so the gooseberries will need to be inside the fruit cage. In May each year mulch the fruit with hay or straw to restrict weeds and retain moisture.

Pruning and Training

BUSH After planting, cut back each leader by about half to an upward or downward bud depending on the growth habit of the variety. Cut out any growth protruding into the centre or arising on the leg.

In the next winter, continue this formative pruning to leave good, strong leaders. Any laterals forming on these are pruned back to three or four buds and the centre is kept clear. Pull off any suckers growing round the base of the bush and keep the leg free of growth.

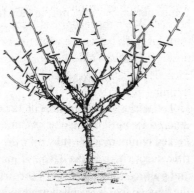

From now on, pruning is done in summer and winter. Summer pruning is not

Winter pruning of a three-year-old bush

essential, but helps greatly in reducing susceptibility to mildew and removing the aphids that often infest the tips. Towards the end of June shorten all new laterals to five leaves, pull out any suckers, but leave leaders unpruned. In winter these laterals are further shortened to three or four buds, weak and crossing shoots are removed and leaders reduced by about a half. After several years, growth can become rather congested and the ageing leaders less productive. Leave suitable laterals nearer the centre to grow on as replacement leaders and prune out the old wood back to these in the following winter.

CORDON Single cordons are treated as single upright branches of a bush for pruning purposes, but need to be tied in to a vertical cane attached to a permanent framework of wires, similar to that used for cordon apples (see p. 147). After planting prune back the centre leader by half and all laterals to three buds. Any shoots less than 15 cm (6 in) from the soil should be removed entirely. Subsequent pruning consists in spur-pruning laterals to three buds and tipping back the leader by a quarter each winter. Summer pruning is carried out as normal. When the leader has reached 1.8 m (6 ft), prune it back each winter to two or three buds or into older wood if it later exceeds its space. Eventually spurs will need thinning or shortening.

GOOSEBERRY – CORDON

Initial pruning

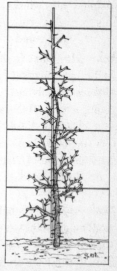

Well established

To make a double cordon allow twice the spacing, three times for a triple cordon. The double cordon is created by training two shoots at 90° to the stem in opposite directions and removing the central leader. In the next winter cut back these shoots to about 15 cm (6 in) at an upward-facing bud. These buds then produce the two stems, all other growth being discouraged. If the centre leader is left intact and the two arms shortened to 30 cm (1 ft), a triple cordon results.

FANS AND ESPALIERS Fans and espaliers are created in much the same way as for apples (see p. 147), but following the pruning methods used for gooseberry cordons adapted to suit the shape. Arms of the espaliers should be 30 cm (12 in) apart.

Pests

Birds, sawfly, aphids.

Diseases

American gooseberry mildew, botrytis.

RECIPE IDEAS

Sweet, ripe fruit can be eaten raw and plain as a dessert fruit, dipped in fondant as a sweetmeat or added to fruit salad mixtures. Smaller, more acid fruit is best stewed for pies and puddings, cooked to a purée for a sauce for oily fish like mackerel; or used in jams and other preserves.

See: **Gooseberry and Raspberry Jam with Sherry.**

Suggested varieties

Early: May Duke (red, susceptible to mildew), Golden Drop (yellow/green, good flavour).
Mid-season: Jubilee (heavy cropper, virus-free stock, best picked green), Crown Bob (red, spreading habit), Whitesmith (large pale fruit, excellent flavour), Invicta (best grown as cordon or espalier, very resistant to mildew; for culinary use).
Late: Captivator (relatively thorn-free; small, sweet red fruit), Lancashire Lad (dark red, some resistance to mildew).

Jostaberry is a cross between blackcurrant and gooseberry, producing a spine-free, vigorous bush with fruits shaped like a large blackcurrant and with the flavour you might expect from such a cross. It is not susceptible to mildew but is attacked by sawfly. The *Worcesterberry* is not a hybrid but an independent species very similar to gooseberry, if rather more vigorous. Fruit is small, purple, abundant and excellent for jam and preserves. Worcesterberry is not usually susceptible to mildew but is attacked by sawfly.

Redcurrants *(and whitecurrants)*

Brightest jewels of the kitchen garden must be the redcurrants. Whitecurrants are simply a white mutant form and are treated in precisely the same way as the red. Redcurrants are tough, reliable, relatively free of pests, virus and disease and usually survive to a venerable age. Advice given for gooseberries (see p. 175) is generally also applicable to redcurrants.

Planting

(*See* Gooseberries.) Space bushes 1.5 m (5 ft), single cordons 40 cm (15 in) and fans 1.8 m (6 ft) apart.

Pruning and Training

Summer pruning of redcurrants is carried out from the last week of June and follows the same principles as for gooseberries (see p. 176). Winter pruning can be more severe than for gooseberries, with spurs pruned back to one or two buds and leaders reduced to 8 cm (3 in) of current season's growth once the established framework is fully formed.

RECIPE IDEAS

Strip from their stems and use raw in fruit salads, tarts, pastries, drinks, punches and cake fillings; use cooked in fools, ice creams, compotes, summer-style puddings and fruit soups; alternatively use to make jams, jellies and other preserves.

See: **Redcurrant Vinegar, Bottled Fruit Salad.**

Pests

Aphids, birds, gooseberry sawfly.

Diseases

Few of importance.

Suggested varieties

Early: Jonkheer van Tets, Laxton's No. 1.
Mid-season: Red Lake.
Late: Rondom, Redstart.

Whitecurrants

White Versailles, White Pearl, White Dutch.

Blackcurrants

Health-conscious gardeners
would do well to find space for a
blackcurrant bush or two. The
berries have an extremely high
vitamin C content and the pips
are now commercially processed
to produce an expensive and
valuable food supplement.

Planting

*(Also see general information on soil
preparation for fruit, p. 140.)* Unlike
redcurrants, blackcurrants fruit
on one-year-old wood, and so
are grown as a stool with
branches initiating mainly from
below soil level. They cannot be
grown as cordons or fans. Since
pruning can be quite hard,

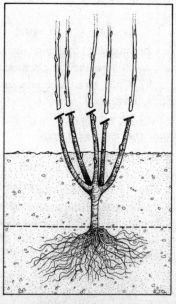

Planting a blackcurrant

blackcurrants need help in producing regular annual supplies of new wood. They may benefit from some additional hoof and horn at planting time at the rate of 125 gm per sq m (4 oz per sq yd), and annual dressings of compost or manure in spring if you are not using any other heavy organic mulch.

Blackcurrants should be planted inside the protection of a fruit cage as the fruit is a great favourite of several species of birds. Certified bushes up to three years old can be bought. Regardless of age they should be planted, preferably in November or December, several centimetres deeper than the previous soil mark to encourage formation of extra roots and branching from below soil level. Distance between plants should not normally be less than 1.5 m (5 ft). It is possible, however, to plant bushes as close as 75 cm (2½ ft) within a row, with rows 1.8 m (6 ft) apart for most varieties. This maximises early yields but needs quite severe pruning to prevent bushes invading each other's space in later years.

Pruning

After planting, cut back all branches to one or two buds above soil level. After this no pruning will be necessary until after the bush carries its first crop in the second summer after planting, except for one-year-olds, which are pruned back to two buds for a second year.

Annual pruning is carried out either directly after fruiting or early in the autumn. With the exception of Malling Jet, which does better with light pruning, bushes benefit from fairly severe treatment. Cut out a quarter to a third of the wood each year, pruning out whole branches to soil level, starting with those lying closest to the soil and continuing with the oldest dark-coloured branches. Any weak or withered shoots

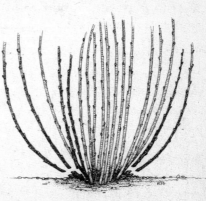

Blackcurrant pruning

181

should be completely removed.

Pests

Big bud mite, aphids, leaf midge.

Diseases

Reversion virus, gooseberry mildew.

Suggested varieties

Mid-season: Ben Nevis (R), Ben Lomond (v. large berries).
Late: Ben More (R), Ben Sarek (R) (compact bush), Malling Jet (R)
(very late – prune only one-fifth of wood each year).

(R) = resistant to gooseberry mildew.

━━━━━━

RECIPE IDEAS

*Strip from their stems and use raw or cooked in fruit salads and compotes;
if sweet, cooked or raw in tarts, pies and pastries; cooked in water ices, ice
creams and sorbets; preserved as jams, jellies, syrups and vinegars; and in
whole host of baked, steamed and boiled fruit puddings.*

See: **Apple and Blackcurrant Jam,
Bottled Fruit Salad,
Blackcurrant Syrup,
Blackcurrant Vinegar.**

━━━━━━

12. Common Pests and Diseases of Fruit

CROP	Pests
	(*For details of pest control and sprays see p. 30.*)

All fruits

Aphids Sap-sucking. Dense clusters under leaves and at shoot tips.
CONTROL Encourage beneficial insects (see p. 20). Choose resistant varieties. Summer prune. *Sprays*: Insecticidal soap, derris, pyrethrum.

Blackcurrants

Big bud mite Microscopic mites cause buds to become round and swollen by winter. Carries reversion virus.
CONTROL Pick off affected buds in winter and burn or prune out whole branches if necessary. Severely affected plants are best replaced. Spraying generally ineffective.

All fruit; gooseberry, cherry & plum buds in winter

Birds Bullfinches may feed on dormant fruit buds, other birds enjoy ripe fruit.
CONTROL Net all fruit. Black cotton thread will protect buds (put in place by January). Protect individual fruits such as apples with muslin or brown paper bags.

Raspberries

Cane midge Areas of dead tissue on lower part of canes show last year's feeding sites. Larvae feed under cracks in bark.

CONTROL Cultivate soil lightly between rows to expose pupae. Malling Jewel and Malling Promise are most susceptible. *Spray*: Derris or pyrethrum in May and again after ten days.

All fruit

Capsid bug Feeds on leaves, leaving tattered holes. Apples show raised bumps and malformations, leaf and bud damage.
CONTROL Pest hard to find but damage seldom disastrous. *Spray*: Derris or pyrethrum if necessary.

Pears, sometimes apples

Leaf blister mites Feed on young leaves causing pink or yellow blisters, turning dark brown later.
CONTROL Pick off affected leaves. Damage can be tolerated.

Blackcurrants

Blackcurrant leaf midge White or orange grubs infest shoot tips, causing distortion and blackening.
CONTROL Avoid susceptible varieties (Wellington XXX, Seabrook's Black, Baldwin). Encourage beneficial predatory anthocorids. *Spray*: Insecticidal soap, but not derris or pyrethrum, which kills anthocorids.

Apples
Pears
Plums

Codling moth Larvae tunnel into maturing fruits (mainly apples) usually from calyx or base in June and July.
CONTROL Use traps (see p. 27). Large catches indicate need to spray. *Spray*: Derris or pyrethrum (see instruction on traps for timing).

Apples
Cherries
Pears
Plums

Winter moth, March moth and plum fruit moth Eggs laid October to March. 'Loopers' hatch to feed on unopened buds, and later on

blossom and young leaves. Wingless females crawl up trunk to lay eggs.
CONTROL Greaseband trunks and stakes in early October and renew if necessary until March. Pick off 'loopers'. *Spray*: Try pyrethrum or *Bacillus thuringiensis* at bud-burst and twice more at fortnightly intervals (more frequently in very wet weather).

Pears

Pear midge Black, distorted fruitlets infested with creamy-coloured larvae fall early. Varieties in flowering groups 2 and 3 most susceptible.
CONTROL Attacks often confined to one or two trees. Pick up and burn affected fruitlets. Mulch below tree canopy with black polythene, cardboard or carpet to prevent adults emerging.

Blackberries
Loganberries
Raspberries

Raspberry beetle Larvae feed on ripening fruit. Common but not inevitable.
CONTROL Spray fruitlets with derris at or after dusk at petal fall and again at pink fruit stage if larvae present the previous year.

Apples
(also plum sawfly on plums)

Apple sawfly Larvae feed on developing fruit, moving from one fruit to another. They leave wet frass round entry hole. Eggs laid April and May.
CONTROL Affected fruitlets fall early. Collect up all fallen fruit after June drop and put in hot compost heap. *Spray*: Derris or pyrethrum at dusk a week after petal fall and again ten days later.

Gooseberry
Jostaberry
Redcurrant
Worcesterberry

Gooseberry sawfly Up to four generations each year. First eggs laid in April in white ribbons under leaves along veins. First signs: leaves towards inside of bush riddled with pin-holes. Larvae later spread to strip whole bushes, developing into large 'caterpillars'.

CONTROL Pick off leaves with eggs or tiny larvae present. Hand-pick larger larvae. Inspect bushes weekly from early April. *Spray*: Derris at first signs of attack. Repeat as necessary.

Apples
Cherries
Pears

Cherry slugworm Small, shiny larvae reminiscent of slugs. Feed on upper surface of leaves, leaving silvered trails. Two hatches: May/June and July/August.
CONTROL Pick off affected leaves if larvae small. *Spray*: Derris or insecticidal soap at first signs of damage.

Strawberries
(and others)

Slugs Mainly feed on fruit trailing on ground and especially strawberries.
CONTROL Keep fruit off soil where possible. Hand-pick slugs after dark. Use traps.

Apples
Pears
Plums

Wasps A nuisance in late summer and early autumn, otherwise beneficial.
CONTROL Find nest and puff derris dust down entrance after dark. Hang jars of sticky juice in trees. Protect individual fruits.

Apples
Pears
Plums

Leaf weevils Large insects with pointed snouts and metallic sheen. Feed on young leaves and blossom in May and June. Not usually serious, but in large numbers can be damaging.
CONTROL Tolerate light damage. Suck up pests with small hand-held vacuum cleaner. *Spray*: Derris at dusk or later.

CROP	# Diseases
Apples	**Bitter pit** Small sunken depressions on the skin and dark patches of inner flesh. Caused by calcium deficiency usually through water shortage or metabolic malfunction. CONTROL Keep trees well mulched. *Spray*: Seaweed foliar feeds may help if problem is recurrent.
Blackberries Gooseberries Raspberries Strawberries and Hybrids	**Botrytis** A rotting disease prevalent in wet seasons, causing (a) brown, rotten fruit (especially strawberries); (b) die-back of branches or bushes (especially gooseberries). CONTROL Do not plant too densely. Remove affected fruit immediately. Prune hard where die-back occurs. Remove and burn severely affected bushes.
Apples Cherries Pears Plums	**Brown rot** Soft brown patches spread over mature fruits, followed by whitish spots. Fruits shrivel and hang on tree all winter. May affect blossom and spur tips. CONTROL Remove and destroy all affected fruit and do not allow 'mummified' fruits to hang on tree. Prune out affected spurs and blossom.
Blackberries Raspberries and Hybrid berries	**Cane spot and purple blotch** Two conditions with similar appearance. Purple-edged grey-white spots on stems and leaves. Loganberry fruits grow one-sided. Premature leaf-fall. CONTROL Raspberry Norfolk Giant and Lloyd George and blackberry Himalayan Giant are susceptible. Damage is seldom severe, but badly affected plants should be removed and burnt.

Spray: Bordeaux mixture (see p. 30) when buds are
1 ½ cm (½ in) long, and again when flower-tips
just visible.

Raspberries

Cane blight Leaves wither, canes die and become
brittle. Often gains entry after cane midge damage
(see p. 183). Disease carried in soil.
CONTROL Lloyd George and Norfolk Giant are
susceptible. Cut out affected canes below soil level
and burn them. Disinfect pruning tool afterwards.
Spray: Bordeaux mixture (see p. 30) as canes grow.

Apples
Pears

Canker Sunken lesions on limbs and spurs, often
surrounding a spur or leaf-scar. Branches can be
girdled. Can be serious.
CONTROL Avoid Lord Lambourne, but Bramley's
Seedling and Newton Wonder have some
resistance. Inspect trees regularly and prune out
diseased tissue back to healthy wood. Burn
prunings and disinfect tools. Paint cuts with
Trichoderma paste (see p. 30).

Cherries
Plums

Bacterial canker Shallow depressions on the
trunk or branches ooze gum, leaves yellow,
branches die back. Secondary symptoms show as
'shot-holing' of leaves.
CONTROL 'Gumming' without other symptoms
does not necessarily indicate bacterial canker.
Victoria and Early Laxton are susceptible.
Marjorie's Seedling and Belle de Louvain are less
susceptible. Rootstock F12/1 for cherries or
Myrobalan for plums gives resistance but both are
very vigorous. Prune out all diseased tissue. Treat
cuts with paste of Bordeaux mixture. *Spray*:
Bordeaux mixture in mid-August, two weeks later
and in early October.

Apples
Pears

Fireblight Devastating. Blossom withers, leaves turn brown-black and hang limply from tree as if scorched. Spreads rapidly. Also affects hawthorn, pyracantha, cotoneaster and other ornamentals.
CONTROL Local MAFF branch must be informed by law. They will advise treatment.

Apples

Apple mildew Powdery coating on young leaves and blossom early in season. May cause eventual defoliation.
CONTROL Choose more resistant varieties. Remove all mildewed wood in winter. Pick off or prune out affected shoots or leaves in spring.

Blackcurrant
Gooseberry

Gooseberry mildew White powdery coating on leaves and shoots turns brown. Eventually affects fruits. First signs may be in April, but usually from June onwards.
CONTROL Use resistant varieties. Do not crowd plantings and summer prune gooseberries. Prune out affected shoots. Do not overfeed bushes. *Spray*: Bicarbonate of soda from just before flowering at weekly or fortnightly intervals until July or later if necessary.

Apples
Pears

Scab Very common on apples, especially old or neglected trees. Brown to dark green discoloured patches appear on leaves, eventually turning black. Leaves may fall prematurely. Fruits covered in dark spots which may crack but do not cause rotting.
CONTROL Grow resistant varieties. Regular pruning and good hygiene important. Run a rotary mower over fallen leaves to speed decomposition and prevent spores returning to tree. (Affected fruit is still edible, although pears may be distorted.)

Cherries
Plums

Silverleaf Silver sheen to leaves starting locally and spreading. Whole tree may be affected. Branches die back and show brown staining of wood.
CONTROL Silvering of leaves is also caused by nutritional disorder (rectify by feeding and mulching). Look for die-back and staining to verify disease. Cut out affected tissue to healthy unstained wood and burn. Grub out and burn severe cases. Avoid pruning from October to April. Paint all wounds with Trichoderma paste. Affected trees may be completely cured with Trichoderma pellets.

Loganberries
Raspberries

Spur blight Purple, spreading blotches of varying size and length appear round buds on new canes from August onwards. They turn silvery-white by winter. Buds may die.
CONTROL Looks worse than it is and crop may not be much reduced. If infection light, prune out affected canes. Keep canes thinned from early on. Malling Admiral and Leo less susceptible.

All fruit

Virus Sickly, weak growth; strange malformations, distortions or discolourations of leaves; poor fruiting.
CONTROL Remove and burn whole plant immediately. Always buy stock that carries a MAFF certificate. Choose resistant or tolerant varieties.

13. The Year in the Garden

This monthly calendar is meant as a rough guide and reminder. There are no precise dates in garden work, and the season will vary throughout the country by as much as a month at either end. Sowings into cold damp soil are much more prone to disease and hungry wildlife than later sowings, which will rapidly catch up anyway. Sowings in the greenhouse can also be too early and plants can be overflowing the benches, begging to go out into an environment which is still too cold and hostile for them.

January

Vegetables
Continue to fill compost trenches.
Check through vegetables in store.
Order seeds and look out for seed potatoes.
Plant out rhubarb crowns if conditions are favourable.
Bring in seakale, witloof chicory and rhubarb for forcing. Cover outdoor plants of seakale and rhubarb with forcing pots. Take seakale cuttings.

Herbs
Complete clearing of dead foliage, etc.

Fruit
Check through stored fruit.
Plant out trees, canes and bushes if conditions are favourable.

Protect susceptible fruit buds from birds. Continue winter pruning in mild spells.

February

Vegetables

Continue to fill compost trenches.

Check through vegetables in store. Continue forcing seakale, chicory and rhubarb.

Set out seed potatoes to chit.

SOWING: IN THE GREENHOUSE – broad beans, greenhouse tomatoes, celeriac, onions, Brussels sprouts, globe artichokes, lettuce.

IN THE GREENHOUSE BORDER OR POLYTUNNEL – spinach, carrots, radish, spring onions.

OUTDOORS – shallots, turnips (protected), garlic.

Fruit

Continue planting out if conditions are favourable.

Renew greasebands and check apples and pears for canker.

Check through stored fruit.

Complete winter pruning in mild spells. Carry out formative pruning of newly planted plums and cherries. Prune out autumn-fruiting and tips of summer-fruiting raspberries.

March

Vegetables

Dress plots with lime, manure or compost as necessary.

Dig in green manures and prepare seedbeds. Sow mustard on vacant land waiting for brassicas.

Cover prepared seedbeds with polythene in dry weather.

Plant out Jerusalem artichokes, early potatoes, onion and shallot sets, autumn-sown cauliflower, asparagus crowns, globe artichokes.

SOWING: IN THE GREENHOUSE – broad beans, peas, lettuce, Brussels sprouts, cabbage, summer cauliflower, multi-sown beetroot, celeriac, onions, skirret, celery, early salads, asparagus.

IN THE GREENHOUSE BORDER – early cutting salads, radish.

OUTDOORS – Brussels sprouts, summer cabbage, kohlrabi, turnip, leeks, carrots, chard, onions, spring onions, parsnips, salsify and scorzonera, spinach, leaf beet, cutting salads, lettuce, radish.

Herbs

If not done in autumn: lift and replant mint and tarragon; chop round sorrel, fennel and lovage roots.

SOW Chives, fennel, lovage, salad burnet, parsley and sorrel.

Fruit

Complete planting out of bushes, canes and trees.

Cut out fruited canes of autumn-fruiting raspberries and tip back summer-fruiting varieties if not done in February.

Complete all winter pruning and prune established acid cherries.

Carry out any feeding or liming necessary.

Start weekly inspections of fruit for pests and diseases.

Spray or pick off as necessary. Spray gooseberries and blackcurrants for mildew just before blossom opens and continue at least fortnightly. Spray canes for cane spot as buds elongate.

Protect blossom in frosty weather.

April

Vegetables

Complete digging in of over-wintered green manures.

Earth up first early potatoes to protect from frost.

Prepare celery trench. Shred or smash brassica stumps for composting.

In the greenhouse, clear away winter salads and fork manure into border soil. Take down insulation.

Erect carrotfly barriers.

PLANT OUT maincrop potatoes, artichokes (globe and Jerusalem), asparagus, seakale, lettuce seedlings, skirret plants, broad beans and peas.

SOWING: IN THE GREENHOUSE – summer cabbage, calabrese, celery, New Zealand spinach, indoor and outdoor cucumbers and gherkins, French and runner beans, peas (all types), sweetcorn, outdoor tomatoes, lettuce, nasturtiums, rhubarb, globe artichokes, seakale, melons, aubergine, Cape gooseberry, early types Chinese cabbage.

OUTDOORS – broccoli, Brussels sprouts, cabbage, calabrese, summer cauliflower, kale, kohlrabi, swede, beetroot, carrots, chard, Hamburg parsley, onions (all types), parsnips, salsify and scorzonera, corn salad, land cress and other cutting salads, endive, lettuce, radish.

Herbs

SOW fennel, all types of marjoram and oregano, basil, sorrel and thyme. Take cuttings of sage, rosemary and thyme.

Fruit

Continue routine inspections. Watch out for: aphids, capsid bugs, winter moth caterpillars, gooseberry sawfly eggs (towards end of month), mildew on apples. Continue spraying gooseberries and blackcurrants for mildew.

Remove blossom on young unformed trees.

Protect blossom in frosty weather where possible.

Remove tied-on greasebands.

PRUNING young plums and cherries, mature acid cherries.

May

Vegetables

Dig in green manure mustard ready for transplanted crop.

Weed and water as necessary, especially seedbeds.

Earth up potatoes and protect from late frosts.

Erect carrotfly barriers, pea supports and bean poles.

Pinch out broad bean tops if affected by blackfly and support plants with canes and string.

Protect brassica seedlings against flea-beetle and pigeons, and young lettuces from sparrows. Watch out for cabbage caterpillars.

PLANT OUT Brussels sprouts, cabbage, leeks, onions from seed, greenhouse tomatoes. After frosts: celeriac, celery, courgettes, marrows, etc, sweetcorn, tomatoes, cucumbers and gherkins, French and runner beans, asparagus peas, nasturtiums, New Zealand spinach.

SOWING: IN THE GREENHOUSE – broccoli, cabbage, cauliflower, kale, cucumbers, melons, Cape gooseberry, aubergine, summer purslane.

OUTDOORS – broccoli, cabbage, cauliflower, kale, kohlrabi, swede, beetroot, chard, florence fennel, Hamburg parsley, spring onions, parsnips, spinach, endive and chicory (witloof), cutting salads, lettuce, radish, broad beans, peas, Chinese cabbage (early types).

Fruit

Mulch all canes, trees and bushes.

Continue routine inspections. Watch out for: capsid bugs, winter moth, leaf weevils, apple and gooseberry sawfly and aphids. Spray for cane blight, cane spot and purple blotch, mildew on blackcurrants and gooseberries. Look out for signs of fireblight. Pick off strawberry fruits affected by botrytis and net the crop. Remove strawberry runners.

At end of month put up codling moth traps.

Deblossom young trees and protect blossom on mature trees from frost.

PRUNING leaders of mature trees in restricted shapes; shoots of fan plum and cherry growing towards or away from the wall; unwanted young raspberry canes.

Start picking gooseberries to thin fruit and pick early strawberries.

June

Vegetables

Weed and water as necessary.

Support peas, broad beans, standard tomatoes, asparagus ferns, artichokes as necessary.

Watch out for early signs of pests and diseases. Protect brassica transplants with rootfly mats.

Earth up maincrop potatoes. Pinch out tomato sideshoots and prune and train indoor cucumbers and melons.

Shade greenhouse.

PLANT OUT broccoli, Brussels sprouts, cabbage, celeriac, celery, courgettes, marrows, other squashes, sweetcorn, outdoor tomatoes, summer purslane, leeks, nasturtiums.

SOWING kohlrabi, pak choy, beetroot, carrots, chard, florence fennel, spring onions, peas, asparagus peas, chicories, endives, cutting salads, radishes, lettuce.

Fruit

Continue regular checks for pests and diseases and check codling moth traps frequently. Keep fruit weeded and watered.

Start thinning pear and plum fruitlets.

Continue thinning gooseberries for cooking.

Thin raspberry canes. Tie in canes of blackberries and hybrid berries. Spray for raspberry beetle if necessary.

Put up fruit-cage netting.

Remove strawberry runners.

PRUNING Summer prune gooseberries and redcurrants. Thin out laterals on fan-trained acid cherries.

PICK strawberries and early raspberries, sweet cherries.

July

Vegetables

Weed and water as necessary. Check for pests and diseases.

Support peas. Tie in and deshoot tomatoes, cucumbers and melons as necessary.

Pinch out the tops of standard outdoor tomatoes at end of month.

Straw down bush tomatoes and mulch crops wherever necessary.

Start harvesting potatoes and self-blanching celery.

Lift, dry and store shallots, over-wintered onions and garlic.

PLANT OUT broccoli, cauliflower, kale, pak choy, leeks.

SOWING spring cabbage, Chinese cabbage, kohlrabi, pak choy, turnips, carrots, chard, florence fennel, leaf beet, land cress, winter purslane, corn salad, endive, lettuce, radish (summer and winter types), peas (early variety), parsley.

Fruit

Continue tying in blackberry canes and trained forms of tree or bush. Keep fruit weeded and watered.

Continue regular checks for pests and diseases. Continue spraying for gooseberry mildew and give second spray for raspberry beetle.

Thin plums, pears and apples after the 'June drop'.

When strawberries are over, remove foliage and runners to compost heap.

PRUNING Start summer pruning pears. Prune out centre leaders of newly planted plums and cherries. Pinch back laterals on trained plums and sweet cherries.

PICK strawberries, raspberries, gooseberries, redcurrants, whitecurrants, blackcurrants, loganberries and hybrid berries, early plums, sweet cherries.

August

Vegetables

Weed and water as necessary. Continue to check for pests and diseases, especially caterpillars on brassicas and blight on potatoes.

Level celery trenches.

Lift and dry onions and garlic.

Pinch out tops of outdoor tomatoes if not done in July.

Continue deshooting and training of greenhouse crops.

PLANT OUT kale, broccoli, winter cauliflower.

SOWING spring cabbage, Chinese cabbage, pak choy, turnips, leaf beet, winter spinach, chicory, land cress, winter purslane, rocket, corn salad, salad mixtures, endive, lettuce (hardy and greenhouse types), winter radish, Japanese onions.

Sow winter tares on vacant land before mid-August.

Herbs

Harvest herbs for drying.

Fruit

Keep fruit weeded and watered. Continue regular checks for pests and diseases. Watch out for scab and bacterial canker. Remove codling moth traps.

Tie down spindle laterals and continue to tie in trees and canes as necessary.

Protect fruit from birds.

Prepare strawberry bed and remove old crowns. Continue to remove any runners. Plant new crowns.

Spray for bacterial canker.

PRUNING raspberries, blackcurrants; summer pruning of apples and pears.

PICK apples, pears, plums, raspberries, gooseberries, Worcesterberries, jostaberries, redcurrants, whitecurrants, blackcurrants, strawberries, blackberries and hybrid berries.

September

Vegetables

Earth up trench celery.

Remove potato haulms early if affected by blight. Lift potatoes on a dry day for storage.

Complete lifting and drying of onions.

Watch out for frosts and cover tender crops. Once leaves withered

by frost, pick remaining sweet corn and courgettes, and remove
marrows and pumpkins to greenhouse to ripen fully before
storing. Bring in green tomatoes to ripen.

Remove and compost all dead or frosted haulms. Cloche late crops.

PLANT OUT spring cabbage, winter lettuce.

SOWING: IN THE GREENHOUSE – mustard and cress, Chinese
mustards, greenhouse lettuce.

IN THE GREENHOUSE BORDER – winter salads, summer spinach,
peas, spring onions, summer radish.

OUTDOORS – hardy lettuce, winter spinach.

Sow grazing rye on vacant land.

Herbs

Harvest herbs for drying.

Take cuttings of sage.

Fruit

Cloche late strawberries and plant new crowns.

Clean boxes ready for fruit storing.

After fruiting, cut out fruited canes of raspberry, blackberry and
hybrid berry and tie in new ones.

Look out for canker and bacterial canker, final hatch of gooseberry
sawfly.

Spray for bacterial canker.

PRUNING plums, sweet cherries, blackcurrants; summer pruning of
apples and pears.

PICK apples, pears, plums, acid cherries, strawberries, raspberries,
blackberries, Worcesterberries.

October

Vegetables

Clear away crop debris to compost heap regularly.

Harvest remaining greenhouse tomatoes, cucumbers, etc, clear away
haulms and growbags. Wash down glass and benches, ventilate the

greenhouse thoroughly and put up insulation. Fork manure or
compost into greenhouse borders.

Earth up celery.

Lift and store carrots, beetroot, turnips and other roots.

Protect celeriac, carrots (if not lifted) and globe artichokes with
straw or bracken.

Lift potatoes if not done in September.

Cloche outdoor winter salads, protect cauliflower curds.

Dig and manure or lime plots where appropriate.

Lift witloof chicory roots for forcing and blanch some endives.

PLANT OUT spring cabbage, garlic, autumn onion sets; indoor
crops of winter salads, pak choy.

SOWING: IN THE GREENHOUSE – summer cauliflower, winter
lettuce.

IN THE GREENHOUSE BORDER – rocket, coriander, fenugreek,
salad rape.

OUTDOORS – broad beans, early peas.

Sow grazing rye on vacant land.

Herbs

Start clearing up plant debris. Lift and replant mint, also marjoram
and tarragon if necessary; bring in some mint roots for early
cropping.

Chop round sorrel and lovage roots. Dress beds with leaf-mould.

Fruit

Bring in apples and pears to store as appropriate, picking all fruit if
severe frost threatens.

Run rotary mower over fallen leaves of top fruit or spray with liquid
manure.

Tidy up strawberry beds and mulch with compost. Complete
planting up of new crowns.

Order new fruit trees and bushes and prepare sites for planting.

Check tree ties. Complete tying in of blackberries and trained fruit.

Check apples and pears for canker, plums and cherries for bacterial
canker.

Before end of month, apply greasebands.

Spray for bacterial canker.

PRUNING blackcurrants, any soft growth following summer
pruning of apples and pears, fruited blackberry canes.

PICK apples, pears, plums, strawberries, raspberries, blackberries.

November

Vegetables

Continue to clear away crop debris, including asparagus ferns and
Jerusalem artichoke stalks.

Lift celeriac if severe frost threatens.

Complete digging and manuring. Apply lime where appropriate.

Final earthing up of celery.

Check vegetables in store.

Protect brassicas and late-sown peas and beans from birds.

PLANT OUT garlic, rhubarb crowns.

SOWING broad beans. Sow field beans for green manure.

Herbs

Complete clearing up (see October).

Fruit

Bring in to store all remaining apples and pears.

Plant out new trees, canes and bushes and prune.

Run rotary mower over fallen leaves or spray with liquid manure.

Check apples and pears for canker.

Complete pruning and tying-in of blackberries.

PRUNING formative pruning of pyramid, fan and espalier apples
and pears; winter pruning of apples, pears, gooseberries and
currants; soft growth following summer pruning of apples and
pears.

December

Vegetables

Lift and store swedes and celeriac. Lift and store some parsnips, salsify and Hamburg parsley for supplies when soil is frosted hard.

Blanch some endive and bring in some witloof chicory to force. Check stored vegetables.

Lift and divide large rhubarb crowns.

Fruit

Check fruit in store. Check apples and pears for canker.

Run rotary mower over fallen leaves or spray with liquid manure.

Plant out new trees, canes and bushes and prune.

Continue winter pruning (see November).

. . . to
Cooking
Pot

14. Cooking Methods for Vegetables

So you've planted, hoed, nurtured, fed, kept pests at bay and now harvested your crop of organic vegetables and fruit. My advice would be first to savour them at their best and simplest, either raw or simply cooked until tender. Then enjoy the delights of all your hard labours by exploring a whole host of cooking methods and recipes that will bring out the best in your fruit and vegetables in terms of variety. You won't be disappointed with the range of possibilities and cooking styles available, and should never have to tire of a vegetable or fruit through familiarity. Methods are as diverse as boiling and baking, sautéing and steaming, braising and roasting, and simmering and deep-frying. Added to which, you can serve most in the 'raw' in a multitude of ways or preserve in countless others for enjoyment the whole year round – you'll see the possibilities are boundless.

Boiling

Boiling is perhaps the most popular method of cooking vegetables. Usually salted water is used, but often this can be replaced with a flavoured stock. Root vegetables should be placed in the pan with their stock or water, then brought to the boil and simmered for the appropriate time, whereas all other vegetables should be added to boiling stock or water, returned to the boil and cooked for the time indicated. Timings are crucial and will depend very much upon the size and type of vegetable being cooked and its maturity. Check after the minimum time stated – the vegetables should be just fork-tender or tender-crisp with some bite and never fallen, limp or soggy. Use the cooking water to make stock, a sauce or gravy if liked.

Vegetable	Preparation and Cooking Time
ARTICHOKES, GLOBE	Cut off the stalks, sprinkle with lemon juice and boil in salted water, with a little vinegar, for 30–45 minutes. Test to see if cooked by pulling out one of the leaves – it should come away easily.
ARTICHOKES, JERUSALEM	Scrub, peel thinly and slice or chop. Sprinkle with lemon juice and boil in salted water for 20–30 minutes, depending on size.
ASPARAGUS	Peel the top of the stems thinly and the bases more thickly. Tie in bundles and boil in salted water, tips uppermost, for 20–35 minutes, depending on size and maturity
ASPARAGUS PEAS	Cook in the minimum of boiling salted water for about 5 minutes.
BEANS, BROAD	Shell, then cook in boiling salted water for 10–12 minutes until tender.
BEANS, DWARF FRENCH	Top and tail, then cook in boiling salted water for 5–10 minutes, depending on size and maturity.
BEANS, RUNNER	Top and tail, remove any stringy edges and slice into diagonal lengths. Cook in boiling salted water for 5–7 minutes.
BEETROOT	Trim the leaf stalks to 2.5 cm (1 in) above the root and do not peel. Cook in boiling salted water for 1–2 hours, depending on size. Plunge into cold water, cut away the stalks and peel or rub away the skin.

BROCCOLI, SPROUTING	Trim the spears free of leaves and excess stalk. Cook in boiling salted water for 8–10 minutes.
BROCCOLI	Trim into even-sized spears free of excess stalk. Cook in boiling salted water for 8–12 minutes.
BRUSSELS SPROUTS	Remove any coarse or damaged outer leaves and excess stalk, then cook in boiling salted water for 8–10 minutes.
CABBAGE, SPRING	Shred and cook in boiling salted water for 5–7 minutes.
CABBAGE, AUTUMN AND WINTER	Shred or cut into wedges and cook in boiling salted water, 5–7 minutes for shredded, 10–12 minutes for wedges.
CABBAGE, RED	Shred or cut into quarters and cook in stock or apple juice or water with a little lemon juice for about 15–25 minutes, depending on size.
CALABRESE	Trim away any coarse outer leaves and long stems, then cook in boiling salted water for 8–10 minutes.
CARROTS	Peel or scrape if necessary, leave whole, slice, quarter or cut into thin julienne strips. Cook in boiling salted water for 5–25 minutes, depending on size and maturity.
CAULIFLOWERS	Trim away the leaves and base and keep whole or divide into florets. Cook in boiling salted water for 10–20 minutes for a whole head or 8–10 minutes for florets.
CELERIAC	Trim away the root end and leaves, then peel for chopping or slicing. Sprinkle with lemon juice, then cook in boiling salted water for 10–15 minutes, depending on size.
CELERY	Trim and cook whole or as individual stems.

Cook individual stems in boiling salted water for 7–10 minutes, or whole hearts for about 20 minutes.

CHARD · Cook the ribs as for celery and the leaves as for spinach.

CHICONS Trim the heads but leave whole, and simmer in stock or water for about 20 minutes.

CHINESE CABBAGE Cook the whole leaves, shredded leaves or whole head. Boil the whole head for about 8 minutes and the leaves for 3–4 minutes.

COURGETTES Cook whole, sliced or cubed in boiling salted water for 4–8 minutes, depending on size and maturity.

CUCUMBER & GHERKINS Cook sliced, chopped or in strips in boiling salted water for 5–8 minutes.

ENDIVE Trim away the root end; leave whole, cut into quarters or tear into large pieces and cook in boiling salted water for 10–12 minutes.

FENNEL, FLORENCE Trim and cut into bite-sized pieces for cooking. Cook in boiling salted water for 10–15 minutes.

KALE Remove the thick stalks and shred coarsely. Cook in boiling salted water for 10 minutes.

KOHLRABI Trim off the stems and leaves, then peel and cut into strips, slices or chunks. Cook in stock or water for 20–25 minutes.

LEEKS Trim away the root end and excess green stem and wash thoroughly. Cook whole stems in boiling salted water for 10–15 minutes, sliced or chopped for 8–10 minutes.

MANGETOUT	Trim and cook the whole pods in boiling salted water for 3–5 minutes.
MARROWS	Peel, halve and remove the seeds, then cut into chunks for boiling. Cook in boiling salted water for 5–8 minutes.
ONIONS	Trim and peel away the papery leaves; then leave whole, slice or cut into quarters. Cook in boiling salted water for 5–20 minutes, depending on size.
PAK CHOY	Shred and cook in boiling salted water for 5–7 minutes.
PARSNIPS	Prepare like carrots and cook in boiling salted water for 10–25 minutes, depending on size and maturity.
PEAS	Shell and cook in boiling salted water for 5–15 minutes, depending on size and maturity.
POTATOES, MAINCROP	Scrub and peel if liked, then cook in boiling salted water for 15–25 minutes, depending on size.
POTATOES, NEW	Scrub and scrape if liked, then cook in boiling salted water for 15–25 minutes, depending on size.
PUMPKIN AND SQUASHES	Peel, remove the seeds and cut into cubes. Cook in boiling salted water for 15–30 minutes, depending on size and type.
RADISHES	Trim and cook whole in boiling salted water for about 10 minutes.
SALSIFY	Remove the tops and bottoms and peel thickly. Cook in boiling salted water with a little lemon juice for 25–35 minutes, depending on whether whole or cut into slices.
SCORZONERA	Prepare and cook as for salsify. Peel after boiling.

SEAKALE	Cook the blanched stalks in boiling salted water for about 10 minutes.
SKIRRET	Scrub the vegetable well and remove any brown threads from the inner flesh if necessary. Boil in the minimum of water for 5–10 minutes, depending on size.
SPINACH	Wash well and cook with just the water clinging to the leaves for 5–8 minutes.
SWEDES	Peel and cut into quarters, cubes or slices. Cook in boiling salted water for 30–40 minutes, depending on size.
SWEETCORN	Cook the prepared kernels in boiling salted water for 6–8 minutes; alternatively cook the whole prepared cob for 8–15 minutes, depending on size and maturity.
TURNIPS	Peel and leave whole or cut into chunks. Cook in boiling salted water or stock for 10–30 minutes, depending on size and maturity.

Steaming

Steaming is a method of cooking vegetables that has always had its devotees and happily is once more coming to the fore. I particularly like it since it ensures crisp vegetables with some bite that are virtually never water-laden or soggy. There are two basic methods, the first perhaps the more popular:

STEAMER METHOD	Place the vegetables in a steaming basket or steamer above boiling salted water or stock, cover tightly and cook for the times in the boiling chart plus an additional 5–10 minutes.
PAN METHOD	Melt about 25–30 g (1–2 oz) butter in a large shallow pan, add the vegetables, shake to coat in

the fat, cover tightly and cook for the times in the
vegetable chart, plus 3–5 minutes, shaking from
time to time. Keeping the temperature at a low
even level is crucial in this method.

Sautéing or shallow frying

This method is best left for young, tender vegetables like
courgettes, mangetout, celeriac and mushrooms. Older vegetables
need to be parboiled until virtually tender, then sautéed in butter to
achieve the right degree of tenderness. The vegetables below are
the ones I consider best for this method of cooking, but you may of
course try others:

Vegetable	Preparation and Cooking Time
AUBERGINE	Cut into cubes or slices and coat in seasoned flour if liked. Sauté in butter until tender, about 5–10 minutes.
CELERIAC	Cut into julienne strips and sauté in butter for 25–30 minutes until tender.
COURGETTES	Cut into thin slices or julienne strips and sauté in butter for 5–8 minutes, tossing frequently.
MANGETOUT	Trim and sauté in butter for 3–5 minutes, tossing and stirring frequently.
MARROW	Cut into slices or chunks and sauté in butter with a few herbs for 8–10 minutes.
MUSHROOMS	Wipe and leave whole or slice. Sauté in a little butter for 3–5 minutes.
ONIONS	Slice or leave small onions whole. Sauté in a little butter until tender – about 5–10 minutes, depending on size.

POTATOES   Parboil until almost tender, then cube or slice or
                  leave baby potatoes whole and sauté in butter and
                  a little oil until golden and crisp.

Deep-frying

Chipped potatoes are not the only vegetables which appreciate the
high heat and fierce cooking of deep-frying – consider cauliflower
florets, leeks and onions too. The temperature of the oil is all-
important here. Fill a pan one-third full with cooking oil and heat to
190°C (375°F) (or when a small cube of bread dropped into the oil
sizzles immediately and will brown in about 45–50 seconds).
Ensure that vegetables are dried before cooking and drained on
absorbent kitchen towel to free them of excess oil after cooking.
Some vegetables are better par-boiled before deep frying and
coated with flour, breadcrumbs or a batter.

Vegetable	Preparation and Cooking Time
ARTICHOKES, JERUSALEM	Parboil for 20 minutes, dry, cut into thick slices, coat in a light batter and deep-fry for 3–5 minutes.
CAULI-FLOWER	Parboil the florets for about 8 minutes. Drain well, then dry and coat in beaten egg and breadcrumbs or batter and deep-fry for 2–3 minutes.
LEEKS	Parboil 5 cm (2 in) lengths for about 5 minutes, drain well then coat in a light batter. Deep-fry for 3–5 minutes.
MUSHROOMS	Coat whole mushrooms in a light batter or egg and breadcrumbs and deep-fry for 3–5 minutes.
ONIONS	Slice into thin rings, dip in milk and flour or a light batter and deep-fry for 3–4 minutes.

PARSNIPS	Cut into paper-thin slices and deep-fry for 3–5 minutes to make crisps for serving with game, etc.
POTATOES	Parboil the whole vegetable and slice into chips if liked for cooking, or cook the chipped potatoes from raw. Deep-fry the raw chips for 4–6 minutes. Drain, then just before serving deep-fry again for 1–2 minutes. Parboiled potato chips should be deep-fried for 2–4 minutes until crisp and golden.

Baking

Vegetables can be baked plainly, with a stuffing, brushed with oil or butter or with a savoury topping, coating or filling. Here are some of my favourite tried and tested methods.

Vegetable	Preparation and Cooking Time
AUBERGINES	Boil whole aubergines for 10 minutes, drain, halve and remove the flesh; then cube or chop and use to make a savoury filling for the aubergine shell. Bake for 20–30 minutes. Alternatively, layer with savoury ingredients and a sauce (as in moussaka) and bake until tender.
BEETROOT	Wrap in buttered paper and bake at 160°C (325°F), Gas Mark 3, for ½–1 hour, depending on size.
CELERY	Parboil, then coat with cheese or a sauce and bake until tender and the top is golden and crisp.
COURGETTES	Hollow out courgettes like small boats and parboil for 5 minutes. Fill with a savoury mixture and bake at 190°C (375°F), Gas Mark 5, for about 20–30 minutes.

CUCUMBERS	Peel and thickly slice or cube the flesh into a baking dish. Dot with butter, sprinkle with herbs and bake at 190°C (375°F), Gas Mark 5, for 25–30 minutes.
MARROW	Stuff a whole marrow or rings with a savoury mixture, place in a buttered baking-dish and bake at 190°C (375°F), Gas Mark 5, for ½–1½ hours, depending on size.
ONIONS	Parboil and hollow out the centres. Fill with a savoury mixture and sprinkle with breadcrumbs. Dot with butter and bake at 190°C (375°F), Gas Mark 5, for 40–60 minutes.
PEPPERS	Core, seed and stuff, surround with a little stock and bake at 180°C (350°F), Gas Mark 4, for 30–50 minutes.
TOMATOES	Cook whole, in halves or slices. Dot with butter and sprinkle with seasonings and breadcrumbs if liked, then bake at 180°C (350°F), Gas Mark 4, for 10–15 minutes.

Roasting

Roots and tubers are mainly used for this method of preparation and cooking. It usually involves cooking around a roast, or at least cooking in meat fat and juices. Often the vegetables are parboiled before roasting (especially if the meat roasting time is short), but most can be roasted from their raw prepared state. All suitable vegetables (other than those detailed below) should be parboiled for 10 minutes, drained, added to the hot fat and roasting juices and cooked for 20–30 minutes, depending on size and maturity.

Vegetable	Preparation and Cooking Time
PARSNIPS	Parboil for 5 minutes, drain well and roast with

the meat joint for 30–60 minutes, depending on size and maturity.

POTATOES Parboil for 5 minutes, then roast around the meat or near the top of the oven in roasting fat and juices for 40–60 minutes, turning over once during the cooking time..

PUMPKIN Cut into bite-size pieces and roast around a joint for at least 45 minutes.

15. Seasonal Availability of Vegetables

(Availability may vary according to local climate)

ARTICHOKES, GLOBE July–September

ARTICHOKES, JERUSALEM November–February

ASPARAGUS May–July

ASPARAGUS PEAS June–September

AUBERGINE August–October

BEANS, BROAD May–August

BEANS, CLIMBING FRENCH July–October

BEANS, DWARF FRENCH June–October

BEANS, RUNNER July–October

BEETROOT June–October and to March from store

BROCCOLI, SPROUTING March–May

BRUSSELS SPROUTS September–March

CABBAGE, SPRING April–May

CABBAGE, SUMMER July–September

CABBAGE, AUTUMN AND WINTER October–February

CABBAGE, RED September–March

CALABRESE July to first frost

CARROTS June–March

CAULIFLOWERS March–December but all year round in warmest parts of UK.

CELERIAC October–November and to March from store

CELERY, SELF-BLANCHING July–September

CELERY, TRENCH November–April

CHARD July–December but may overwinter with protection

CHICORY FOR WINTER SALADS December–April

CHICORY, HEADING August–December or through winter if protected

CHINESE CABBAGE September–November

COURGETTES July–September

CUCUMBERS AND GHERKINS July–September

CUTTING SALADS All year round

ENDIVE June–November and through winter if protected

FENNEL, FLORENCE July–October

GARLIC August and all year round from store

KALE November–May

KOHLRABI May–October

LEEKS October–April/May

LETTUCE May–September and all year round with protection

MARROWS September/October and to December from store

ONIONS July–April from store

ONIONS, PICKLING July/August

ONIONS, SPRING March–October

PAK CHOY August/September and to April with protection

PARSNIPS November–March

PEAS June–August

PEPPERS July–September

POTATOES, MAINCROP August onwards and to April from store

POTATOES, EARLY June–September but from May with protection

PUMPKINS AND SQUASHES July–September and to December from store

RADISHES May–October and through winter to April with protection

SALSIFY, SCORZONERA October onwards

SEAKALE December–April

SHALLOTS July and to April from store

SKIRRET November–March

SPINACH May–November and into spring with protection

SPINACH, PERPETUAL All year round

SWEDES October–April

SWEETCORN August–September

TOMATOES June–October and later from store

TURNIPS June–December and later from store.

Seasonal Availability of Fruits

APPLES August–April (from store)

BLACKBERRIES August–November

CHERRIES, SWEET June/July

CHERRIES, ACID August–October

CURRANTS, BLACK June–August

CURRANTS, RED AND WHITE July–August

DAMSONS September–October

GOOSEBERRIES May–August

LOGANBERRIES AND OTHER HYBRIDS July/August

MELONS August–October

PEARS August–April with good storage

PLUMS AND GAGES August–September

QUINCE October and from store through winter

RASPBERRIES July–October

RHUBARB March/April to end May

STRAWBERRIES June–October

16. Storing & Preserving Home-grown Fruit & Vegetables

Making your own preserves and storing away surplus fruit and vegetables is often a necessity for the home gardener, but thankfully it's great fun and a few shelves of really individual and fresh-flavoured jams, jellies and fruit cheeses – as well as pickles, chutneys and ketchups – are an infinite source of satisfaction the whole year round. There is nothing more beguiling or rewarding than an unusual pot of jam or jelly at breakfast or mid-afternoon tea, a laden jar of juicy fruit for a pudding or pie, a spoonful of home-made pickle or chutney to cheer up a cold joint, a dash of flavoured oil or vinegar to give a lift to a salad or its dressing, or a tureen of summer-picked fresh vegetables in the depths of a cold winter. And, just like the fresh produce from which they are made, they make a welcome and economical change from the bland assortment of commercially-produced foods on offer. An added bonus is that some preserves, when packed decoratively, also make super gifts. The cost savings and lack of waste speak for themselves.

Most preserving methods are based on the more traditional forms of preserving using sugar, vinegar or alcohol and sterilisation to maintain foods in prime condition. Others include drying, salting, freezing and, of course, chilling or keeping at optimum low temperatures. All work on more or less the same principle of removing, keeping out or prohibiting the growth of spoilage microorganisms. These techniques are all explained in the following pages.

The art of preserving and storing has no special season – indeed there is a preserve and a vegetable or fruit to store during every month of the year – but there is well-rehearsed timetable that coincides with peak-time harvest. You will find this handy chart on pp. 215–16 of the book.

Jams

'The rule is, jam yesterday and jam tomorrow – but never jam today.' (*Alice in Wonderland* by Lewis Carroll).

Thankfully this is true only in the children's story, for today it is possible to have jam on the same day as making, thanks to the remarkable impact of the microwave, pressure cooker, commercial pectin and other short-cut speedy solutions.

Basic rules

Choose fruit that is sound and just ripe.

Check the pectin level or acid level of fruit before you begin to ascertain if extra pectin or acid are needed (see below).

Gather all the equipment you need – including a good range of clean, sound jars for potting.

Warm the jars while the fruit is cooking so that you are ready to pot when the jam has reached setting point.

Always follow the initial cooking stage faithfully – it is perhaps the most important stage, determining jam quality.

Fruit selection

Pectin is what makes jam set and some fruits have more of it than others. Jam will only set if there are sufficient and agreeable quantities of pectin, acid and sugar present. Fruits that lack pectin or acid require the addition of a fruit that is rich in these; in such cases, either mix a poor with a good level fruit, add lemon juice, home-made pectin extract or as a last resort a commercially-prepared bottled pectin (according to the manufacturer's instructions).

Pectin content of fruits used in jam making

GOOD Quince, most plums, damsons, gooseberries, redcurrants, blackcurrants, cooking apples, barberries, loganberries, rowan berries.

MEDIUM Dessert apples, apricots, bilberries, blueberries, acid cherries, greengages, raspberries, some plums, mulberries, blackberries.

LOW Strawberries, figs, melons, nectarines, peaches, pears, rhubarb, grapes.

Acid content of fruits used in jam making

GOOD Blackcurrants, damsons, gooseberries, greengages, plums, redcurrants, rhubarb.

MEDIUM Apples, apricots, blackberries, cherries, grapes, loganberries, mulberries, raspberries.

LOW Figs, melons, nectarines, peaches, pears, quince, strawberries.

Step-by-step golden guide to jam making

1. Prepare the fruit according to variety. Wash and place in a preserving pan or large, heavy-based saucepan.
2. Add the required amount of water or fruit juice. Bring to the boil, reduce the heat and simmer until tender.
3. Test for the pectin level at this point if necessary (see p. 220).
4. Warm sugar in the oven, add to fruit and stir well to dissolve. Bring to the boil and cook until setting point is reached.
5. Test for a set about 2–3 minutes after boiling, or according to the recipe instructions, by placing a small amount of the jam on a cold saucer. Allow to cool, push with the finger when cold and if the surface wrinkles a set has been reached. Alternatively, use a sugar thermometer – jam sets at 105°C (221°F).
6. Skim the surface of the jam to remove any foam or stones and discard.
7. Using a jug, ladle or funnel, pour the hot jam into clean, hot jars right up to the neck.
8. Cover while still very hot (or when cold) with waxed discs, waxed-sides down, and dampened cellophane rounds.
9. Secure with elastic bands or string. Label and store until required in a cool dry, dark place.

Storage

Store jams in a cool, dry, dark place for up to one year.

Testing for pectin content

1. Test after the first stage process when the fruit has been simmered until tender. Place 1 teaspoon of the fruit juice in a glass and leave to cool.
2. Add 1 tablespoon methylated spirits and mix well.
3. If after 2 minutes the mixture forms a jelly-like clot, there is sufficient pectin.
4. If the mixture clots into a few blobs, boil the fruit mixture further to evaporate more liquid and test again.
5. If the mixture still does not form a complete jelly-like clot, then additional pectin is required.
6. Either add 100 ml (4 fl oz) commercial liquid pectin (e.g. Certo) to each 450 g (1 lb) fruit used; or 150 ml (¼ pint) fruit juice rich in pectin and acid (e.g. redcurrant juice) to each 450 g/1 lb fruit used.

For home-made pectin

Pectin can be made at home from apples, gooseberries or redcurrants. Apples are perhaps the easiest to use and the most readily available:

1. Cut up 900 g (2 lb) cooking apples but do not peel or core. Remove any blemishes if necessary.
2. Cover with 900 ml (1½ pints) water and cook gently for about 50 minutes until pulped.
3. Strain through a jelly-bag or piece of muslin.
4. Use about 150 ml (¼ pint) home-made pectin to set 1.2 litres (2 pints) low pectin fruit pulp or juice.

Jellies

Tantalisingly sweet or temptingly savoury, jellies with their crystal-clear appearance and fresh fruity taste are delightful served with rich sweet concoctions or succulent meat roasts. A little more time-consuming to make than jams, their culinary use is perhaps more varied. Made purely from juice, the fruit pulp straining may seem lengthy but the fruit preparation is especially simple since no tiresome peeling and coring is required with the majority of fruits.

Fruit choice

Only fruits with a high pectin content (see p. 218) are really suitable for jelly-making, although it is possible to stretch the choice if you use home-made or commercially produced pectin. Ideal fruits include apples, redcurrants, gooseberries, blackcurrants and quince.

Step-by-step golden guide to jelly-making

1. Prepare the fruit by simply coarsely chopping. There is no need to remove skin, pips and cores.
2. Place in a preserving pan or large, heavy-based saucepan with the water and cook gently until very tender.
3. Place the fruit pulp in a jelly-bag, suspend and leave to drip into a bowl for at least 12 hours or overnight.
4. Measure the juice and calculate the sugar required, remembering 600 ml (1 pint) extracted juice needs 450 g (1 lb) sugar. Place the sugar and water in the pan and bring gently to the boil, stirring well to dissolve the sugar.
5. Boil rapidly until setting point is reached. Test for set (as for jams).
6. Skim quickly and pour into clean, hot jars.
7. Cover with waxed discs, waxed-sides down, and dampened cellophane rounds or preserving skin and secure. Label and store in a cool, dry, dark place out of direct sunlight.

Storage

Store jellies in a cool, dry dark place for up to one year.

Fruit Cheeses, Butters and Curds

Deliciously rich, thick and fruity, cheeses, butters and curds are the traditional sisters of jams often neglected today. This is surprising really, for they have a wide variety of uses with which jams can never hope to compete: they make super fillings for cakes and pastries; make splendid bases for fruity puddings; or can be eaten alone or with cream for an after-dinner treat. Many will also compete admirably with jellies as a roast accompaniment especially with rich meats like pork, goose and game.

Fruit cheeses are very thick fruit preserves – so thick in fact that they can be turned out of a mould for slicing to serve. Today they are the savoury use option of the trio since they are excellent for serving with roasts, curries and cold meats instead of – or in addition to – pickles, chutneys and relishes. They are greedy on fruit so are ideally made with glut or windfall fruits like apples, apricots, blackberries, damsons and quince.

Fruit butters have a softer texture than cheeses – more like jam – and are spread like butter for serving. Usually less sweet than cheeses, they are used more as a sweet or dessert; for filling cakes, spreading on to bread for a teatime treat or making a fruity sauce for a sponge pudding or ice-cream dessert.

Curds are the rich members of this threesome since the sweetened fruit mixture is enriched with butter and eggs. For this reason they do not keep as well as cheeses or butters, so are best made in small quantities.

Step-by-step golden guide to making fruit cheeses

1. Pick over and wash the fruit and cut into large pieces without removing any skin, cores or pips.
2. Place in a pan with just enough water to cover and cook until very soft and pulpy.
3. Sieve to remove skin, pips & cores, measure & return to the pan.
4. Add 350–450 g (12–16 oz) sugar per 600 ml (1 pint) fruit purée. Heat gently to dissolve, then cook until very thick, about 45–60 minutes.

5. Spoon into clean, hot jars and cover with waxed discs (waxed-sides down) and dampened cellophane rounds. Secure with string and label.
6. Alternatively, brush small, warmed, clean moulds with olive oil or glycerine and fill with the hot cheese mixture. Cover with waxed discs and cellophane rounds or melted paraffin wax to a depth of 3 mm (⅛ in). Store.

Step-by-step golden guide to making fruit butters

1. Pick over and wash the fruit and cut into large pieces without removing any skin, cores or pips.
2. Place in a pan with just enough water to cover and cook until very soft and pulpy.
3. Sieve to remove any skin, pips and cores, measure and return to the pan.
4. Add 225–350 g (8–12 oz) sugar per 600 ml (1 pint) fruit purée. Heat gently to dissolve, then cook until very thick and no excess liquid remains, about 20–30 minutes.
5. Spoon into clean, hot jars and cover with waxed discs (waxed-sides down) and dampened cellophane rounds. Secure with string and label.

Step-by-step golden guide to making fruit curds

1. Place the fruit juice, rind, butter and sugar in a heavy-based pan, double saucepan or bowl over a pan of simmering water. Cook until the butter melts.
2. Add the beaten eggs, blending well.
3. Cook very gently, stirring constantly until the mixture will coat the back of a wooden spoon. Do not allow to boil or the mixture will curdle.
4. Strain the cooked curd through a fine sieve. Ladle or spoon into clean, hot jars. Cover with waxed discs (waxed-sides down) and dampened cellophane rounds. Secure with string and label.

Storage
Store cheeses, butters and curds in a cool, dry, dark place. With

their high sugar content cheeses will store for up to one year; butters for three–six months; and curds for up to two weeks (or, if kept in a refrigerator, for up to two months).

Fruit Juices, Syrups, Drinks and Liqueurs

There are probably few things more rewarding than a cool, ice-chinked glass of squash or fruit syrup on a hot summer's day; sipping a home-made liqueur by the fireside when cold winds blow outside; or giving a present of a carefully prepared fruit gin or brandy to a friend for a celebratory surprise.

All these are quite easy to make, prove economical on the pocket and resources, and can be made during the peak autumn harvest to enjoy during the Christmas festivities.

Fruit juices and squashes are made from ripe fruits and are diluted with water, mineral water, lemonade or soda water for drinking. They will store admirably for up to eight weeks if unopened.

Liqueurs are fruit-infused spirits that need about three months' storage to mature before sampling. The bonus is that they offer two preserves in one, since the fruits may also be eaten as a dessert.

Drinks like damson brandy are made in a similar way to liqueurs; probably the only difference in their classification may be in their strength or serving – they are usually drunk in larger quantities (but with care!).

Step-by-step golden guide to making a fruit juice or squash

1. Place the fruit rind, sugar and water in a pan. For most recipes this is a citrus rind. Heat gently to dissolve the sugar, bring to the boil and cook for one minute.
2. Strain through a sieve into a large jug. Add the fruit juices and citric acid if used, blending well.
3. Pour into sterilised bottles and seal with sterilised corks or sterilised screw caps; if using corks, these must be secured with wire or string after filling so that they do not blow or explode during the sterilising process.

4. Wrap each bottle in a cloth or newspaper and stand upright in a deep pan on a rack.
5. Fill up to the corks or caps with warm water and heat to 88°C (190°F) or simmering point. Maintain this for 30 minutes.
6. Remove from the pan and push down the corks or tighten the screw caps and leave until warm.
7. If using corks, dip each cork-top in melted sealing or paraffin wax to make airtight. Leave until cold.
8. Label and store in a cool, dry, dark place.

Step-by-step golden guide to making a fruit liqueur or drink

1. Prepare the fruit according to variety. If the fruit has a tight membrane, as in cherries for example, then prick first with a needle and place in a large glass jar.
2. Add the chosen spirit with sugar. Cover tightly and shake to dissolve the sugar.
3. Leave at room temperature in a dark place to mature (shaking occasionally to dissolve the sugar) for about two to three months.
4. Strain off the liqueur through muslin and bottle. Store in a cool, dry, dark place. The fruit may be eaten.

Step-by-step golden guide to making fruit syrups

1. Place the fruit rind (if used), fruit or fruit juice, water and flavourings in a pan. Bring to the boil and cook for 1 minute.
2. Pour into a jelly-bag and leave to strain over a bowl for 8–12 hours.
3. Place the juice in a pan and add the sugar, blending well. Heat to dissolve, bring to the boil and cook according to the recipe instructions.
4. Pour into sterilised bottles, seal and process as for fruit juices or squashes (see above).
5. Store in a cool, dry, dark place after labelling.

Storage

Fruit juices, cordials and squashes will keep for about eight weeks unopened if stored in a cool, dry, dark place. Once opened, use within two weeks and store in the refrigerator.

Fruit syrups should be stored in a cool, dry, dark place for up to two months.

Fruit liqueurs and drinks should be stored in a cool, dry place to mature for about three months before sampling. Once strained of their fruit and bottled, they will keep for several years.

Pickles

Whereas jams, jellies and conserves use sugar, pickles use vinegar as their preservative. It is therefore important to use a good quality vinegar with an acetic acid content of at least 5 per cent. For good insurance, look for a pickling vinegar that is labelled as such – as a bonus it may have been flavoured with spices and herbs.

Also choose the vinegar carefully so as to suit the end product. Pearl-white baby onions, for example, look better in distilled white vinegar, whereas larger plumper pickling onions appreciate a good malt flavour from a darker vinegar.

Fruit and vegetables suitable for pickling include onions, cauliflower, cabbage, peaches, peppers, cucumbers, beetroot, carrots, marrow, gherkins, apples, beans, pears, damsons and apricots.

Step-by-step golden guide to pickling

1. Prepare the vegetables or fruit according to variety. Peel onions, cut cauliflower into florets, shred cabbage and top and tail beans, for example.
2. If dry brining, layer the prepared vegetables in a bowl with salt, allowing 1 tablespoon salt per 450 g (1 lb) vegetables. Cover and leave overnight. This is a suitable method for preparing cucumbers, marrows, tomatoes and red cabbage.
3. If wet brining, place the vegetables in a bowl and cover with the brine solution, made by dissolving 50 g (2 oz) salt in 600 ml (1 pint) water. Cover with a plate to keep immersed and leave

overnight. This is the ideal method to use for cauliflowers and onions.

4. Rinse the vegetables thoroughly in cold water and pack into pickle jars.
5. Cover with hot spiced vinegar right to the tops.
6. Cover with a vinegar-proof cap and seal. Label and store in a cool, dark place.

To make spiced vinegar

Place 600 ml (1 pint) vinegar in a pan. Add 1 stick cinnamon, 6 allspice berries, 6 white or black peppercorns, 4 whole cloves and a bay leaf. Bring very slowly to the boil, remove from the heat, cover and leave to stand for 2–3 hours. Strain to use.

Storage

Pickles should be left in a cool, dry, dark place for about two to three months to mature – the exception being red cabbage which only needs one to two weeks. Store for up to six months; red cabbage for two to three weeks.

Chutneys and relishes

Chutneys and relishes offer the best of both worlds to the 'preserving' cook since they can be made with fruit and/or vegetables yet – depending upon choice and mixture – can appear so deliciously different every time.

The age-old question on this topic seems to be in defining the difference between a chutney and a relish. It is largely a question of texture – chutneys are deemed such because they have a smoother, less chunky texture than relishes, which have been made from bite-sized pieces of fruit and vegetables. The dividing line is a narrow tightrope to walk, so take your pick and call your own creation what you like.

Step-by-step golden guide to making chutneys

1. Prepare the vegetables and/or fruits according to variety, then

finely mince, slice or chop according to the recipe instructions.
2. Place in a pan with the vinegar, sugar, spices and seasonings.
3. Simmer gently until very thick and no excess liquid remains, about 1–4 hours, stirring occasionally.
4. Pour into clean, hot, sterilised jars and seal with vinegar-proof tops. Label and store.

Step-by-step golden guide to making relishes

1. Prepare the vegetables and/or fruits according to variety, then slice or chop into bite-sized pieces according to the recipe instructions.
2. Place in a pan with the vinegar, sugar, spices and seasonings.
3. Simmer gently until the vegetable or fruit pieces are tender but still whole, according to the recipe instructions.
4. Pour into clean, hot, sterilised jars and seal with vinegar-proof tops. Label and store.

Storage

Store most chutneys and relishes for about 2–3 months to mature before eating. Store in a cool, dry, dark place for up to two years.

Sauces, Ketchups, Oils and Vinegars

Home-made sauces, ketchups, oils and vinegars are rarely anything like the shop-bought, commercially-bottled variety – and all are better for being so. Rich and fruity, sweet or savoury, herb-flavoured or spicy, they offer delicious and unusual food accompaniments or cooking aids to the traditional or experimental cook.

Sauces are almost like chutneys and relishes which have been sieved to pouring consistency, whereas ketchups are usually thinner, clearer fruit and vegetable mixtures that are strained after cooking.

Oils are infused delicacies which make delicious ingredients for salad dressings; vinegars are the same, but can also make refreshing summer drinks when diluted with water.

Step-by-step golden guide to making sauces and ketchups

1. Prepare the fruit and/or vegetables according to the recipe instructions. This may involve a brining process overnight or softening in oil by sautéeing.
2. Place in a preserving pan with the vinegar, sugar, herbs and seasonings. Bring to the boil and simmer until tender according to the recipe instructions.
3. Purée sauces in a blender or pass through a sieve; sieve or strain ketchups.
4. Return to the pan, bring to the boil, then pour into hot, sterilised bottles, leaving a 2.5 cm (1 inch) headspace. Seal with sterilised corks or screw-tops (if using corks they must be secured with wire or string after filling so that they do not blow or explode during the sterilising process).
5. Wrap each bottle in cloth or newspaper and stand upright in a deep pan with an upturned plate or rack on the base.
6. Top up with warm water to reach the necks of the bottles and heat to 88°C (190°F) simmering point. Maintain this for 30 minutes.
7. Remove from the pan and push down the corks or tighten the screw-tops and leave until warm.
8. If using corks, dip each cork-top in melted sealing or paraffin wax to make airtight. Leave until cold. Label and store.

Step-by-step golden guide to making a flavoured oil

1. Place the oil in a screw-topped jar or decorative bottle as liked.
2. Add a few sprigs of herbs (rosemary, bay leaves, tarragon and thyme make good additions), and/or a mixture of spices.
3. Shake well to mix then seal tightly, label and leave to mature for 2–3 weeks in a cool, dark place.

Step-by-step golden guide to making a fruit vinegar

1. Prepare the fruit according to variety, wash well and place in a large bowl. Crush and bruise with a wooden spoon, slowly adding the vinegar.

2. Cover and leave to stand for 4–5 days, stirring occasionally.
3. Strain through muslin into a pan. Bring to the boil, add any sugar or spirits if used and cook for 10 minutes.
4. Strain again if the recipe indicates or pour into hot sterilised bottles or jars. Seal with sterilised corks, screw-tops or vinegar-proof lids and seal with hot wax if necessary. Label and store until required.

Storage

Sauces and ketchups should be stored in a cool, dark place for one month to mature before using, and for up to one year. Oils should be stored in a cool, dark place for two to three weeks before using, and for up to one year. Fruit vinegars should be stored in a cool, dark place for two weeks before using, and for up to one year.

Bottling

Preserving by bottling is very simple and has been especially popular since the invention of the Kilner jar at the turn of the century. It an inexpensive, easy and, moreover, healthy way of preserving fruit.

Bottling is preserving by sterilisation and is an excellent way to preserve fruit, but should *not* be used for vegetables since the temperatures reached in home bottling cannot be guaranteed high enough to kill their bacteria. This is true even with a pressure cooker. There are three basic methods by which to preserve fruit: the oven method, the water bath method, and the pressure cooker method.

Fruit may be preserved in either syrup or water. The sugar syrup is made from 225 g (8 oz) sugar to 600 ml (1 pint) water. Generally fruit is packed, layer by layer, in clean preserving jars, then filled up with syrup or water before or after processing.

The oven method

You can choose between the wet-pack or dry-pack method:

WET PACK METHOD Preheat the oven to 150°C (300°F, Gas Mark 2). Warm the jars and fill with prepared fruit. Fill jars to within 2.5 cm (1 in) of the tops with either boiling syrup or water. Fit the rubber rings around the inside of the glass lids and place on the jars, ensuring that the rubber rings lie evenly all round. Do not fix screwbands or metal clips. Place the jars 5 cm (2 in) apart in the centre of the oven on a baking tray lined with sheets of newspaper and cook for the time recommended in the chart (pp. 234–5). Remove from the oven, wipe any excess syrup from the necks of the jars, check the rings and lids are in place, screw on plastic screwbands tightly, leave for 2–3 minutes then re-tighten, or secure the metal clips. Label and store.

DRY PACK METHOD Preheat the oven to 130°C (250°F, Gas Mark ½). Warm the jars and fill with prepared fruit but no syrup or water. Put on glass lids but not rubber rings, screwbands or metal clips. Place the jars 5 cm (2 in) apart in the centre of the oven on a baking tray lined with sheets of newspaper and cook for the time recommended in the chart. Remove and fill up jars with boiling syrup or water. Fit the rubber rings around the insides of the glass lids and place on the jars, ensuring the rubber rings lie evenly all round. Screw on plastic screwbands tightly or secure metal clips. Label and store.

The water bath method

You can choose between the slow or the quick method:

SLOW METHOD Warm the jars and fill with prepared fruit. Fill jars to within 2.5 cm (1 in) of the tops with cold syrup or water. Fit the rubber rings around the insides of the glass lids and place on the jars ensuring the rubber rings lie evenly all round. Secure the metal clips or screw on the plastic screwbands, then turn the screwbands back a quarter-turn. Place in large vessel with a false bottom (a metal grid or folded coarse cloth is ideal), about 5 cm (2 in) deeper than the height of the jars. Cover with cold water up to their necks. Heat gently to 54°C (130°F) on the hob for 1 hour. Then heat to the recommended temperature for the recommended time given in the chart. Remove the jars with tongs and tighten the plastic screwbands immediately. Label and store.

QUICK METHOD This is a good method to use if you do not have a thermometer. Warm the jars and fill with prepared fruit and hot syrup or water to within 2.5 cm (1 in) of the tops. Fit the rubber rings around the insides of the glass lids and place on jars ensuring the rubber rings lie evenly all round. Secure the metal clips or screw on the plastic screwbands, then turn the screwbands back a quarter-turn. Place in large vessel with a false bottom (a metal grid or folded coarse cloth is ideal), about 5 cm (2 in) deeper than the height of the jars. Cover with warm water up to their necks. Bring the water to simmering point in 25–30 minutes, and keep simmering for the times stated in the chart. Remove the jars with tongs and tighten the plastic screwbands immediately. Label and store.

The pressure cooker method

Use a pressure cooker with a low (5-lb) pressure control. Any pressure cooker will take the 500 ml jars, but you will need a cooker with a domed lid when using the larger jars.

Layer the fruit into warmed jars and cover with boiling syrup or water to within 2.5 cm (1 in) of the tops. Fit the rubber rings around the insides of the glass lids and place on jars ensuring the rubber rings lie evenly all round. Secure the metal clips or screw on the plastic screwbands, then turn the screwbands back a quarter-turn. Heat the jars by standing in a bowl of hot water.

Put the inverted trivet into the pressure cooker and add 900 ml (1 1/2 pints) water and 1 tablespoon vinegar. Bring the water to the boil, pack the jars into the pressure cooker – packing a little newspaper between each to prevent them from touching – and fix the lid in place. Heat without pressure until steam comes out of the vent. Put on the low (5-lb) pressure and bring to pressure. Reduce and maintain pressure for the time recommended in the chart. Remove the pressure cooker from the heat and reduce the pressure at room temperature for about 10 minutes before taking off the lid. Remove jars with tongs, tighten plastic screwbands immediately, label and store.

Basic rules for bottling

Good results with preserving depend on following a few basic rules before you start:

Before use, check all jars and fittings for any flaws.

Check that jars are absolutely clean, wash them well and rinse in clean, hot water.

Soak the rubber rings in hot water for a few minutes, then bring them to the boil before use.

Don't use a rubber ring more than once – spares can be bought easily and cheaply at your equipment stockist.

Don't attempt to preserve vegetables by bottling, even in a pressure cooker. The temperatures reached are not high enough for safe preservation.

Choose fruit that is fresh, blemish-free, clean and properly ripe – neither too soft nor too hard.

Choose fruits of a similar shape, size and ripeness for any one jar.

Step-by-step golden guide to bottling

1. You will need preserving jars with plastic screwbands or metal clips to secure glass discs. Prepare the fruit by washing, peeling, coring, stoning or chopping as liked. Always select blemish-free fruits.

2. Make the syrup if used. Add 225 g (8 oz) sugar to each 300 ml (½ pint) water. Boil for 1 minute, then add the same amount of water again.

3. Pack the fruit into the jars, using the handle of a wooden spoon to push down the fruit firmly.

4. Pour over the syrup or water for all methods except dry-pack oven method. Release any air bubbles with a carefully inserted knife.

5. Fit a rubber ring around the inside of the glass lid and place on the jar, ensuring the rubber ring lies evenly all round.

6. OVEN METHOD Place jars 5 cm (2 in) apart in middle of oven on baking tray lined with sheets of newspaper.

7. WATER BATH METHOD Process jars by slow or quick method

233

covered with water up to their necks in a large pan with a false bottom (a metal grid or folded cloth placed on bottom of pan is ideal).

8. PRESSURE COOKER METHOD Process jars in hot water in a pressure cooker, keeping jars separate with newspapers or cloths.

9. Remove jars from oven with oven gloves or from water bath or pressure cooker with tongs.

10. DRY PACK METHOD Remove jars from the oven and fill up with boiling syrup or water. Fit the rubber rings around the lids, screw on screwbands or secure metal clips.

11. Test the seal when the jars are cold; check that a vacuum has formed by removing the screwband or clip carefully and lifting the jar by its lid. If the seal fails, use the contents immediately or re-process.

12. Wipe any stickiness from the jars and screw on plastic screwbands if not in place. Label with contents and date. Store in a cool, dark place.

Conserves and Fruits in Alcohol

Cooked for the minimum amount of time, conserves and fruits in alcohol are in general the preserves which

Bottling processing chart

Fruit	Oven method		Water bath method			Pressure cooker method
	Wet pack in minutes	Dry pack in minutes	Temperature	Sterilising time in minutes from simmer		Bring to pressure at 5 lb then process in minutes
				Slow	Fast	
APPLES, SLICED	30–40	N/R	74°C (165°F)	10	2	1
APRICOTS, HALVED	50–60	N/R	82°C (180°F)	15	10	1

APRICOTS, WHOLE	40–50	N/R	82°C (180°F)	15	10	1
BLACKBERRIES	30–40	45–55	74°C (165°F)	10	2	1
CHERRIES, WHOLE	40–50	55–70	82°C (180°C)	15	10	1
CURRANTS	30–40	45–55	74°C (165°F)	10	2	1
DAMSONS, WHOLE	40–40	55–70	82°C (180°F)	15	10	1
FIGS	60–70	80–100	88°C (190°F)	30	40	1
GAGES, WHOLE	55–70	N/R	82°C (180°F)	15	10	1
GOOSEBERRIES	45–60	60–75	74°C (165°F)	10	2	1
LOGANBERRIES	45–60	60–75	74°C (165°F)	10	2	1
MULBERRIES	45–60	60–75	74°C (165°F)	10	2	1
NECTARINES, HALVED	65–80	N/R	82°C (180°F)	15	20	1
PEACHES, HALVED	65–80	N/R	82°C (180°F)	15	20	1
PEARS	60–70	N/R	88°C (190°F)	30	40	5
PLUMS, HALVED	65–80	N/R	82°C (180°F)	15	20	1
PLUMS, WHOLE	55–70	N/R	82°C (180°F)	15	10	1
RASPBERRIES	45–60	60–75	74°C (165°F)	10	2	1
RHUBARB	40–50	55–70	74°C (165°F)	10	2	1
STRAWBERRIES	50–60	N/R	74°C (165°F)	10	2	N/R
TOMATOES, WHOLE	60–70	80–100	88°C (190°F)	30	40	5

*Lower figure is for up to 4 litre quantities, higher figure for up to 10 litres quantities.

*Times given for 1 litre jars; if 2 litre jars are used, add 5 minutes to times.

N/R = Not Recommended

most closely resemble their original fruits and flavour.

Conserves are cousins of jams and could loosely be described as fruits suspended in a sugar syrup base. Many are made from whole fruits – strawberries and raspberries are favourites, but you could use chopped or sliced peaches, plums, rhubarb or apples equally well.

Though often thought of as those opulent jars of whole fruit steeped in brandy, kirsch, bourbon or other spirits, fruits in alcohol can also be as simple as plums in a sherry syrup.

Step-by-step golden guide to making a conserve

1. Prepare the fruit according to variety or to the specific recipe instructions. Sometimes the fruit is left whole or it may be sliced, chopped or minced.
2. Place in a pan with any additional liquid and spices and cook gently until softened.
3. Add the warmed sugar and heat gently to dissolve. Bring to the boil, reduce the heat and cook gently until thickened.
4. Allow to cool for about 15 minutes so that the sugar base has thickened sufficiently to hold the fruit pieces suspended in it.
5. Spoon into clean hot jars, cover with waxed discs – waxed-sides down – and dampened cellophane rounds or preserving skin. Label and store until required.

Step-by-step golden guide to making fruits in alcohol

1. Prepare the fruit according to variety or to the specific recipe instructions. For example, this may mean halving and stoning for cherries.
2. Place in a pan with the prepared sugar syrup and poach gently until tender.
3. Remove with a slotted spoon and arrange attractively in clean, hot preserving jars.
4. Add any remaining sugar to the syrup and heat gently to dissolve.
5. Stir in the chosen spirit or liqueur, blending well and pour over the fruit to cover.
6. Cover with a vinegar-proof cap and seal. Label and store in a cool, dry place.

Storage

Conserves and fruits in alcohol should be stored in a cool, dry, dark place for up to one year.

Salting

Salting is one of those age-old methods of preserving which has lost favour over the years and been replaced with the more modern freezing process. Nevertheless, it is still a splendid method of preserving nuts, beans and cucumbers.

Used in the past as a method of preserving summer food for winter consumption, today it is appreciated more for its flavouring technique. Many of us enjoy a crisp salted nut, a specially stored and then simmered bean or pea, or sauerkraut with spiced sausages - the traditional German speciality.

Salt

The choice of salt in this method of preservation is all-important. Do not use refined table salt, iodised salt or specially-flavoured salts since they are usually too fine and have chemicals added to ensure free flow. They are also expensive.

Common cooking or block salt is ideal, as is coarse-grained – but not crystal – sea salt. Crystal sea salt can be used for wet salting but not dry.

Step-by-step golden guide to salting vegetables

1. Prepare vegetables according to variety by topping and tailing, peeling and slicing, coring, seeding and slicing or shredding, for example.
2. To dry salt (ideal for beans, onions, turnips and peas), place a 1 cm (½ in) layer of salt in the base of an earthenware crock, preserving jar or wooden barrel. Top with a 2.5 cm (1 in) layer of the prepared vegetables. Continue to layer in this way, finishing with a layer of salt.

3. Weight the top with a saucer or plate to keep the vegetables immersed in the salt and leave for 2–3 days.
4. During this time the vegetables will settle, leaving enough room for another layer of vegetables and salt. Weight again for 2–3 days, then cover with waxed paper or a screw-top and seal.
5. To wet salt (ideal for cauliflower, onions and peppers), place the prepared vegetables in an earthenware crock, preserving jar or wooden barrel. Cover with a brine solution made by dissolving 100 g (4 oz) salt per 600 ml (1 pint) water. Weight down to keep the vegetables immersed and leave for 4–5 weeks.
6. Check every week to make sure the vegetables are immersed and top up if necessary with fresh brine solution. Cover with waxed paper or a screw-top and seal.

Storage

Store salted vegetables in a cool, dark place for up to six months.

Drying and Storing

Drying was probably the earliest method of preservation known and used by man. Drying in the sun, by the wind or by smoke was a simple affair and is still popular in many tropical countries today. In Britain we mainly dry produce indoors, using a controlled temperature with adequate ventilation. Fresh food is dried in a cool oven over several hours – the drying temperature must be constant, between 50°–60°C (120°–150°F), any hotter and the food cooks; any cooler and it simply rots. In general, gas ovens are not suitable for drying as a sufficiently low temperature cannot be maintained. You could also try drying produce in an airing cupboard.

Some fruits and vegetables are more suited to drying than others – suitable fruits include apples, apricots, grapes, pears, plums and peaches. Beans, onions, mushrooms and herbs are ideal vegetables.

Storing fruit and vegetables to preserve their quality is perhaps one of the simplest methods open to the organic fruit and vegetable gardener. It can be as simple as wrapping apples in tissue paper before storing in a box, or involve a more complicated peat-layering process for root vegetables. All methods have their devotees and degrees of success.

Step-by-step golden guide to drying fruit

1. Prepare fruit according to variety – peel, core and slice apples into rings; peel, core and halve pears; halve and stone apricots; or separate grapes into individual berries for example.
2. Dip in lemon juice or salt water to prevent the fruit turning brown if necessary.
3. Dry on absorbent kitchen paper and thread on to long skewers to fit the oven shelving or to fit across a large deep baking tin.
4. Alternatively, place on muslin-lined trays or racks, spacing evenly.
5. Place in a cool oven, 50–60°C (120–150°F) until dry, about 4–6 hours.
6. Remove from the oven and leave to cool completely for at least 12 hours, before storing in airtight tins or jars.

Step-by-step golden guide to drying vegetables

1. Prepare the vegetables according to variety or special recipe instructions.
2. Blanch in boiling water for the recommended time. Drain, rinse in cold water and dry on absorbent kitchen paper.
3. Place on muslin-lined trays, spacing evenly, and dry in a cool oven, 50–65°C (120–150°F) for the recommended time.
4. If drying mushrooms the caps may be threaded on to string, tying a knot between each mushroom so that they do not touch when hung to dry.
5. Remove from the oven and leave to cool completely for at least 12 hours, before storing in airtight tins or jars.

Storage

Most dried fruits and vegetables will keep for up to six months if stored in an airtight container in a cool, dry place out of direct sunlight.

Storing organically grown fruit and vegetables

FRUIT OR VEGETABLE	PREPARATION AND STORING
Apples	*Wrap individually in specially oiled paper, tissue paper or newspaper. Stack in fibre trays, greengrocer's discarded wooden boxes or in punctured polythene bags. Keep varieties separate and check fruit regularly to ensure one rotten apple doesn't affect the rest. Store in a cellar, frost-proof garage or garden shed with temperature about 4°C (40°F). Apples can be pulped and frozen or dried in rings.*
Beetroot	*Lift and shake off excess earth, twist off tops leaving leaf ends attached to prevent bleeding, but do not remove or damage roots. Place a layer of damp sand, earth or peat in a box. Top with a layer of beetroot, cover with a layer of sand and repeat as necessary. Keep the sand damp but not wet. Store in a frost-proof shed or garage.*
Carrots	*Lift and shake off excess earth, twist off tops close to the crowns. Store in boxes of damp sand, packing closely together with roots head to tail.*
Celeriac	*Lift and remove foliage. Store in boxes of sand or peat in a cool shed or cellar. Celeriac can be protected with straw in the ground till hard frosts.*
Cucumbers	*Store in a cool, dry place on racks.*
Kohlrabi	*Lift and shake off excess earth, twist off tops but do not damage roots. Store in layers in damp sand in a frost-proof shed or garage.*
Marrow	*Hang in nets in an airy, frost-free place.*
Onions	*Thoroughly dry before storing. Place in slatted wooden trays or bind to a length of rope to hang freely. Alternatively, remove tops and store in nets in a frost-free shed.*

Parsnips   *Best to leave in the ground and pull as required. If not possible, dig up and layer in damp soil in a cold place.*

Pears   *Place in a single layer, unwrapped, on a tray or shelf, making sure they do not touch. Store in a cold room or shed. Final ripening is achieved by bringing the fruit into a warm room.*

Potatoes   *Place in dark, well-ventilated containers such as hessian or paper sacks or boxes topped with straw. Store in a cool, dry, frost-free place.*

Pumpkin   *As for marrow.*

Winter   *Lift and store, layered, in boxes of sand. Store in a cool, radishes   well-ventilated place.*

Salsify   *As for parsnips.*

Scorzoneras   *As for parsnips.*

Shallots   *As for onions. Not suitable for roping.*

Swedes   *As for beetroot. Swedes can also be left in the ground and covered with straw or bracken.*

Tomatoes   *Wrap firm, green tomatoes individually in newspaper in a tray or drawer. Store indoors. A few ripe tomatoes in the boxes will speed the ripening process. Or, lift the whole plant and hang upside down in a greenhouse or frost-free shed.*

Turnips   *As for beetroot.*

Storage times

Storage times for fruit and vegetables depend largely on their condition when initially stored, the storage area and weather conditions. Check frequently, since times for some items such as tomatoes may be as little as two weeks, whereas potatoes may be stored for up to six months.

Drying herbs

There is nothing better than a fresh herb for flavouring a dish whether it be a simple marinade or an exotic sauce, but it isn't always possible to have fresh herbs all the year round. So it does seem sensible to have to hand a least a handful of popular dried herbs. All the evergreen varieties like bay, thyme and rosemary can be picked at any time, so they are best left alone, but marjoram, parsley, sage and mint for example are suitable for drying. Alternatively chop and freeze away in small bags or in ice cube-trays with a little water for all-year-round use.

Harvest herbs for drying while relatively young and certainly before they flower – early to mid-summer is the best time. Pick the herbs in the mid-morning after the dew has evaporated from them, choosing only choice specimens and discarding any damaged or diseased leaves. Large-leaved herbs like sage should be stripped from their stems, while feathery herbs such as fennel should be left whole.

I dry most of my herbs above my Aga cooker since the heat is dry and constant, but there are other methods which are just as good and reliable. An airing cupboard, well-ventilated larder or warm but airy garden shed is a good substitute for my way, but you can of course use the oven itself.

AGA METHOD Collect the herbs in bunches of the same type and tie to secure. Hang upside down well above the cooker (or in the airing cupboard, larder or shed) and leave for 5–10 days until completely dry. Wrap in muslin or thin paper bags if the area is dusty, but never in polythene since this will cause them to sweat and become mouldy. Store as bunches, or crumble the leaves from the dried bunches and store in small airtight jars out of direct sunlight. If you have a very warm airing cupboard or warming drawer to your cooker then the herbs may be placed on a baking tray and dried here for about 2–3 days then stored as above.

OVEN METHOD Place the well washed and dried leaves or whole branches of herb on a baking tray lined with muslin. Bake in the oven at the lowest possible setting, keeping the door slightly ajar to allow moisture to escape. The process will take about 1 hour and the leaves should be turned over or rearranged once during this time – say after 30–40 minutes. When dry, turn off the oven and leave the herbs to cool there until cold, then crumble and store as above.

Remember that whichever method you use, dried herbs are more potent in terms of flavouring power than their fresh counterpart. Use only half the recommended amount of fresh herb in a recipe.

Freezing

Freezing is probably the best way of preserving most fresh fruit and vegetables and is suitable – by one method or another – for virtually every type with just a few notable exceptions. Most vegetables simply need blanching before freezing, although if you only plan to store short-term it really isn't worth the bother; and fruits can be frozen in an unsweetened dry pack, dry sugar pack, in syrup, as fruit purée or plain free-flow according to variety and desired end use.

For best results plan your schedule carefully before freezing.

Aim to pick and freeze on the same day, and work quickly but carefully in manageable quantities.

Choose the method of preparation and have the ingredients prepared or close at hand.

Remember to freeze only food in good condition – freezing won't improve it!

Any foods which have been blanched or cooked should be cooled quickly and thoroughly before freezing.

Pack into suitable freezer-proof containers such as heavy-duty foil, freezer- and vapour-proof polythene, rigid containers, freezer film, etc.

Exclude as much air as possible from the boxes or packets as you can prior to freezing so that packages take up as little space as possible.

If adding quite a few packs to the freezer, switch to fast freeze at least 1 hour before use.

Try to follow the rules on labelling and storing – once the contents are frozen it is difficult to check if a pack contains chopped apples or baby queen scallops! It can be a bore but try to keep a freezer record for good rotation of stock and variety.

Unless you plan to feed a crowd quite frequently, freeze in meal-size or manageable quantities.

Blanching

This is necessary for long-term storage to retard the activity of natural enzymes in vegetables. To blanch, fill a blanching basket or wire basket with about 450 g (1 lb) prepared vegetables. Immerse in a large pan of boiling water – use about 4 litres (7 pints). Return quickly to the boil, then time accurately according to the chart from the moment the water returns to the boil. Remove the vegetables from the water and plunge at once into iced water. Drain and pack. Use this blanching water up to 6 times, then replace with new.

Freeze as a solid block or free-flow. To freeze for free-flow, lay the blanched vegetables on a tray in the freezer and freeze until firm, making sure they do not touch each other. When solid, pack into freezer bags, seal, label and store.

Freezing fruit

Choose one of the following methods for freezing fruit:

UNSWEETENED DRY PACK This is useful for people on sugar-free diets and is perhaps the simplest method. Wash and drain the fruit, dry as much as possible then pack into cartons, seal, label and freeze.

DRY SUGAR PACK Wash, drain and dry the fruit, then either mix fruit and sugar in a bowl (450 g (1 lb) sugar to 1.4 kg (3 lb) fruit) or pack fruit in layers with the sugar. Leave 1 cm (½ in) headspace in all cases to allow room for the fruit to expand when it freezes. Seal, label and freeze.

SYRUP PACK Make a sugar syrup using 900 g (2 lb) sugar to 1.2 litres (2 pints) water; the sugar must be completely dissolved in boiling water, then cooled before use. Pack the fruit into containers and cover with syrup, leaving a 1–2.5 cm (½–1 in) headspace. To prevent freezer burn a piece of cellophane should be pressed down over the fruit into the syrup (to make it airtight) before sealing the container.

POACHING First simmer the fruit in a little sugar syrup. Pour the fruit and syrup into a container and allow to cool completely before freezing. Seal, label and freeze.

FRUIT PURÉE Cook the fruit in a little water and sieve or simply purée in a blender, sieving after to remove any pips if liked. Sweeten to taste before freezing if preferred.

Fruit freezing chart

FRUIT	SUITABLE METHODS
Apples	*Dry pack, dry sugar pack, syrup pack, poach or purée.*
Apricots	*Dry sugar pack, syrup pack, poach or purée.*
Blackberries	*Dry pack, dry sugar pack, syrup pack or poach.*
Blueberries	*Dry pack, dry sugar pack or syrup pack.*
Cherries	*Dry pack, dry sugar pack or syrup pack.*
Currants – all types	*Dry pack, dry sugar pack or purée.*
Damsons	*Dry pack, dry sugar pack, syrup pack, poach or purée.*
Figs	*Dry pack or syrup pack.*
Gooseberries	*Dry pack, dry sugar pack, syrup pack or purée.*
Grapes	*Syrup pack.*
Greengages	*Dry pack, dry sugar pack, syrup pack, poach or purée.*
Loganberries	*Dry pack, dry sugar pack, syrup pack or purée.*
Melons	*Syrup pack.*

continued p.252

Vegetable freezing chart

Those vegetables not mentioned are considered unsuitable for freezing.

Vegetable	Selection	Preparation for freezing	Blanching time	Storage time
ARTICHOKES, GLOBE	Small young chokes that are not fully open.	Remove coarse outer leaves. Trim stalk level with base. Cut off pointed top and spiky tops to leaves. Freeze whole or as hearts. Cook hearts before freezing.	whole: 5 to 7 minutes hearts: no need	12 months 6 months
ARTICHOKES, JERUSALEM	Choose firm tubers.	Scrub, peel thinly and slice or dice.	2 minutes	3 months
ASPARAGUS	Choose young tender stalks. Reject any with woody or withered stems.	Grade according to thickness. Trim off thick end and any scales. Sort into equal bundles.	2 to 4 minutes	12 months
AUBERGINES	Choose firm ripe fruits with smooth shiny skins.	Slice or cube according to later use. Degorge and rinse.	cubes: 4 minutes slices: 3 minutes	9 months
BEANS BROAD	Small young pods.	Shell or if very young leave whole.	1½ to 2 minutes	12 months
BEANS, FRENCH	Choose small tender beans not longer than 10 cm (4 in).	Top and tail. Slice if large.	whole: 3 minutes slices: 2 minutes	12 months

BEANS, RUNNER	Young crisp beans.	Top and tail, remove strings. Leave whole or slice.	whole: 3 minutes slices: 2 minutes	12 months
BEETROOT	Select small beetroot about 7.5 cm (3 in) in diameter.	Twist off leaves. Wash carefully. Cook before freezing.	—	6 months
BROCCOLI	Bright green, purple or white compact heads with tender stalks.	Grade for size and cut into even-sized pieces.	2 to 4 minutes	12 months
BRUSSELS SPROUTS	Choose small very firm and tight buds.	Wash, trim the base and remove any outer damaged leaves. Grade according to size.	1½ to 3 minutes	12 months
CABBAGE, SUMMER, AUTUMN, WINTER, SAVOY AND RED	Select firm heads with a good colour and firm texture.	Remove and discard outer leaves. Cut into quarters and remove woody triangles at base. Shred finely.	1 minute	12 months
CABBAGE, SPRING	Young dark green leaves.	Separate leaves. Trim away any hard ends. Leave whole or cut into strips.	1½ minutes	6 months
CARROTS	Choose young spring carrots of even shape.	Remove tops and scrub or peel thinly. Freeze whole or sliced.	3 minutes	12 minutes
CAULIFLOWERS	Choose white, firm cauliflowers with green leaves and fresh appearance.	Divide into florets about 5 cm (2 in) in diameter. Grade according to size.	2 to 3 minutes	6 months

[Vegetable freezing chart (continued)]

Vegetable	Selection	Preparation for freezing	Blanching time	Storage time
CELERIAC	Choose firm small roots.	Peel and wash then cut into cubes, thick slices or grate.	cubes and slices: 1 to 2 minutes grated: 1 to 1½ minutes	12 months
CELERY	Select firm large heads that are fresh and green.	Scrub and slice into 5 cm (2 in) lengths.	3 minutes	9 months
CHICORY	Choose conical, tightly-packed heads.	Trim bases and remove any outer damaged leaves.	4 minutes	5 months
CHILLIS	Firm, shiny chillis without wrinkles	Cut in half, remove stalks and seeds. Open freeze on trays. Double wrap.	—	12 months
COURGETTES	Small young courgettes.	Trim the ends and leave whole, slice or cube.	whole: 2 minutes slices or cubes: 1 minute	9 months
CUCUMBERS	Firm straight cucumbers.	Peel, chop and purée. Freeze leaving 2 cm (¾ in) headspace.	—	2 months
FENNEL	Choose firm, tight heads with white leaf bases.	Trim and cut each head into quarters.	3 to 5 minutes	6 months

	Selection	Preparation	Blanching time	Storage time
HORSERADISH	Young roots that show no signs of woodiness.	Trim, clean thoroughly then grate. Sprinkle with wine vinegar. Pack in rigid containers.	—	6 months
KOHLRABI	Choose small stems with a firm texture.	Remove leaves and peel thinly. Slice or leave small whole.	whole: 3 minutes slices: 2 minutes	12 months
KALE	Choose young leaves with a good bright green colour.	Pull the leaves from the stems like spinach. Wash.	3 minutes	12 months
LEEKS	Choose firm, young leeks with a fresh green colour.	Trim away root and the topmost green leaves. Wash thoroughly and leave whole or slice.	3 to 4 minutes	6 months
LETTUCE	Select tight lettuce hearts that are crisp and firm.	Remove any damaged or wilted leaves.	2 minutes	6 months
MARROWS	Choose only small to medium marrows.	Peel if liked. Halve and scoop out seeds. Cut into 2.5 cm (1 in) dice.	2 minutes	6 months
MUSHROOMS & FUNGI	Choose firm undamaged mushrooms with no trace of damp.	Wipe and trim stalks if necessary. Leave raw or sauté in butter. Open freeze whole uncooked mushrooms. Pack sauteéd mushrooms into rigid containers.	—	whole uncooked: 1 month sauteéd: 3 months

[Vegetable freezing chart (continued)]

Vegetable	Selection	Preparation for freezing	Blanching time	Storage time
ONIONS	Firm onions of all varieties with crisp, papery skins.	Trim, top, tail and peel. Grade according to size. Leave whole or slice.	whole, button or shallots: 2 to 4 minutes sliced: 1 to 2 minutes	6 months 6 months
OKRA	Small pods about 5 cm (2 in) long.	Trim the stems.	3 minutes	12 months
PARSNIPS	Young parsnips that are crisp and bright in colour.	Trim and wash. Peel thinly and core and slice.	4 minutes	12 months
PEAS, PODDED	Young and tender pods.	Shell.	1 minute	12 months
PEAS, MANGETOUT	Flat shiny pods.	Top and tail.	½ to 1 minute	12 months
PEPPERS	Firm shiny peppers without wrinkles.	Core, deseed and slice or chop. No need to blanch for 6 months storage.	3 minutes	12 months
POTATOES	Undamaged tubers without signs of decay or disease.	Scrub *new potatoes* and remove skins. Cook until tender. Freeze. For *chips* – cook in hot oil for 2 to 3 minutes. Drain and open freeze.		3 months

PUMPKIN	Choose firm fruit without too many blemishes.	Peel and remove seeds. Cut into chunks and cook until soft. Drain and mash. Pack in rigid containers leaving 2 cm (6 in) headspace.	—	12 months
RADISHES, WINTER	Choose firm undamaged roots.	Trim, scrub and peel thinly, then grate or dice.	2 minutes	6 months
SALSIFY & SCORZONERA	Choose firm young roots that are fresh in appearance.	Trim off leaves and scrub but do not peel. Blanch for 2 minutes then remove skins. Cut into 7.5 cm (3 in) pieces.	—	6 months
SPINACH	Young fresh green crisp yet tender leaves.	Snap off stalks, wash each leaf individually.	2 minutes	12 months
SWEDES	Small roots that show no signs of woodiness.	Top, tail and peel thinly. Cut into 2 cm (¾ in) dice.	2 minutes	12 months
SWEETCORN	Choose cobs that are just ripe with plump, pale-coloured kernels which are even-sized.	Pull away leaves and silks. Trim stems level with base of cobs. Alternatively remove kernels after blanching.	2 to 6 minutes	12 months
TOMATOES	Chose firm, medium-sized ordinary tomatoes, under rather than over ripe.	Prepare whole or as pureé. Pack in rigid containers leaving a 2 cm (¾ in) headspace.	—	12 months
TURNIPS	Choose small to medium turnips that have bright green tops.	Top and tail then peel thinly. Leave small whole or cut into 2 cm (¾ in) dice.	2 to 3 minutes	12 months

Mulberries	*Dry pack, dry sugar pack, syrup pack or purée.*
Peaches and Nectarines	*Dry sugar pack, syrup pack or purée.*
Pears	*Syrup pack.*
Plums	*Dry sugar pack, syrup pack or purée.*
Quince	*Poached.*
Raspberries	*Dry pack, syrup pack or purée.*
Rhubarb	*Dry pack, syrup pack or purée.*
Strawberries	*Dry pack, syrup pack or purée.*

Recipes

17. Beautiful Beginnings: Soups & Starters

Chilled Cucumber Soup

This cold soup takes only 15 minutes to prepare and involves no cooking; therefore it is ideal for those who do not want to waste the precious days of sunshine in the kitchen. It is great for picnics too – carry it in a vacuum flask to keep it icy cold.

(SERVES 4–6)

1 large cucumber
100 g (4 oz) garlic cheese (or other soft lightly whipped cheese flavoured with garlic and herbs)
250 ml (8 fl oz) thick natural Greek-style yoghurt
1 tablespoon lemon juice
salt and freshly ground black pepper
a few fresh mint leaves or thinly sliced cucumber to garnish

Wash and dry the cucumber, then coarsely grate into a bowl. Gradually blend the cheese into the yoghurt until smooth, then stir into the grated cucumber with the lemon juice. Season to taste with salt and pepper and chill for at least 1 hour.

Thin the soup if necessary with a little milk. Serve garnished with whole or chopped mint leaves or a few paper-thin slices of cucumber. Serve with crusty bread.

Carrot and Lentil Revival Soup

This welcoming and reviving carrot and lentil soup is subtly flavoured with a garlic and herb cheese. Don't be tempted to omit the croûtons – they provide a delicious crunchy contrast to the medley of vegetables in the soup itself. Hearty and nourishing, it's ideal for a winter lunch or supper dish.

(SERVES 4–6)

450 ml (¾ pint) boiling water
50 g (2 oz) red lentils
50 g (2 oz) butter or margarine
1 large onion, peeled and chopped
2 sticks celery, chopped
225 g (8 oz) carrots, peeled and grated
600 ml (1 pint) vegetable or chicken stock
½ teaspoon dried mixed herbs
1 tablespoon cornflour
150 ml (¼ pint) milk
100 g (4 oz) tub Danish Castello Bouquet cheese with garlic and herbs
   (or other soft garlic and herb cheese)
4 slices wholemeal bread, cubed

Pour the boiling water over the lentils and leave to soak for 1 hour. Meanwhile, melt half the butter or margarine in a large pan, add the onion and celery and fry gently for 5 minutes. Stir in the carrots and cook for a further 2 minutes. Add the lentils with their water, the stock and herbs. *Stir well, bring to the boil, lower the heat and simmer for 45 minutes, or until the lentils are tender. Remove from the heat.*

Blend the cornflour to a smooth paste with a little of the milk. Add the rest of the milk and half of the cheese. Blend until smooth, then stir into the soup. Return the pan to the heat and bring to the boil, stirring constantly, then cook for 1 minute.

To make the croûtons, melt the remaining butter or margarine and cheese in a frying pan. Add the bread cubes and fry until crisp and brown, tossing frequently. Remove with a slotted spoon and drain on absorbent kitchen paper. Serve the soup hot, topped with the warm croûtons.

Aubergine Pâté

This thick, tasty aubergine purée has also been described as 'poor man's caviar'. It is delicious served with crisp crackers and toast or a selection of vegetable crudités such as carrot sticks, celery strips, cauliflower florets, whole mushrooms and pepper slices.

(SERVES 4)

450 g (1 lb) aubergines
4 tablespoons olive oil
1 small onion, peeled and finely chopped
½ green pepper, cored, seeded and finely chopped
225 g (8 oz) tomatoes, peeled and chopped
1–2 garlic cloves, peeled and crushed
2 tablespoons white wine
lemon juice
salt and freshly ground black pepper
chopped parsley, to garnish

Trim the caps from the aubergines, prick well and place on a baking tray. Bake in a preheated moderate oven (180°C (350°F, Gas Mark 4)), for about 1 hour until soft. Allow to cool.

Heat the oil in a heavy based pan, add the onion and pepper and cook until softened – about 5 minutes. Add the tomatoes and simmer over a gentle heat until pulpy, about 10–15 minutes.

Meanwhile, halve the aubergines and scoop out the soft flesh with a spoon. Add to the tomato mixture with the garlic and wine. Mix well, season to taste with salt and pepper and continue to cook until very thick. Allow to cool.

Beat the cooled mixture to a thick purée and stir in lemon juice to taste, about 1 tablespoon. Spoon into a serving dish and sprinkle with chopped parsley. Chill thoroughly before serving.

Crudités with Dips

Crudités with dips are the perfect starter to a summer meal or appetiser with drinks before a winter dinner; they also make wonderful party fare. Use the best of crudité vegetables in season; below are just a selection of ideas.

(SERVES 6–8)

Crudités:
5 cm (2 in) lengths of cucumber, carrot and pepper strips
florets of broccoli or cauliflower
whole baby mushrooms, tomatoes and sweetcorn
trimmed spring onions
slices of cucumber and fennel

Spicy Cheese Dip:
200 g (7 oz) skimmed milk soft cheese
3 tablespoons mayonnaise or salad cream
2 teaspoons tomato paste
1 teaspoon chilli sauce

Curry Dip:
6 tablespoons mayonnaise or salad cream
2 tablespoons curry paste
1 teaspoon mango chutney

Avocado Dip:

1 large ripe avocado, peeled and stoned

1 teaspoon lemon juice

2 tablespoons mayonnaise or salad cream

salt and freshly ground black pepper

dash of chilli sauce

To make the spicy cheese dip, mix all the ingredients together and place in a small bowl.

For the curry dip, mix all the ingredients together, blending well, and place in a small bowl.

To make the avocado dip, either whizz all the ingredients together in a blender or food processor or mash the avocado with the lemon juice and then stir in the remaining ingredients. Place in a small serving bowl.

Place the three bowls of dips in the centre of a large serving platter and surround with a selection of the freshly prepared crudité vegetables. Chill lightly and serve as soon as possible.

Melon and Orange Caprice

This is one of those magical dishes which can be served as either a starter or a dessert. The melons are stuffed with melon balls, orange segments and small spoonfuls of cream cheese mixed with hazelnuts and ground ginger.

(SERVES 4)

2 small ripe melons

4 oranges, peeled, pith removed and segmented

1 tablespoon clear honey

100 g (4 oz) low fat cream cheese

¼–½ teaspoon ground ginger

25 g (1 oz) hazelnuts, finely chopped

mint sprigs to garnish

Cut the melons in half and remove the seeds. Using a small spoon or melon baller, scoop out the flesh in balls and place in a bowl. Add the orange segments and mix well. Reserve any juice from the oranges and mix with the honey.

Mix the cheese with the ginger, form into small balls and roll in the hazelnuts. Fill the empty melon shells with the prepared fruit and cheese balls. Spoon over the honey mixture and decorate with sprigs of mint to serve.

Celeriac and Apple Rémoulade

This has been a great favourite of mine ever since I first tasted it at one of my favourite restaurants, Pennyhill Park. They always tell me that it is made with organically grown celeriac and apples from a 'good' local source, so there's not a hint of pesticide in sight! It is usually on the menu as a starter adorned with thin slices of pink lamb, but is equally good served alone with a sprinkling of herbs.

(SERVES 4)

1 medium celeriac
1 tart eating apple
1 tablespoon lemon juice
3 tablespoons mayonnaise
2 tablespoons whipped cream
½ teaspoon Dijon mustard
salt and pepper
4 teaspoons snipped chives, parsley and tarragon

Peel the celeriac and peel and core the apple. Cut both into thin slices and then thin julienne strips. Toss in the lemon juice to prevent turning brown.

Mix the mayonnaise with the cream, mustard and salt and pepper to taste. Fold the celeriac and apple pieces into the sauce to coat. Spoon on to serving plates and sprinkle with the chives, parsley and tarragon.

Cheese and Carrot Oaties

(MAKES 12)

75 g (3 oz) peanut butter
50 g (2 oz) butter or soft margarine
75 g (3 oz) wholemeal plain flour
40 g (1½ oz) medium oatmeal
75 g (3 oz) Cheddar cheese, grated
2 carrots, grated

Rub the peanut butter and butter or margarine into the flour and oatmeal. Stir in the cheese and one grated carrot and mix to a dough. Knead lightly, then press into a 20 cm (8 in) round flan ring placed on a lightly oiled baking tray.

Bake in a preheated moderately hot oven at 190°C (375°F, Gas Mark 5) for about 25 minutes. Remove from the flan ring, then cut into 12 wedges while still warm. Serve warm or cold with grated carrot on top.

Courgette and Peanut Quiche Wedges

These tasty quiche wedges make the perfect start to a light main meal but can also be served as picnic, lunch-box or late supper fare.

(SERVES 4–6)

Pastry:
50 g (2 oz) plain white flour
50 g (2 oz) wholemeal flour
25 g (1 oz) butter or margarine
2 tablespoons crunchy peanut butter
cold water to mix

Filling:
1 teaspoon oil
225 g (8 oz) courgettes
225 g (8 oz) cottage cheese
2 tablespoons crunchy peanut butter
2 eggs, beaten

4 tablespoons milk
grated Parmesan cheese
paprika pepper

To make the pastry, mix the flours together in a bowl. Rub in the butter or margarine and peanut butter until the mixture resembles fine breadcrumbs. Stir in enough water to bind to a firm but pliable dough. Roll out thinly on a floured surface and use to line an 18 cm (7 in) loose-bottomed French flan tin. Bake 'blind' in a preheated moderately hot oven at 200°C (400°F, Gas Mark 6) for 25 minutes.

Meanwhile, heat the oil in a pan, add the courgettes and cook for about 4 minutes. Drain on absorbent kitchen paper, then arrange in the partly cooked pastry case. Beat the cottage cheese with the egg, milk and peanut butter and pour over the courgettes. Dust liberally with Parmesan cheese, then sprinkle with paprika pepper. Return to the oven and bake for a further 30 minutes.

Serve warm or cold cut into wedges.

Courgette and Tomato Bake

This crunchy vegetable dish of courgettes and tomatoes makes a good hot starter, or it can be served as part of a vegetarian style meal.

(SERVES 4)

450 g (1 lb) courgettes, trimmed and thickly sliced
1 tablespoon vegetable oil
1 onion, peeled and chopped
1 garlic clove, peeled and crushed
1 carrot, coarsely grated
225 g (8 oz) tomatoes, sliced
1 teaspoon chopped fresh marjoram

Topping
4 tablespoons mayonnaise or salad cream
4 tablespoons single cream
salt and freshly ground black pepper

Place the courgettes in a pan of water, bring to the boil and cook for 1 minute. Drain thoroughly.

Heat the oil in a pan, add the onion, garlic and carrot and cook until tender, about 5–10 minutes. Arrange half the courgettes and tomatoes on the base of a shallow ovenproof dish. Cover with the onion mixture, spreading well, then sprinkle with the marjoram and season to taste with salt and pepper. Top with the remaining courgettes and tomatoes.

To make the topping, mix the mayonnaise or salad cream with the single cream. Drizzle over the courgette and tomatoes. Cover and bake in a preheated moderately hot oven at 190°C (375°F, Gas Mark 5) for about 30 minutes.

Remove from the oven and toss the vegetables together to coat with the creamy sauce. Serve at once.

Eggs Florentine

The most successful starters are often those which are quick and easy to prepare yet still look good. This simple recipe certainly fits the bill and moreover is economical.

(SERVES 4)

900 g (2 lb) fresh spinach, trimmed, washed and chopped
salt and freshly ground black pepper
4 eggs
4 teaspoons mayonnaise
grated nutmeg

Cook the spinach in about 4 tablespoons water until tender, about 4–6 minutes. Drain thoroughly by squeezing with the back of a spoon through a sieve. Divide between 4 lightly greased ramekin dishes, making deep hollows in the centres.

Crack an egg into each hollow and top with a teaspoon of the mayonnaise and a sprinkling of nutmeg.

Bake in a preheated moderately hot oven at 200°C (400°F, Gas Mark 6) for 12–15 minutes or until the whites have set but the yolks are still runny. Serve at once.

Crunchy Cheese with Cherry Sauce

This tasty, crunchy fried cheese with cherry sauce accompaniment is ideal for a cheese and wine party dish, an unusual starter or a savoury at the end of a meal.

(SERVES 4)

150 g (5 oz) disc Dania (or other Brie-type) cheese
15 g (½ oz) flour
1 egg, beaten
40 g (1½ oz) fresh white breadcrumbs
oil for deep frying

Sauce:
225 g (8 oz) cherries, stoned
150 ml (¼ pint) dry white wine or water
1½ teaspoons arrowroot powder
2 teaspoons sugar (optional)

Cut the cheese into 4 equal wedges. Dip each into the flour and shake off the excess. Dip into the beaten egg and finally into the breadcrumbs. Place on a plate and chill for at least 30 minutes.

Meanwhile, to make the sauce, cook the cherries in the wine or water until just tender. Mix the arrowroot with a little water to make a paste and then stir into the cherries, blending well. Cook until smooth, clear and thickened. Add the sugar if necessary to sweeten the sauce to taste.

Heat the oil in a deep fat fryer to 180°C (350°F) then lower the cheeses, two at a time, into the hot fat and fry for ½–1 minute or until the coating is golden. Remove from the pan and drain on absorbent kitchen towel.

Serve the cheese wedges at once with the cherry sauce.

18. Side Lines:
Vegetables & Salads

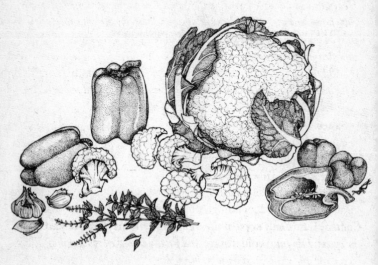

Gingered Cauliflower Medley Stir-Fry

This is an unusual but flavoursome way to serve cauliflower with an interesting medley of vegetables and seasonings. Make sure your timings are accurate so that the vegetables stay tender-crisp for serving.

(SERVES 4)

2 tablespoons oil
1 slice root ginger, very finely chopped
1 garlic clove, peeled and crushed
1 medium cauliflower, trimmed and broken into small florets
1 green or red pepper, cored, seeded and sliced
100 ml (4 fl oz) vegetable stock

1 teaspoon chopped fresh basil

1 teaspoon chopped fresh oregano

3 tomatoes, peeled, seeded and chopped

75 g (3 oz) fresh young peas

salt and freshly ground black pepper

Heat the oil in a large frying pan or wok. Add the ginger and garlic and cook for ½ minute. Add the cauliflower and stir-fry for 2 minutes. Stir in the red (or green) pepper, stock, basil and oregano, blending well. Cover and steam for 3 minutes.

Add the tomatoes and peas with salt and pepper to taste and stir-fry for a further 3–5 minutes or until the vegetables are all cooked tender-crisp. Serve at once.

Kitchen Garden Rice

Whenever we tire of potatoes or pasta I cook this tasty vegetable rice or a version of it (depending upon what vegetables are in season or to hand). I usually serve it hot as a vegetable accompaniment but it is equally as good cold, tossed with a little salad dressing.

(SERVES 4)

175 g (6 oz) French or dwarf beans, trimmed and cut into 2.5 cm (1 in) lengths

100 g (4 oz) fresh peas

100 g (4 oz) broccoli, divided into small florets

2 courgettes, trimmed and thickly sliced into strips

175 g (6 oz) long-grain rice

50 g (2 oz) butter or margarine

3 tomatoes, skinned, seeded and chopped

1 garlic clove, peeled and crushed (optional)

100 g (4 oz) button mushrooms, wiped and sliced

50 g (2 oz) pine nuts (optional)

salt and freshly ground black pepper

2 tablespoons chopped fresh parsley

Cook the beans, peas, broccoli and courgettes in boiling salted water until barely tender, about 4–5 minutes. Drain and set aside.

Meanwhile, cook the rice in boiling salted water according to the packet instructions and rice type until tender. Drain thoroughly.

Melt the butter in a large, deep frying pan, add the tomatoes, garlic and mushrooms and sauté for 3 minutes. Stir in the pine nuts, if used, with the cooked vegetables and rice. Add salt and pepper to taste and stir well to mix. Heat through until the mixture is piping hot, about 1–2 minutes, then spoon into a warmed serving dish. Sprinkle liberally with the parsley and serve at once.

Cauliflower Fritters

(SERVES 4)

  100 g (4 oz) plain flour
  pinch of salt
  150 ml (¼ pint) milk
  1 tablespoon oil
  1 egg, separated
  100 g (4 oz) Cheddar cheese, grated
  1 cauliflower, divided into florets
  oil for deep frying

Sift the flour with the salt into a bowl. Gradually add the milk, oil and egg yolk, mixing well to make a smooth batter. Chill for 30 minutes.

Stir the cheese into the batter. Whisk the egg white until stiff, then fold in with a metal spoon.

Steam the cauliflower florets for 10 minutes, then drain well. Dust in a little flour, then coat in the batter. Deep-fry in hot oil for about 2 minutes until crisp and golden. Drain on absorbent kitchen paper.

Serve hot. Delicious with tartare sauce.

Salsify au Gratin

This vegetable dish makes a good accompaniment to roast or grilled meats, or can be served with other vegetable dishes as part of a vegetarian meal.

(SERVES 4–6)

1.25 kg (2½ lb) salsify
3 tablespoons lemon juice
40 g (1½ oz) butter or margarine
2 shallots, peeled and finely chopped
40 g (1½ oz) plain flour
450 ml (¾ pint) milk
100 g (4 oz) Cheshire cheese, grated
½ teaspoon wholegrain mustard
4 tablespoons double cream
2 egg yolks
salt and freshly ground black pepper
3 tablespoons dried breadcrumbs

Scrape the skins from the salsify, then cut the flesh into chunks about 5 cm (2 in) long. Place in a pan with cold water and the lemon juice and cook for 10–15 minutes until just tender.

Meanwhile, melt the butter in a pan. Add the shallots and cook until softened. Add the flour and cook for 1 minute, then gradually stir in the milk. Bring to the boil, stirring constantly, until smooth, glossy and thickened. Remove from the heat and stir in three-quarters of the cheese. Mix the cream with the egg yolks and stir into the hot cheese sauce, blending well. Cook over a gentle heat for 1 minute but do not allow to boil.

Drain the salsify thoroughly and mix into the hot sauce. Spoon into an ovenproof dish. Mix the breadcrumbs with the reserved cheese and sprinkle over the top.

Bake in a preheated moderately hot oven at 200°C (400°F, Gas Mark 6) for about 25–30 minutes until golden and bubbly. Serve at once.

Variations

SCORZONERA AU GRATIN *Prepare and cook as above but use scorzonera instead of the salsify.*
SKIRRET AU GRATIN *Prepare and cook as above but use skirret instead of the salsify. Scrub or scrape the skirret as for salsify, but leave whole and*

cook until just beginning to soften but not quite tender; it will finish cooking in the sauce, but if it is cooked too much during the first stage it will tend to dissolve into the sauce.

Pear Waldorf Salad

This variation of the classic apple-based Waldorf Salad makes a splendid late summer main meal lunch dish – add 175 g (6 oz) diced, cooked chicken to make a little more substantial if preferred. Serve with warm wholemeal bread.

(SERVES 4)

1 lettuce, washed and shredded
2 sticks celery, sliced
1 red pepper, cored, seeded and sliced
25 g (1 oz) walnuts, chopped
2 pears, peeled, cored and sliced

Dressing:
4 tablespoons mayonnaise
2 teaspoons chopped fresh mint
2 tablespoons grated cucumber
salt and freshly ground black pepper
unpeeled pear slices, to garnish

Mix the lettuce with the celery, pepper, walnuts and peeled pear slices in a serving bowl, tossing gently to mix.

To make the dressing, mix the mayonnaise with the mint, cucumber and salt and pepper to taste, blending well. Fold into the pear mixture to coat lightly.

Serve lightly chilled, garnished with unpeeled pear slices.

Curly Endive and Citrus Chicken Salad

(SERVES 4)

1 round lettuce, washed
½ curly endive or frisée lettuce, washed
50 g (2 oz) corn salad, lamb's lettuce or watercress, washed
¼ cucumber, sliced
2 grapefruit, peeled, pith removed and cut into segments
350 g (12 oz) cooked chicken, cut into thin strips
1 pepper, cored, seeded and sliced

Dressing:
150 ml (¼ pint) thick natural Greek-style yoghurt
2 tablespoons grapefruit or lemon juice
salt and freshly ground black pepper
croûtons, to garnish

*Tear the lettuce and endive or frisée lettuce into bite-sized pieces and place
in a salad bowl with the corn salad, lamb's lettuce or watercress. Add the
cucumber, grapefruit, chicken and pepper and toss lightly to mix. Cover and
chill for 30 minutes.*

*To make the dressing, mix the yoghurt with grapefruit juice or lemon
juice and add salt and pepper to taste, blending well.*

*Just before serving, sprinkle the salad with the croûtons to garnish.
Serve the dressing separately with the salad.*

Spinach and Mushroom Salad

(SERVES 4)

225 g (8 oz) fresh young spinach leaves
175 g (6 oz) firm button mushrooms, wiped and thinly sliced
4 tablespoons mayonnaise
2 tablespoons walnut oil
1 tablespoon lemon juice
2 teaspoons chopped fresh parsley

269

salt and freshly ground black pepper

50–75 g (2–3 oz) feta cheese, crumbled (optional)

Trim and wash the spinach leaves, then dry thoroughly. Place in a salad bowl with the mushrooms, tossing gently to mix.

To make the dressing, mix the mayonnaise with the walnut oil, lemon juice, parsley and salt and pepper to taste, blending well.

Just before serving, pour the dressing over the salad and toss lightly to coat. Serve at once, sprinkled with the crumbled feta cheese if liked.

Best-ever Potato Salad

This is the best potato salad I know. The bacon is optional but the lovage is something of a must – though don't be tempted to add too much, as lovage has a strong distinctive flavour which could overwhelm if not used cautiously. When lovage is unavailable, use chopped celery leaf instead.

(SERVES 4–6)

1 kg (2 lb) new potatoes, scrubbed

salt and freshly ground black pepper

6 tablespoons walnut or other salad oil

75 g (3 oz) smoked bacon, rinded and chopped (optional)

2 shallots, peeled and thinly sliced

3 tablespoons wine vinegar

pinch of castor sugar

1 teaspoon chopped fresh lovage

2 tablespoons snipped fresh chives

3 tablespoons natural thick-set yoghurt

Cook the potatoes in their skins in boiling salted water until tender, about 20–30 minutes, depending on size. Slice thickly into a serving bowl. Season generously with salt and pepper.

Heat the oil in a frying pan, add the bacon (if used) and cook until crisp and golden. Add the shallots and cook for ½ minute, then add the vinegar and sugar, stirring well to mix. Pour over the potatoes, add the lovage, chives and yoghurt and toss gently to coat. Serve warm or cold.

Pink Winter Salad

The natural colour of the red cabbage and beetroot in this salad turns the dressing a delicate shade of pink – a warm colour for cold winter nights.

(SERVES 4–6)

200 g (7 oz) (about ¼ small) red cabbage, finely shredded
200 g (7 oz) can red kidney beans, drained
2–3 cooked beetroot, cubed
4 tablespoons mayonnaise
100 g (4 oz) streaky bacon, cut into strips
salt and freshly ground black pepper
1 tablespoon sunflower seeds

Mix the shredded red cabbage with the kidney beans and beetroot. Stir in the mayonnaise and toss lightly until the dressing turns pink.

Fry the bacon in a non-stick pan until crisp and brown. Drain on absorbent kitchen paper and scatter over the salad. Season with salt and pepper to taste, then toss again lightly. Sprinkle with sunflower seeds and serve at once.

Cut-and-Come-Again
Stilton and Peach Salad

This is a favourite salad to make with the seemingly endless supply of cutting salad mixture that we grow. The mixtures can contain corn salad, celery leaf, coriander, summer purslane, rocket and chop-suey greens. I always add a sprinkling of cress cut from the children's windowsill 'garden' to this salad too!

(SERVES 4)

1 small Lollo Rosso lettuce
2 large handfuls of cutting salad mixture
3 ripe peaches, peeled, stoned and thinly sliced
175 g (6 oz) Stilton cheese, thinly sliced

Dressing:
6 tablespoons olive oil
1 tablespoon mild coarse grain mustard
2 tablespoons clear honey
2 tablespoons white wine vinegar
salt and freshly ground black pepper

Separate the lettuce into leaves, tearing any larger ones into small bite-sized pieces. Arrange on a large salad plate or in a shallow bowl with the washed and trimmed cutting salad mixture, tossing well to mix. Cover with the sliced peaches and Stilton, arranged attractively.

To make the dressing, beat the oil with the mustard, honey, vinegar and salt and pepper to taste until well blended. Dribble it over the salad and serve at once.

Hot Pasta and Vegetable Salad

This is the perfect spring-time salad to make when vegetables are young and need 'stretching' with pasta. Tossed in a light coating of mayonnaise and mint it makes a complete light meal in itself, or it can be served with a meat or poultry accompaniment. It is equally delicious served cold.

(SERVES 4)

175 g (6 oz) dried multi-coloured pasta shapes
100 g (4 oz) baby corn on the cob or sweetcorn
100 g (4 oz) broccoli, divided into small florets
1 medium courgette, trimmed and sliced
1 red pepper, cored, seeded and cut into thin strips
1 teaspoon oil

272

4 tablespoons mayonnaise
1 tablespoon chopped fresh mint
freshly ground black pepper

Cook the pasta in a large pan of boiling salted water for 10 minutes or according to the packet instructions.

After 5 minutes, bring a large pan of salted water to the boil, add the sweetcorn and simmer for 2 minutes. Add the broccoli, courgette and red pepper and simmer for a further 3 minutes.

Drain the pasta and vegetables and place in a warmed bowl with the oil, tossing gently to mix. Carefully stir in the mayonnaise and mint and season with pepper to taste. Spoon into a serving dish and serve at once.

Spring Cabbage or Pak Choy Salad

(SERVES 4)

2 tablespoons oil
1 spring cabbage or medium bunch of pak choy, cored and shredded
1 onion, peeled and sliced
1 garlic clove, peeled and crushed
1 tablespoon lemon juice
150 ml (¼ pint) thick natural Greek-style yoghurt
2 teaspoons creamed horseradish

Heat the oil in a large frying pan or wok. Add the cabbage or pak choy, onion and garlic. Fry for 5–10 minutes until just tender but still firm.

Meanwhile, mix the lemon juice with the yoghurt and horseradish. Drain the cabbage mixture and toss in the horseradish mixture to serve.

Salad Crunch

This is a salad which just sort of 'happened' and has remained a firm favourite with the family ever since. It really has more style than the usual coleslaw offerings.

(SERVES 4–6)

350 g (12 oz) white cabbage, finely shredded
4 carrots, coarsely grated
1 apple, cored and chopped
50 g (2 oz) dates, stoned and chopped
25 g (1 oz) Brazil or other nuts, chopped
1 tablespoon raisins
1 tablespoon chopped fresh coriander

Dressing:
3 tablespoons olive oil
1 tablespoon lemon juice
2 teaspoons clear honey
1 teaspoon mild wholegrain mustard
salt and freshly ground black pepper

*Mix the cabbage with the carrots, apple, dates, nuts, raisins and coriander
in a large salad bowl.*

*To make the dressing, beat the oil with the lemon juice, honey, mustard
and salt and pepper to taste, blending well. Pour over the salad, toss gently
and serve.*

Greek Summer Salad

Ripe, fat tomatoes all the better for slicing and crumbly feta cheese
together conjure up images of summer and sunshine. If you do not
have a liquidiser, blender or food processor, then chop the fresh
basil, put all the ingredients in a screw-topped jar and shake well to
blend. If ewe's milk feta is a little strong-tasting for you, look out for
Danish feta made from pasteurised cow's milk.

(SERVES 4)

3 large 'beef' tomatoes
225 g (8 oz) feta cheese
10 black olives, drained

4 spring onions, trimmed and chopped

1 small lettuce (Lollo Rosso, for example)

Dressing:

100 ml (4 fl oz) sunflower oil

50 ml (2 fl oz) red wine vinegar

a few leaves of fresh basil

1 teaspoon tomato purée

1 teaspoon castor sugar

1 teaspoon French mustard

garlic salt and freshly ground black pepper

Blanch the tomatoes in boiling water to remove their skins, then slice. Crumble the feta into a bowl and add the tomatoes, black olives and spring onions.

To make the dressing, place all the ingredients with salt and pepper to taste in a liquidiser, blender or food processor and blend for a few seconds.

Pour the dressing over the tomato mixture and leave for 30 minutes to allow the flavours to develop.

Wash and dry the lettuce leaves and arrange on a serving dish or plate. Spoon the feta and tomato salad into the centre, garnish with fresh basil or parsley leaves if liked and serve with rolls for a light lunch or as a first course.

Mediterranean Salad

Recreate the salad mixtures of the Mediterranean with this stunning dish of beans, tomatoes, onions and peppers tossed with crisp lettuce heart and flaked tuna.

(SERVES 4)

1 garlic clove, peeled and halved

100 g (4 oz) French beans, trimmed

4 large tomatoes, cut into wedges

1 small onion, peeled and thinly sliced

1 yellow or green pepper, cored, seeded and sliced
1 lettuce heart, cut into wedges
8 black olives
200 g (7 oz) can tuna, drained and flaked

Dressing:
4 tablespoons natural yoghurt
1 tablespoon snipped chives
salt and freshly ground black pepper

Rub a large salad bowl with the cut clove of garlic. Cook the beans in boiling salted water until tender-crisp, drain and allow to cool.

Place the beans, tomatoes, onion, pepper, lettuce, black olives and tuna in the bowl and toss lightly to mix.

To make the dressing, mix the yoghurt with the chives and salt and pepper to taste. Pour over the salad mixture and toss lightly to coat. Serve as soon as possible.

Spring Spinach and Rice Salad

(SERVES 4)

225 g (8 oz) long-grain rice
1 bay leaf
1 teaspoon turmeric
2.5 cm (1 in) piece root ginger, peeled
100 g (4 oz) grated carrot
1 bunch spring onions, trimmed and chopped
100 g (4 oz) fresh spinach, trimmed, washed and chopped
3–4 tablespoons seafood mayonnaise or sauce
lemon wedges to garnish

Cook the rice in boiling salted water with the bay leaf, turmeric and ginger for 10–15 minutes until tender. Drain and allow to cool.

Add the carrots, spring onions and spinach, mixing well. Place in a serving bowl and spoon the sauce over the top. Garnish with wedges of lemon.

Chinese Leaf Salad Pitta Pockets

Some years ago I wrote *The Giant Sandwich Book*, which was great fun to develop since I have long been an enthusiast for the nutritious sandwich. I really thought there were no more fillings left to discover until my daughter came up with this idea recently. We love its unique taste and are sure you will enjoy the fish and fruit flavourings. We like to serve the salad in a pitta bread pocket but it can also be served alone.

(MAKES 8)

5 Chinese cabbage leaves, shredded
200 g (7 oz) can tuna in brine, drained and flaked
¼ cucumber, diced
¼ red pepper, diced
4 ripe apricots, stoned and chopped
1 tablespoon olive oil
2 tablespoons lemon juice
salt and freshly ground black pepper
8 mini pitta breads

Mix the Chinese cabbage with the tuna, cucumber, pepper and apricots. Beat the oil with the lemon juice and salt and pepper to taste, then add to the filling and toss gently to coat.

Split open each pitta at one end to form a pocket. Fill the pockets with the salad mixture. Serve as soon as possible, or wrap in foil or cling-film until required.

Gingered Corn Relish

This is an 'instant' relish not intended for long-term storage which makes a wonderful accompaniment or side dish to boiled bacon or cooked ham.

(SERVES 4–6)

25 g (1 oz) butter
1 tablespoon soft brown sugar
3 tablespoons marmalade
1 tablespoon distilled vinegar
1 teaspoon ground ginger
salt
225 g (8 oz) sweetcorn kernels, cooked

Melt the butter in a small pan. Add the sugar and cook over a moderate heat until dissolved. Gradually add the marmalade, vinegar, ginger and salt to taste, mixing well. Cook, stirring constantly, for about 2 minutes or until the mixture becomes smooth.

Add the cooked sweetcorn kernels, mixing well. Serve hot or cold as required.

19. The Main Event: Main Courses

Spare-rib of Pork Braised with Cabbage and Prunes

(SERVES 6–8)

1 medium white cabbage, cored and shredded
2 onions, peeled and sliced
100 g (4 oz) pre-soaked prunes, chopped
2 teaspoons fresh chopped sage
salt and freshly ground black pepper
150 ml (¼ pint) dry white wine
1.5 kg (3 lb) spare-rib pork joint, boned and rolled

Place the cabbage, onions and prunes in an ovenproof casserole. Add half of the sage and salt and pepper to taste, mixing well. Pour over the wine and place the pork joint on top, sprinkling with the remaining sage. Cover with foil and a tight-fitting lid. Cook in a preheated moderate oven at 180°C (350°F, Gas Mark 4) for 3–4 hours, or until the meat is very tender

To serve, remove the pork from the dish and slice thickly. Thicken the cooking liquor if liked with a little cornflour. Serve the sliced meat with the braised vegetables and their juices.

Rabbit or Pork with Normandy Sauce

(SERVES 4)

25 g (1 oz) butter or margarine
1 teaspoon oil
450 g (1 lb) rabbit fillets or pork fillet, cubed
2 tablespoons seasoned flour
1 onion, peeled and sliced
2 cooking apples, peeled, cored and sliced
2 leeks, trimmed and sliced
2 sprigs fresh thyme
300 ml (½ pint) chicken or light stock
300 ml (½ pint) milk
salt and pepper

Melt the butter and oil in a flameproof casserole dish. Toss the rabbit or pork fillet in the flour, then cook in the fat until lightly coloured on all sides. Add the onion, apples, leeks, thyme, stock, milk and salt and pepper to taste. Bring to the boil.

Remove from the heat and place in a preheated moderate oven at 180°C (350°F, Gas Mark 4) for 1–1¼ hours or until the meat is tender and the vegetables are cooked. Serve with rice and green vegetables.

Spicy Lamb Kebabs

Cook these kebabs outside on the barbecue when the weather permits, or cook under a preheated hot grill, turning and brushing frequently with the marinade.

(SERVES 4)

675 g (1½ lb) boned leg of lamb
1 large corn on the cob
8 shallots, peeled
150 ml (¼ pint) natural yoghurt
1 garlic clove, peeled and crushed
2 bay leaves, crumbled

1 tablespoon lemon juice

1 tablespoon vegetable oil

1 teaspoon ground allspice

1 tablespoon coriander seeds, lightly crushed

salt and freshly ground black pepper

450 g (1 lb) courgettes, sliced

8 tomatoes, halved

lemon wedges to garnish

Cut the lamb into 2.5 cm (1 inch) cubes. Cut the corn into 8 slices and blanch in boiling salted water, then drain thoroughly. Blanch the shallots in boiling salted water, then drain well.

To make the marinade, mix the yoghurt with the garlic, bay leaves, lemon juice, oil, allspice, coriander seeds and salt and pepper to taste.

Thread the lamb cubes on to 8 skewers with the courgettes, tomatoes, corn and shallots. Place in a shallow dish and cover with the marinade. Cover and leave to marinate in the refrigerator for 2–3 hours, turning twice to coat with the mixture during this time.

Barbecue or grill the kebabs over or under a moderate heat for about 15–20 minutes, turning and brushing with the marinade frequently. Serve hot on a bed of crisp salad leaves, garnished with lemon wedges.

Leave-to-cook Casserole

This casserole was given its name by my children, who quickly caught on to the fact that it was always produced when we went out for the day yet needed something tasty and hot to come home to. It really doesn't need any last-minute or mid-cooking attention – I simply place it in the slow-cooking oven of my Aga or set the automatic timer of my ordinary oven if we are out for a long time and leave well alone.

(SERVES 4)

8 middle neck lamb chops

4 leeks or onions, trimmed or peeled and sliced

550 g (1¼ lb) ripe tomatoes, skinned and chopped, *or* 2 400 g (14 oz)
   cans
2 bay leaves
salt and freshly ground black pepper

*Place all the ingredients in a casserole dish with salt and pepper to taste. If
using fresh tomatoes, it may be necessary to add 4 tablespoons stock, water
or wine if they are not very ripe. Cover tightly and cook in a preheated
moderate oven at 180°C (350°F, Gas Mark 4) for 1½–2 hours.*

Serve hot with creamed potatoes, cooked rice or boiled noodles.

Leek and Bean Hot-Pot

I often use baked beans in hot-pots, especially to 'stretch' the meat
content to the barest minimum, and they taste so good with winter
root vegetables and leeks. This is a quick, nutritious and warming
meal, extra good for winter time.

(SERVES 4)

2 teaspoons oil
225 g (8 oz) bacon or gammon, diced
225 g (8 oz) carrots, peeled and chopped
225 g (8 oz) leeks, washed and sliced
450 g (1 lb) can baked beans
450 g (1 lb) potatoes, peeled and thinly sliced
15 g (½ oz) butter or margarine, melted

*Heat the oil in a heavy-based pan, then fry the bacon or gammon until
browned. Add the carrots and cook for a few minutes. Add the leeks and
baked beans and warm through. Transfer half of the mixture to an
ovenproof dish and top with half of the potatoes. Cover with the remaining
mixture and arrange the remaining potatoes on top.*

*Brush with the melted butter and cover the dish with greaseproof paper.
Bake in a preheated moderately hot oven at 200°C (400°F, Gas Mark 6)
for about 1 hour, or until the top is golden and the potatoes are tender.*

Sunny Stir-fried Liver and Vegetables

(SERVES 4)

2 oranges
225 g (8 oz) lambs' liver, cut into thin strips
1 tablespoon walnut or soya oil
1 spring onion, trimmed and finely chopped
1 garlic clove, peeled and crushed
2 courgettes, trimmed and sliced
1 pepper, cored, seeded and sliced
100 g (4 oz) baby corn on the cob or bean sprouts
50 g (2 oz) asparagus peas, trimmed
50 g (2 oz) mushrooms, wiped and halved
1 ½ teaspoons soy sauce
1 teaspoon dry sherry
1 teaspoon cider vinegar
pinch of sugar

Remove the zest from half of one orange and set aside to garnish the cooked dish. Remove the rind and the pith from the oranges and cut into segments over a bowl to catch any juice. Reserve the orange segments.

Add the liver strips, half of the oil, the spring onion and garlic to the orange juice, mixing well. Cover and leave to marinate for about 45 minutes.

Heat the remaining oil in a wok or large frying pan and fry the liver in small batches for about 2–3 minutes, tossing constantly. Remove from the pan with a slotted spoon and place on a warmed plate. Cover and keep warm while frying the remaining liver.

Add the courgettes and pepper to the pan and stir-fry for 2 minutes. Add the corn or bean sprouts, asparagus peas and mushrooms and stir-fry for a further 4 minutes.

Add the liver, soy sauce, sherry, vinegar and sugar, mixing well. Stir-fry for a further 2 minutes or until all the ingredients are hot and crisp. Serve at once garnished with the reserved strips of orange zest.

Beanfeast Dumplings

(SERVES 4)

675 g (1½ lb) root vegetables (carrots, turnips, parsnips, onions and
    swedes for example)
3 tablespoons vegetable oil
2 sticks celery, chopped
2 tablespoons plain flour
salt and freshly ground black pepper
600 ml (1 pint) vegetable stock
150 g (5 oz) canned red kidney beans
175 g (6 oz) sweetcorn kernels
200 g (7 oz) can baked beans in tomato sauce

Dumplings:
350 g (12 oz) minced beef
2 teaspoons chopped fresh mixed herbs
dash of Worcestershire sauce
1½ teaspoons yeast extract
225 g (8 oz) self-raising flour
125 g (4½ oz) shredded suet

Peel and dice the root vegetables. Heat the oil in a heavy-based frying pan, add the vegetables and celery and sauté for 15 minutes. Stir in the flour and season to taste with salt and pepper. Gradually add the stock, mixing well. Bring to the boil, then add the kidney beans, sweetcorn and baked beans. Transfer to a cooking dish, cover and place in a moderately hot oven at 190°C (375°F, Gas Mark 5) while preparing the dumplings.

To make the dumplings, mix the minced beef with the herbs, Worcestershire sauce and yeast extract. Divide and shape into 8 small balls. Roll in a little flour, then fry in non-stick pan until browned on all sides.

Meanwhile, mix the flour with the suet, salt to taste and enough water to make a firm dough. Divide into 8 pieces and, on a lightly floured surface, press each to a round flat shape. Place a meatball in the centre of each piece of dough, then mould the dough around the meatball to enclose it completely.

Place the prepared dumplings on top of the vegetable mixture and cook for a further 20–30 minutes, or until the dumplings are cooked and are crunchy golden-brown. Serve at once.

Sea Bass with Fennel and Tomato Bake

I adore plainly grilled sea bass, often cooking it on the barbecue during the summer. When the weather is a little chilly I like to serve the fish with a baked fennel and tomato dish instead of a crisp, light salad. The fennel dish freezes beautifully and after thawing can be reheated in a moderate oven for about 30 minutes.

(SERVES 4)

Sea Bass
1.8 kg (4 lb) sea bass, cleaned and scaled
fresh fennel sprigs
salt
freshly ground black pepper
juice of 2 lemons
2 tablespoons olive oil

Fennel and Tomato Bake
1 tablespoon olive oil
4 shallots or 1 onion, peeled and chopped
1–2 garlic cloves, peeled and crushed
1 lb ripe tomatoes, peeled, seeded and chopped
150 ml (¼ pint) dry white wine
2 teaspoons chopped fresh parsley
4–6 heads of fennel, trimmed and halved lengthways

Using a sharp knife, cut diagonal slashes into the flesh of the bass and insert sprigs of fresh fennel. Season the inside of the fish with salt and pepper and stuff with more fresh fennel. Season the outside of the fish with salt and pepper and squeeze over half of the lemon juice and olive oil. Then leave to stand while preparing the fennel and tomato bake.

Heat the oil in a pan, add the shallots and garlic and fry for 5 minutes.

Stir in the tomatoes, wine and parsley with salt and pepper to taste, mixing well. Bring to the boil, reduce the heat, cover and simmer for 30 minutes. Remove the lid and cook for 10 minutes or until thick and pulpy.

Cook the fennel in a pan of boiling salted water for 8–10 minutes or until just tender. Drain and place in an ovenproof dish. Spoon over the tomato mixture. Cook, uncovered, in a preheated moderate oven at 180°C (350°F, Gas Mark 4), for 30–35 minutes.

Meanwhile, grill the bass on the barbecue or under a preheated hot grill until the flesh is cooked, about 5–10 minutes. Turn over carefully and sprinkle with the remaining lemon juice and olive oil. Continue to grill until the flesh is cooked and tender, about 5–8 minutes.

Serve the cooked sea bass with the fennel and tomato bake.

Sizzling Stir-Fry Scallops

(SERVES 2)

1 tablespoon sesame or sunflower oil
1 garlic clove, peeled and crushed
2.5 cm (1 in) piece root ginger, peeled and coarsely grated
8 scallops, cleaned and sliced
6 spring onions, trimmed and sliced
50 g (2 oz) asparagus peas, trimmed
1 tablespoon lemon juice
salt and freshly ground black pepper

Heat the oil in a frying pan or wok and sauté the garlic and ginger for 2 minutes.

Add the scallops, spring onions and asparagus peas and stir-fry for 3–4 minutes. Add the lemon juice and salt and pepper to taste, blending well. Serve at once.

Ratatouille Pasta

A delicious vegetable, cheese and pasta main meal dish that can be made in under half an hour. Serve with a mixed green salad accompaniment.

(SERVES 4)

25 g (1 oz) butter or margarine
1 large onion, peeled and chopped
2 garlic cloves, peeled and crushed
450 g (1 lb) aubergines, trimmed and sliced
225 g (8 oz) courgettes, trimmed and sliced
1 green or red pepper, cored, seeded and chopped
350 g (12 oz) ripe tomatoes, peeled and chopped **or** 425 g (15 oz) can
    chopped tomatoes
1 teaspoon chopped fresh mixed herbs (e.g. basil, parsley and marjoram)
salt and freshly ground black pepper
225 g (8 oz) dried plain or wholemeal pasta (e.g., penne, spirals, shells or
    wheat ears)
100 g (4 oz) Danish Mycella cheese

*Melt the butter or margarine in a large heavy-based pan, add the onion
and garlic and fry gently until soft, about 5 minutes. Add the aubergines,
courgettes and pepper and cook until just softened, about 5–8 minutes.*

*Add the tomatoes with their juice and the herbs, mixing well. Cook,
uncovered, over a gentle heat for about 20 minutes, or until the vegetables
are tender and the juices are slightly thickened. Season to taste with salt
and pepper.*

*Meanwhile, cook the pasta in boiling salted water according to the
packet instructions. Drain well and place in a warmed serving dish.
Crumble the cheese over it and toss lightly so that the cheese begins to melt.*

*Serve the pasta immediately with the ratatouille sauce and a crisp green
salad.*

Summer Vegetable Curry

(SERVES 4)

2 tablespoons sunflower oil
1 tablespoon cumin seeds
2 cloves
1 small cinnamon stick

2 cardamoms

2 teaspoons ground turmeric

few drops of Tabasco sauce

2 large onions, peeled and sliced

175 g (6 oz) long-grain rice

100 g (4 oz) lentils (red or green), rinsed

750 ml (1 ¼ pints) vegetable stock

175 g (6 oz) broccoli spears, trimmed

175 g (6 oz) French beans, trimmed

175 g (6 oz) courgettes, trimmed and sliced

175 g (6 oz) mangetout, trimmed

Heat the oil in a large heavy-based pan. Add the cumin seeds, cloves, cinnamon and cardamoms and fry for 2 minutes. Add the turmeric, Tabasco sauce, onions and rice and fry, stirring frequently, for 5 minutes.

Stir in the lentils and stock, cover and cook over a gentle heat for 30 minutes.

Meanwhile, blanch the broccoli, beans and courgettes in boiling salted water until tender-crisp. Drain thoroughly. Add to the rice mixture with the mangetout and mix well. Re-cover and cook for a further 5 minutes.

Fluff up the rice to serve. A delicious dish either hot or cold.

Layered Vegetable and Cheese Pie

This is one of those hearty main meal dishes that is particularly welcome during the cold winter months – also especially welcome at the end of the week or the month when the purse-strings are stretched to their limit!

(SERVES 6–8)

Pastry:

225 g (8 oz) plain wholemeal or wheatmeal flour

100 g (4 oz) butter or margarine

1 ½ tablespoons sesame seeds

1 ½ tablespoons cold water

Filling:

225 g (8 oz) potatoes, scrubbed

225 g (8 oz) carrots, peeled and grated

225 g (8 oz) cooked spinach, finely chopped

175 g (6 oz) Cheddar cheese, grated

2 medium tomatoes, sliced

salt and freshly ground black pepper

1 teaspoon chopped mixed fresh herbs

Glaze:

1 small egg, beaten

seasame seeds

To make the pastry, sift the flour into a bowl, adding any bran left in the sieve. Rub in the butter or margarine until the mixture resembles fine breadcrumbs. Stir in the sesame seeds and the water and mix to a firm but pliable dough. Chill while preparing the filling.

Cook the potatoes in boiling water until just cooked, about 15–20 minutes. Drain, then slice thinly and allow to cool.

Roll out two-thirds of the pastry and use to line the base and sides of a deep 20 cm (8 in) round, loose-bottomed tin. Arrange the potatoes over the pastry and top with the grated carrot, spinach, cheese and finally the tomatoes, seasoning between each layer with salt, pepper and herbs.

Roll out the remaining pastry to make a lid for the pie. Dampen the edges of the pie with water and cover with the pastry lid. Seal, trim and flute the edges of the pie and make a slit in the centre. Use any of the pastry trimmings to make leaves to decorate the pie.

Glaze with beaten egg and sprinkle liberally with sesame seeds. Bake in a preheated moderately hot oven at 200°C (400°F, Gas Mark 6) for 40 minutes. Serve hot.

Broccoli and Mushroom Gratin

A wonderful light lunch or supper dish to serve with warm wholemeal rolls. When broccoli is not available, try this with cauliflower, potatoes, carrots or green beans.

(SERVES 4)

50 g (2 oz) butter or margarine
2 onions, peeled and finely chopped
1 teaspoon cumin seeds
40 g (1½ oz) plain flour
450 ml (¾ pint) milk
300 ml (½ pint) vegetable stock
few drops of Tabasco sauce
1 bay leaf
350 g (12 oz) broccoli, cut into even-sized pieces
100 g (4 oz) mushrooms, wiped and quartered
salt and freshly ground black pepper
2 eggs, soft-boiled

Topping:

25 g (1 oz) wholewheat breadcrumbs
50 g (2 oz) Parmesan cheese, finely grated
2 tablespoons chopped fresh parsley

Melt the butter or margarine in a large pan. Add the onions and cumin seeds and fry gently until softened but not browned. Stir in the flour and cook for 1 minute. Gradually add the milk, stock and Tabasco and bring to the boil, stirring constantly until boiling, smooth and thickened. Add the bay leaf, broccoli, mushrooms and salt and pepper to taste. Partially cover the pan and cook over a low heat until the broccoli is just tender, about 15–20 minutes.

Roughly chop the eggs and stir into the broccoli mixture, then transfer to a shallow flameproof dish. Mix the breadcrumbs with the cheese and parsley and sprinkle evenly over the broccoli and mushroom mixture.

Place the dish under a preheated hot grill and cook until crisp and lightly browned. Serve at once with warm wholemeal rolls.

Savoury Carrot Bake

(SERVES 4)

450 g (1 lb) carrots, peeled and grated
150–250 ml (5–8 fl oz) vegetable stock
2 tablespoons chopped fresh parsley
1 teaspoon soy sauce
2 tablespoons unsweetened orange juice
1 teaspoon grated orange rind
350 g (12 oz) cooked long-grain rice (100 g (4 oz) uncooked)
1 tablespoon sunflower oil
1 tablespoon flour
200 ml (7 fl oz) milk
2 eggs, beaten
75 g (3 oz) Edam cheese, grated
salt and freshly ground black pepper

Cook the carrot in the stock until really tender, about 15 minutes. Add the parsley, soy sauce, orange juice and orange rind, mixing well. Spread a little in the base of a medium ovenproof dish and cover with a layer of the cooked rice. Continue layering in this way until all the rice and carrot mixture has been used, finishing with a layer of rice.

Heat the oil in a pan, add the flour and cook for 1 minute. Stir in the milk and then bring to the boil, stirring constantly, and cook for 2 minutes. Remove from the heat and beat in the eggs and half of the cheese. Season to taste with salt and pepper and pour over the rice mixture.

Sprinkle with the remaining cheese and bake in a preheated moderate oven at 180°C (350°F, Gas Mark 4), for 45 minutes, or until firm and golden-brown. Serve immediately.

Noodles with Creole Sauce

The sweet and fiery tomato sauce in this recipe also tastes delicious with meat loaves and grilled meats and poured over cooked long-grain rice. The sauce reflects the Creole food style, which is a mixture of every ethnic group which has ever been in the city of New Orleans, including Indian, French, Spanish and African cuisine.

(SERVES 4)

2 tablespoons olive oil
1 onion, peeled and thinly sliced
1 garlic clove, peeled and crushed
450 g (1 lb) ripe tomatoes, chopped
1 green pepper, cored, seeded and chopped
2 teaspoons capers
1 teaspoon soft brown sugar
Tabasco sauce
1 tablespoon lemon juice
salt
450 g (1 lb) dried pasta noodles

Heat the oil in a large heavy-based pan, add the onion and fry gently until soft, about 5 minutes. Add the garlic, tomatoes, pepper and capers, mixing well. Bring to the boil, stirring constantly.

Add the sugar, a good shake of Tabasco sauce, lemon juice and salt to taste. Reduce the heat and simmer until thick and pulpy, about 10–15 minutes.

Meanwhile, cook the pasta in boiling salted water according to the packet instructions. Drain and place in a warmed serving dish. Spoon over the hot Creole sauce and toss lightly before serving. Serve with a crisp green salad.

Savoury Apple and Cheese Quiche

This quiche may be served warm or cold. A green salad or some boiled new potatoes or fresh bread make the ideal accompaniment.

(SERVES 4)

Pastry:
100 g (4 oz) butter or margarine
225 g (8 oz) plain flour
water to mix

Filling:
150 g (5 oz) Blue Brie cheese
1 Cox's-type eating apple
75 g (3 oz) smoked ham, chopped
1 tablespoon snipped chives
1 large egg
150 ml (¼ pint) single cream
salt and freshly ground black pepper

To make the pastry, rub the butter into the flour until the mixture resembles fine breadcrumbs. Add sufficient water to bind to a firm but pliable dough. Roll out on a lightly floured surface and use to line a 20 cm (8 in) flan ring standing on a baking tray.

To make the filling, thinly pare the rind from the cheese and slice. Peel, core and slice the apple. Arrange the cheese, ham and sliced apple in the pastry case and sprinkle with the chives.

Beat the egg with the cream and salt and pepper to taste and pour over the filling. Bake in a preheated moderate oven at 180°C (350°F, Gas Mark 4) for about 45 minutes, until the filling is set and the pastry is crisp. Serve warm or cold.

20. Sweet Suggestions: Puddings, Desserts & Sweet Baked Fare

Country Apple and Orange Pie

There is no pie more famous in Britain than the apple pie. This is a delicious variation using potted orange curd, although lemon is just as good.

(SERVES 4–6)

350 g (12 oz) shortcrust pastry
675 g (1½ lb) cooking apples
50 g (2 oz) sugar
25 g (1 oz) cornflour
100 ml (4 fl oz) orange curd
icing sugar to dust

Roll out half of the pastry on a lightly floured surface and use to line a deep 20 cm (8 in) pie-plate.

Peel, core and thickly slice the apples and mix with the sugar and cornflour. Place one-third of the apples in the pie and dot with half of the orange curd. Cover with a further one-third of the apples and dot with the remaining orange curd. Finally top with the remaining apples. Roll out the remaining pastry on a lightly floured surface and use to make a lid for the pie. Seal the edges firmly and crimp or flute to decorate. Use any pastry trimmings to make leaves or shapes to decorate the pie.

Bake in a preheated moderately hot oven at 200°C (400°F, Gas Mark 6) for 30 minutes. Reduce the oven temperature to a moderate 180°C (350°F, Gas Mark 4) and cook for a further 15 minutes. Serve warm or cold dusted with icing sugar.

Autumn Fruit Layer Pudding

This is a colourful version of the traditional British suet pudding using apples, pears, blackberries and plums. Serve with a honey or golden syrup sauce.

(SERVES 4–6)

225 g (8 oz) self-raising flour
100 g (4 oz) shredded suet
cold water to mix
100 g (4 oz) blackberries, hulled
100–175 g (4–6 oz) demerara sugar
3 Conference-type pears, peeled, cored and sliced
225 g (8 oz) plums, halved and stoned
3–4 dessert apples, peeled, cored and sliced

Sift the flour into a bowl and mix in the suet. Add sufficient water to make a soft but not sticky dough. Roll out the pastry on a lightly floured surface to 5 mm (¼ in) thick. Cut out a large round to fit the top of a 900 ml (1½ pint) pudding basin; three intermediate rounds to fit one-quarter, half-way and three-quarters up the basin; and a small round to fit the bottom of the basin.

Place the small round in the bottom of the greased pudding basin and cover with the blackberries and a little sugar to taste. Cover with the second circle of pastry and layer with sliced pears and sugar to taste. Cover with the third round and layer of plums with sugar to taste. Add the fourth pastry round with sliced apples and remaining sugar, then finish with the remaining pastry round and seal the edges with water.

Tie on a greased and pleated foil cap and steam over simmering water for 2 hours, topping up with water if necessary. Allow to shrink slightly before turning out on to a warmed serving dish.

Pears au Gratin

(SERVES 4)

4 ripe, firm pears
3 tablespoons lemon juice
200 g (7 oz) quark or low fat soft cheese
8 teaspoons demerara sugar
orange and lemon slices to decorate

Peel the pears and cut in half. Remove the cores. Brush the pears with lemon juice to prevent them turning brown.

Fill the pear cavities with the quark or cheese and sprinkle with the sugar. Cook under a preheated hot grill until the sugar melts and begins to caramelise.

Serve hot, decorated with orange and lemon slices.

Pear and Orange Custard Tart

(SERVES 6–8)

Pastry:

50 g (2 oz) butter or margarine
50 g (2 oz) wholemeal flour
50 g (2 oz) plain white flour
grated rind 1 orange
cold water to mix

Filling:

450 g (1 lb) pears, peeled, halved and cored
300 ml (½ pint) thick custard
1 tablespoon clear honey
1 large orange, peeled, pith removed, and cut into segments

Glaze:

1 tablespoon arrowroot powder
150 ml (¼ pint) water
5 teaspoons clear honey

Rub the butter or margarine into the flours until the mixture resembles fine breadcrumbs. Stir in the orange rind and sufficient water to bind to a firm but pliable dough. Roll out thinly, on a lightly floured surface, to a round large enough to line the base and sides of a 20 cm (8 in) round fluted flan ring placed on a greased baking tray. Bake 'blind' in a preheated moderately hot oven at 200°C (400°F, Gas Mark 6) for 20 minutes.

Meanwhile, poach the pear halves in a little water until just tender. Drain thoroughly. Pour the custard into the cooked flan case, then arrange the pear halves and orange segments on top in a decorative pattern.

To make the glaze, blend the arrowroot with a little of the water, then gradually stir in the remainder. Bring to the boil, stirring constantly, until clear and thickened. Stir in the honey, then carefully spoon over the fruit in the tart. Chill before serving cut into wedges.

Peach and Orange Rulle Flans

Quick and easy to assemble, these flans rely on the sweetness of ripe peaches and the luxury of Orange Rulle cheese. A soft cheese, Orange Rulle is laced with orange liqueur and orange rind and rolled in hazelnuts. You can make this more luxurious by using meringue nests in place of the sponge flans. Make sure that the cheese is well chilled so that you can slice it thinly – or freeze it for 30 minutes before slicing.

(SERVES 4)

4 individual sponge flan cases
2 tablespoons Grand Marnier liqueur
2 tablespoons fresh orange juice
2 ripe peaches
125 g (4 oz) packet Orange Rulle cheese, well chilled

Glaze:
1 teaspoon arrowroot powder
150 ml (¼ pint) fresh orange juice

Place the sponge cases on one large or 4 individual serving plates. Blend the Grand Marnier with the orange juice, sprinkle some over each flan and leave to soak in.

Peel the peaches if liked, stone and then cut them into thin slices. Thinly slice the Orange Rulle cheese. Arrange the peach and cheese slices in the sponge cases.

To make the glaze, blend the arrowroot until smooth with a little of the juice. Add the remaining juice, bring to the boil and cook until thick and glossy, stirring constantly. Allow to cool.

Spoon a little of the glaze over each flan to coat the peach and cheese slices thinly. Chill until ready to serve (not more than 24 hours). Serve with cream or ice cream.

Strawberry and Kiwi Pavlova

The secret to getting a good crisp pavlova with a soft fluffy inside is in adding just the right amount of cornflour and vinegar to the beaten egg-white mixture. The recipe below is absolutely foolproof and all the better for being topped with sliced fresh strawberries mixed with kiwi fruit. If you can't find organically grown kiwi fruit, then use sliced ripe pears instead.

(SERVES 8–10)

4 egg whites
¼ teaspoon salt
225 g (8 oz) castor sugar
4 teaspoons cornflour
½ teaspoon vanilla essence
2 teaspoons vinegar
300 ml (½ pint) whipping cream
225 g (8 oz) strawberries, hulled and halved
3 kiwi fruit, peeled and sliced

Whisk the egg whites with the salt until stiff. Whisk in the sugar, a teaspoonful at a time, and continue whisking until the mixture is very stiff. Beat in the cornflour, vinegar and vanilla essence.

Spoon the mixture on to a baking tray lined with non-stick baking paper and marked with a 23 cm (9 in) circle, building up the sides and hollowing out the centre of the circle slightly. Bake in a preheated cool oven at 140°C (275°F, Gas Mark 1) for 1¼ hours. Leave to cool.

Fill the pavlova just before serving. Whip the cream until thick, then fold in half of the strawberries and kiwi fruit. Peel the pavlova away from the paper and place on a serving dish. Top with the cream and fruit and decorate with the remaining strawberries and kiwi fruit. Cut into wedges to serve.

Rhubarb and Apple Ice Cream

Unless you happen to have a larder groaning under the weight of fruit syrups, then make this delicious ice cream with ready-made apple and grenadine syrup. Serve with crisp light wafers or thin dessert biscuits.

(SERVES 6)

450 g (1 lb) rhubarb
6 dessertspoons apple syrup
6 dessertspoons grenadine syrup
150 ml (¼ pint) whipping cream
150 ml (¼ pint) natural yoghurt

Trim the rhubarb and cut into small pieces. Place in a heavy-based pan with the apple and grenadine syrups. Cover and cook over a gentle heat until soft, about 10 minutes. Allow to cool, then mash with a fork.

Whip the cream until it stands in soft peaks and fold into the rhubarb mixture with the yoghurt, mixing well. Pour into a freezer container and freeze until half-frozen and mushy. Beat well with a spoon or whisk to break down any large ice crystals, then freeze until firm.

Remove the ice cream from the refrigerator about 30 minutes before serving to soften slightly. Scoop into chilled glasses to serve.

Honey and Carrot Cake

(MAKES 1 18CM (7 INCH) ROUND SANDWICH CAKE)

175 g (6 oz) butter or margarine
25 g (1 oz) castor sugar
4 tablespoons clear honey
2 eggs, separated
1 tablespoon lemon juice
225 g (8 oz) plain wholemeal flour
1 tablespoon baking powder
½ teaspoon ground cinnamon

1 teaspoon freshly grated coconut
2 carrots, peeled and finely grated

Icing:
40 g (1½ oz) butter or margarine
1 tablespoon clear honey
1 tablespoon lemon juice
225 g (8 oz) icing sugar, sifted
angelica leaves, to decorate

Lightly grease and base-line two 18 cm (7 in) round sandwich tins. Cream the butter or margarine with the sugar and honey until light and fluffy. Beat in the egg yolks and lemon juice. Stir in the flour, baking powder, spices and carrot and mix well. Whisk the egg whites until they stand in stiff peaks, then fold into the cake mixture with a metal spoon. Divide the mixture evenly between the prepared cake tins and level the surface. Bake in a preheated moderate oven at 180°C (350°F, Gas Mark 4) for 20–25 minutes, or until cooked and light and springy to the touch. Allow to cool, then turn out on to a cooling rack.

To make the icing, melt the butter or margarine, honey and lemon juice together in a bowl over a saucepan of hot water. Remove the bowl from the pan and stir in the icing sugar, beating well until thick and creamy. Use one-third of the icing to sandwich the cakes together, then spread the remaining icing over the top of the cake, swirling to give a decorative effect. Quickly decorate with angelica leaves before the icing sets. Store in an airtight tin for up to one week until required.

Oatmeal and Apple Crunch Bars

These are the perfect healthy lunch-box or biscuit-tin treat – they're also ideal for 'no-time' breakfasts for people on the move!

(MAKES 15)

450 g (1 lb) cooking apples, peeled, cored and sliced
100 g (4 oz) raisins
grated rind and juice 1 orange

3 tablespoons water

150 g (5 oz) soft brown sugar

175 g (6 oz) plain wholemeal flour

100 g (4 oz) oatmeal

100 g (4 oz) butter or margarine

demerara sugar for sprinkling

Place the apples in a pan with the raisins, orange rind, orange juice and water. Simmer, covered, for about 10 minutes or until pulpy. Remove from the heat and stir in 50 g (2 oz) of the sugar, mixing well.

Place the flour and oatmeal in a bowl; rub in the butter or margarine until the mixture resembles fine breadcrumbs. Stir in the remaining sugar. Sprinkle half of this dry mixture over the base of a greased 28×18 cm (11×7 in) shallow tin, pressing down lightly. Spread the apple mixture evenly over the top. Cover with the remaining dry mixture and press down lightly.

Bake in a preheated moderately hot oven at 190°C (375°F, Gas Mark 5) for 35 minutes until lightly browned.

Sprinkle with demerara sugar and leave to cool in the tin. When cool cut into three down lengths and five across to make 15 squares. Store in an airtight tin for up to one week until required.

Coconut and Apple Knobbles

(MAKES 18)

100 g (4 oz) butter or margarine

225 g (8 oz) wholemeal self-raising flour

50 g (2 oz) demerara sugar

75 g (3 oz) desiccated coconut

1 cooking apple, weighing about 175 g (6 oz) , peeled, cored and grated

3 tablespoons clear honey

1 egg, beaten

Rub the butter or margarine into the flour. Stir in the sugar, coconut, apple, honey and egg and mix well.

Place about 18 spoonfuls on to lightly greased baking trays. Bake in a preheated moderately hot oven at 190°C (375°F, Gas Mark 5) for about 20 minutes. Cool on a wire rack.

21. Off the Shelf: Perfect Preserves

Tudor Damson Jam

We inherited little in terms of a kitchen or fruit garden when we moved into our present house, Tudor Court, save a wonderful damson tree. Year after year it never fails to give us a huge basketful of fruit, which we nearly always make into jam. 'Tudor Court Jam' therefore has something of a reputation amongst friends and family! Try it – you won't be disappointed.

MAKES ABOUT 4.5KG (10 LB)

2.1 kg (4¾ lb) damsons
900 ml (1½ pints) water
2.7 kg (6 lb) preserving sugar
knob of butter

Wash the damsons and place in a large pan with the water. Bring to the boil, reduce the heat and simmer until tender, about 20–30 minutes.
  Add the sugar, mixing well. Heat gently to dissolve the sugar, stirring

occasionally. Add the butter to reduce foaming. Bring to the boil and boil rapidly until setting point is reached, about 10–20 minutes. Remove the damson stones with a slotted spoon and discard. Remove from the heat and skim if necessary.

Spoon into clean, hot jars, cover with waxed discs, waxed-sides down, and dampened cellophane rounds. Label and store in a cool, dry dark place for up to a year.

Piquant Raspberry Jam

This is a delicious raspberry jam to make when the harvest of raspberries is not too large – the apple pulp helps to 'stretch' the raspberries to produce an excellent, inexpensive preserve. You can of course use any of the other hybrid berries such as loganberries, boysenberries and tayberries.

MAKES 1.5 KG (3½ LB)

450 g (1 lb) peeled, cored and chopped Bramley apples
150 ml (¼ pint) water
450 g (1 lb) raspberries, hulled
900 g (2 lb) preserving or granulated sugar

Place the apples in a large pan with the water. Bring to the boil, reduce the heat and simmer until tender, about 15 minutes.

Add the raspberries, mixing well, and cook for 2–3 minutes. Stir in the sugar, mixing well. Heat gently to dissolve the sugar, stirring occasionally. Bring to a full rolling boil and boil rapidly until setting point is reached, about 15 minutes. Skim if necessary.

Spoon into clean, hot jars, cover with waxed discs, waxed-sides down, and dampened cellophane rounds. Label and store in a cool, dry, dark place for up to a year.

Apple and Blackcurrant Jam

A good versatile jam for tea-time spreading or using in baked pastries. Vary the ingredients (see variations below) to make the most of your soft fruit produce.

MAKES 1.5 KG (3½ LB)

450 g (1 lb) peeled, cored and chopped Bramley apples
450 g (1 lb) blackcurrants, topped and tailed
300 ml (½ pint) water
900 g (2 lb) preserving or granulated sugar

Place the apples in a large pan with the blackcurrants and water. Bring to the boil, reduce the heat and simmer until tender, about 15 minutes.

Stir in the sugar, mixing well. Heat gently to dissolve the sugar, stirring occasionally. Bring to a full rolling boil and boil rapidly until setting point is reached, about 15 minutes. Skim if necessary.

Spoon into clean, hot jars cover with waxed discs, waxed-sides down, and dampened cellophane rounds. Store in a cool, dry, dark place for up to a year.

Variations

APPLE AND BLACKBERRY JAM Prepare and cook as above, but use 450 g (1 lb) hulled blackberries instead of the blackcurrants. Cook with 4 tablespoons water.

APPLE AND GINGER JAM Prepare and cook as above, but add 1 teaspoon ground ginger and omit the blackcurrants. Cook with only 450 g (1 lb) sugar as above.

Gooseberry and Raspberry Jam with Sherry

Definitely a jam worth giving – pot in attractive jars, label and add a ribbon or bow for the final luxurious touch!

MAKES ABOUT 3.25 KG (7 LB)

900 g (2 lb) gooseberries, topped and tailed
5 tablespoons water
5 tablespoons sherry
900 g (2 lb) raspberries, hulled
2.75 kg (6 lb) preserving sugar
200 ml (7 fl oz) liquid pectin

Place the gooseberries in a large pan with the water and sherry. Bring to the boil, reduce the heat, cover and simmer for 15 minutes or until the fruit skins are tender, stirring occasionally.

Crush the raspberries and add to the gooseberry mixture, mixing well. Add the sugar and heat gently to dissolve, stirring occasionally. Bring to a full rolling boil and boil rapidly for 2 minutes. Remove from the heat and stir in the liquid pectin, mixing well.

Allow to cool slightly to prevent the fruit from floating. Stir well, then spoon into clean, hot jars, cover with waxed discs, waxed-sides down, and dampened cellophane rounds. Label and store in a cool, dry, dark place for up to a year.

Spiced Blackberry Jam

MAKES 1.5 KG (3½ LB)

1.25 kg (2½ lb) blackberries, hulled
50 ml (2 fl oz) water
50 ml (2 fl oz) lemon juice
¾ teaspoon ground cinnamon
¾ teaspoon ground mixed spice
1.3 kg (2¾ lb) sugar
100 ml (4 fl oz) liquid pectin

Crush the blackberries slightly and place in a large pan with the water. Bring to the boil, reduce the heat and simmer, uncovered, for 10 minutes.

Sieve the fruit and return the purée to the pan. Add the lemon juice, cinnamon, mixed spice and sugar, mixing well. Heat gently to dissolve the sugar, stirring occasionally.Bring to a full rolling boil and boil rapidly for 1 minute. Remove from the heat and stir in the liquid pectin, mixing well. Skim if necessary.

Spoon into clean, hot jars, cover with waxed discs, waxed-sides down, and dampened cellophane rounds. Label and store in a cool, dry, dark place for up to a year.

Quince Jelly

This is one of the most fragrant jellies I know – serve it with game or mix it with fruit-pie fillings for a luxurious lift. It is impossible to give a precise guideline for the yield to this recipe, since much will depend upon the ripeness of the fruit and the 'dripping' time.

1.75 kg (4 lb) quinces, washed and coarsely chopped
3 litres (5 pints) water
grated rind and juice 2 lemons
sugar (see method)

Place the quinces in a preserving pan or large saucepan with the water, lemon rind and juice. Bring to the boil, reduce the heat, cover and simmer until very tender, about 1 hour, stirring occasionally. Spoon into a jelly-bag and leave to strain into a bowl for at least 12 hours.

Measure the juice and return to the pan. Add 450 g (1 lb) warmed sugar for each 600 ml (1 pint) measured juice. Heat gently to dissolve the sugar, bring to the boil and boil rapidly until setting point is reached, about 10 minutes.

Skim if necessary and spoon quickly into clean, hot jars. Cover with waxed discs, waxed-sides down, and dampened cellophane rounds. Label and store in a cool, dry, dark place for up to a year.

Rosemary Jelly

This is a family favourite to serve with roast lamb, grilled fish and game birds – it is also one of the first preserves to sell out on charity and school fête days!

MAKES ABOUT 3.25 KG (7 LB)

2.25 kg (5 lb) cooking apples
600 ml (1 pint) water
4 tablespoons fresh rosemary leaves, washed and dried
250 ml (8 fl oz) distilled vinegar
sugar (see method)

Coarsely slice or chop the apples (without coring) into a preserving pan or large saucepan. Add the water and half of the rosemary, mixing well. Bring to the boil, reduce the heat and simmer gently until very soft, about 40–50 minutes. Add the vinegar, mixing well, and boil for a further 5 minutes.

Spoon into a jelly-bag and leave to strain into a bowl for at least 12 hours.

Measure the juice and return to the pan. Add 450 g (1 lb) warmed sugar for each 600 ml (1 pint) measured juice. Heat gently to dissolve the sugar, bring to the boil and boil rapidly until setting point is reached, about 10 minutes.

Skim if necessary, stir in the remaining rosemary and mix well. Allow to cool slightly, stir well and spoon into clean, hot jars. Cover with waxed discs, waxed-sides down, and dampened cellophane rounds. Label and store in a cool, dry, dark place for up to a year.

Bramble Cheese

This is a delicious very thick preserve which is especially good with game meats and duckling. If liked the cheese can be set in one large or several small moulds (instead of being stored in jars) for turning out to serve.

MAKES 900 G (2 LB)

900 g (2 lb) blackberries or other 'hybrid' berries, hulled
450 g (1 lb) cooking apples, peeled, cored and finely chopped
600 ml (1 pint) unsweetened apple juice or water
1 teaspoon ground cinnamon
sugar (see method)

Place the blackberries in a pan with the apples, apple juice or water and cinnamon. Cook over a gentle heat until tender and pulpy, about 30 minutes. Pass through a fine nylon sieve, measure the purée, return to the pan and add 350 g (12 oz) sugar for each 600 ml (1 pint) fruit purée, blending well. Bring slowly to the boil to dissolve the sugar, then boil rapidly until thick and stiff, about 30 minutes, stirring frequently to prevent scorching.

Spoon into clean, hot jars or lightly-oiled moulds, cover with waxed discs, waxed-sides down, and dampened cellophane rounds. Store in a cool, dry, dark place for up to a year.

Damson and Plum Butter

MAKES ABOUT 1.25 KG (2½ LB)

1.4 kg (3 lb) ripe damsons and plums, mixed
grated rind and juice 1 lemon
450 ml (¾ pint) water or unsweetened red grape juice
sugar (see method)

Stone the damsons and plums and place in a pan with the lemon rind, lemon juice and water or red grape juice. Cook over a gentle heat until tender and pulpy, about 15–20 minutes.

Purée in a blender, then pass through a fine nylon sieve. Measure the purée, return to the pan and add 350 g (12 oz) sugar for each 600 ml (1 pint) fruit purée, blending well. Bring slowly to the boil to dissolve the sugar, then boil rapidly until the mixture is thick and no excess liquid remains, about 20–25 minutes, stirring frequently.

Spoon into clean, hot jars, cover with waxed discs, waxed-sides down, and dampened cellophane rounds. Label and store in a cool, dry, dark place for 3–6 months.

Blackberry and Apple Curd

This is the ideal recipe to make the most of the autumn blackberries and apples – it also makes a delicious change from the traditional lemon curd. Don't make too large a batch, as the addition of butter and eggs to the fruit means that the curd will only keep for about a month. Store in a cool place and, once opened, in the refrigerator.

MAKES ABOUT I KG (2 LB)

350 g (12 oz) blackberries, hulled
1 cooking apple, peeled, cored and sliced
juice 1 lemon
100 g (2 oz) butter
450 g (1 lb) golden granulated sugar
4 eggs

Place the blackberries and apple in a large pan. Cook slowly until tender, about 15–20 minutes. Pass through a fine nylon sieve.

Return the fruit purée to the pan with the lemon juice, butter and sugar. Heat gently until the butter melts and the sugar dissolves, stirring occasionally.

Beat the eggs lightly and slowly add to the fruit mixture, stirring constantly. Cook over a gentle heat until the curd coats the back of a wooden spoon, stirring constantly. DO NOT ALLOW TO BOIL OR THE MIXTURE WILL CURDLE.

Strain the cooked curd through a fine nylon sieve and spoon into clean, hot jars. Cover with waxed discs, waxed-sides down, and dampened cellophane rounds. Label and store in a cool, dark, dry place for up to a month. Serve with plain and sweet breads or as a topping for ice cream.

Blackcurrant Syrup

This is a refreshing any-time-of-the-year drink – to serve, use 1 part blackcurrant syrup to 2 parts water. Alternatively use undiluted as a dessert sauce or topping – especially good with ice cream.

MAKES ABOUT 600 ML (1 PINT)

450 g (1 lb) blackcurrants, topped and tailed
600 ml (1 pint) water
350 g (12 oz) cube sugar

Place the blackcurrants and water in a pan. Bring to the boil and boil rapidly for 1 minute. Remove from the heat and crush with the back of a wooden spoon. Spoon into a jelly-bag and leave to strain over a bowl for at least 12 hours.

Place the juice in a pan and add the sugar. Heat gently to dissolve the sugar, stirring constantly. Pour into small sterilised bottles, seal with sterilised corks or sterilised metal or plastic screw-caps. Wrap each bottle in a cloth and place in a deep pan on a metal rack. Fill up to the corks or caps with warm water and bring to simmering point or 80°C (180°F) for 30 minutes.

Remove from the pan and if using corked bottles then dip corks in melted wax to seal. Store in a cool, dry place for up to two months.

Cherry Brandy

MAKES ABOUT 750 ML (1¼ PINTS)

450 g (1 lb) cherries
600 ml (1 pint) brandy
75–100 g (3–4 oz) castor sugar

Remove the cherry stalks and wash thoroughly. Prick each cherry with a needle and place in a large glass jar. Add the brandy and sugar, cover tightly and shake to dissolve the sugar.

Leave at room temperature in a dark place for 2–3 months, shaking occasionally to dissolve the sugar.

After 2–3 months the fruit will have become very soft and should be strained off for eating. Bottle the liqueur and store in a cool, dry, dark place until required.

Piccalilli

MAKES 1.4 KG (3 LB)

1 medium cauliflower, broken into small florets
225 g (8 oz) cucumber, chopped
225 g (8 oz) green tomatoes, chopped
2 onions, peeled and sliced
1 small marrow, seeded and chopped
225 g (8 oz) celery, scrubbed and chopped
16 French beans, topped and tailed and cut into 2.5 cm (1 in) lengths
175 g (6 oz) salt
1.75 litres (3 pints) water
100 g (4 oz) sugar
1½ teaspoons mustard powder
½ teaspoon ground ginger
1 garlic clove, peeled and crushed
750 ml (1½ pints) distilled vinegar
25 g (1 oz) plain flour
1 tablespoon ground turmeric
pinch of chilli powder
pinch of ground allspice

Place the cauliflower, cucumber, tomatoes, onion, marrow, celery and beans in a large bowl, sprinkling between each layer with salt. Add the water, cover and leave to stand for 24 hours.

Drain, rinse and again drain the vegetables. Place in a large pan with the sugar, mustard, ginger, garlic and 600 ml (1 pint) of the vinegar. Bring to the boil, reduce the heat, cover and simmer until cooked but crisp, about 20 minutes.

Blend the flour, turmeric, chilli and allspice with the remaining vinegar.

Gradually add to the vegetable mixture, mixing well. Bring to the boil, stirring constantly, and cook for 2 minutes.

Spoon into clean, hot, wide-necked pickle or preserving jars. Cover with airtight, vinegar-proof tops. Label and store for 2–3 months before eating.

Sweet and Sour Peaches

MAKES ABOUT 900 G (2 LB)

675 g (1½ lb) small ripe peaches, peeled
350 ml (12 fl oz) white wine vinegar
175 g (6 oz) granulated sugar
1 large cinnamon stick
6 whole cloves

Pack the peaches into a large jar, as closely together as possible.

Place the vinegar, sugar, cinnamon and cloves in a pan. Heat gently to dissolve the sugar and bring to the boil.

Pour over the peaches and cover at once with an airtight vinegar-proof top. Label and store in a cool place for 1 month before eating.

Apple and Orange Chutney

Chutneys have an oriental origin: the word comes from the Hindustani *chatni* meaning a strong sweet relish. The following recipe is a good basic one which lends itself to simple variations.

MAKES 1.5–1.75 KG (3½–4 LB)

450 g (1 lb) peeled and finely chopped onions
275 ml (9 fl oz) malt vinegar
1 teaspoon pickling spice
25 ml (1 fl oz) unsweetened orange juice
900 g (2 lb) peeled and sliced cooking apples
350 g (12 oz) brown or castor sugar
½–1 teaspoon salt

100 g (4 oz) sultanas
1–2 teaspoons ground ginger

Place the onions in a large pan with half the vinegar. Simmer gently for 10 minutes, stirring occasionally.

Tie the spices in a piece of muslin and add to the pan with the orange juice and apples. Simmer gently until the apples are a soft pulp, about 20–30 minutes.

Stir in the remaining vinegar and sugar, mixing well. Heat gently until the sugar dissolves. Add salt to taste, the sultanas and ginger as liked. Boil rapidly until the chutney is thick and pulpy and no excess liquid remains. Remove and discard the spices in muslin.

Pour into clean, dry, pre-heated jars and cover at once with vinegar-proof lids. Label and store for 2–3 months before eating.

Variations

APPLE AND MINT CHUTNEY Prepare and cook as above, omitting the ginger. Just before potting, stir 2 tablespoons of finely chopped mint leaves into the chutney.

APPLE AND RED PEPPER CHUTNEY Prepare and cook as above, but replace 450 g (1 lb) of the peeled and sliced apples with 450 g (1 lb) chopped red pepper. Omit the ginger and use 1 teaspoon ground mixed spice instead.

APPLE AND TOMATO CHUTNEY Prepare and cook as above, but replace 675 g (1½ lb) of the peeled and sliced apples with chopped green tomatoes.

Pickled Red Cabbage and Onion

MAKES ABOUT 1.75 KG (4 LB)

1.4 kg (3 lb) red cabbage, cored and finely shredded
2 large onions, peeled and thinly sliced
4 tablespoons salt
about 1.8 litres (3 pints) cold spiced vinegar

Place the red cabbage and onion in a bowl, sprinkling salt between each layer. Cover and leave to stand overnight.

Drain, rinse and drain again thoroughly. Pack into wide-necked pickle jars and pour over the spiced vinegar to cover. Cover with airtight vinegar-proof caps. Label and store in a cool place for 2–3 weeks to mature before eating. Eat within 2–3 months.

Mint Sauce

It is essential to use only young, tender fresh mint leaves for this preserve. Wash the leaves, discarding the stalks, dry on absorbent kitchen paper and then chop finely on a board with a sharp knife or, for speed, in a food processor.

MAKES ABOUT 600 ML (I PINT)

225 g (8 oz) fresh mint, washed, dried and finely chopped
450 g (1 lb) granulated sugar
600 ml (1 pint) vinegar

Pack the mint into dry, wide-necked small preserving jars. Place the sugar and vinegar in a pan and heat slowly to dissolve the sugar, then bring to the boil.

Pour over the mint and seal with airtight covers. Store in a cool, dry place for 1 month before using and for up to 1 year.

To use, remove from the jar about 1 tablespoon of the mint sauce per person, and place in a bowl. Add a little extra vinegar and salt and pepper to taste, blending well. Serve in a sauce-boat – a favourite with lamb.

Home-made Tomato Sauce

This is just the sauce to make with those slightly over-ripe tomatoes when you have a glut. It is a home-made must for hamburgers, grills, meat-loaves and barbecue fare – much nicer than the commercial offerings!

MAKES ABOUT 1 LITRE (1¾ PINTS)

50 ml (2 fl oz) oil
12 shallots, peeled and chopped
1.4 kg (3 lb) ripe tomatoes, peeled, seeded and chopped
1 tablespoon tomato purée
150 ml (¼ pint) red wine vinegar
25 g (1 oz) soft brown sugar
2 teaspoons salt
1 teaspoon freshly ground black pepper

Heat the oil in a large pan. Add the shallots and cook gently until softened, about 8 minutes.

Add the tomatoes, tomato purée, vinegar, sugar, salt and pepper, mixing well. Bring to the boil, reduce the heat and simmer for 15–20 minutes, stirring occasionally. Purée in a blender or pass through a fine nylon sieve. Return to the pan and bring to the boil.

Pour into clean, warm bottles, leaving a 2.5 cm (1 in) headspace, and seal with sterilised corks or screw-tops. Wrap in cloth or newspaper and stand upright in a deep pan with an upturned plate or rack on the base. Top up with warm water to reach the necks of the bottles and heat to 88°C (190°F) or simmering point. Simmer at this temperature for 30 minutes.

Remove from the pan and push down the corks or tighten the screw-tops and leave until warm. If using corks, dip each cork in melted paraffin wax to make airtight. Leave until cold. Label and store in a cool, dark place for 1 month before using, and for up to 1 year.

Redcurrant Vinegar

This is a fruity vinegar which is delicious to use in salad dressings or diluted to make a refreshing drink.

MAKES ABOUT 600 ML (1 PINT)

450 g (1 lb) ripe redcurrants, topped and tailed
600 ml (1 pint) malt, wine or distilled vinegar
450 g (1 lb) white or brown sugar

Wash the fruit and place in a large bowl. Crush with the back of a wooden spoon and add the vinegar, mixing well. Cover and leave to stand for 4–5 days, stirring occasionally.

Strain through muslin into a saucepan and add the sugar, mixing well. Heat gently to dissolve, then bring to the boil and boil gently for 10 minutes.

Allow to cool, strain again and pour into clean warm bottles, leaving a 2.5 cm (1 in) headspace. Add a few whole washed berries to the bottle if liked. Seal securely with vinegar-proof tops, label and store in a cool, dark place for up to 2 weeks before using.

Variations

BLACKBERRY VINEGAR *Prepare and cook as above, but use 450 g (1 lb) hulled blackberries instead of redcurrants.*

RASPBERRY VINEGAR *Prepare and cook as above, but use 450 g (1 lb) hulled raspberries instead of redcurrants.*

BLACKCURRANT VINEGAR *Prepare and cook as above, but use 450 g (1 lb) topped and tailed blackcurrants instead of redcurrants.*

Herb Vinegars

Splendid in salad dressings, sauces and pickles, herb vinegars are attractive enough to present as a gift. Use herbs freshly gathered just before they flower – favourites include tarragon, sage, rosemary, mint, basil, thyme, marjoram and dill. Use a mixture or just one type for success.

MAKES ABOUT 600 ML (1 PINT)

about 150 g (5 oz) freshly gathered herbs, washed
about 600 ml (1 pint) white wine or red wine vinegar

Strip the leaves from the stems of the herbs and bruise with the back of a wooden spoon. Place in a large jar or bottle and top up with the wine vinegar. Cover and leave in a cool, dry place for 3–4 weeks.

Strain through muslin, pour into clean bottles and add a fresh sprig of the chosen herb, or a small bunch of mixed herbs if liked. Seal with airtight vinegar-proof tops and leave to mature for 2–3 weeks before using.

Bottled Fruit Salad

I am not suggesting that you make only one jar of this bottled fruit salad. To make as many as you like, simply double, treble or quadruple the ingredients below, or make up a mixture of your own soft berry fruits and follow the basic cooking instructions.

MAKES I × I LITRE (1¾ PINT) JAR

100 g (4 oz) cherries, stoned
100 g (4 oz) loganberries, hulled
100 g (4 oz) blackcurrants, topped and tailed
100 g (4 oz) redcurrants, topped and tailed
175 g (6 oz) strawberries, hulled
175 g (6 oz) sugar
450 ml (¾ pint) water

Rinse the fruit and layer attractively in a 1 litre (1¾ pint) warmed preserving jar, packing the fruit closely together.

Place the sugar and water in a pan. Heat gently to dissolve, bring to the boil and boil rapidly for 1 minute. Pour over the fruit to within 2.5 cm (1 in) of the top of the jar. Fit the rubber ring around the inside of the glass lid and place on the jar, ensuring that the rubber ring lies evenly all round. Secure the metal clip or screw on the plastic screwband, then turn the screwband back a quarter-turn. Place in a large vessel with a false bottom (a metal grid or folded coarse cloth is ideal), about 5 cm (2 in) deeper than the height of the jar. Cover with warm water up to the neck of the jar. Bring the water to simmering point in 25–30 minutes, and keep simmering for 2 minutes. Remove the jar with tongs and tighten the plastic screwband (if used) immediately.

Store in a cool, dark place for up to 1 year.

Greengages in Honey Syrup

MAKES I × I LITRE (1¾ PINT) JAR

about 12–16 ripe greengages (enough to fill the jar)
75 g (3 oz) sugar
75 g (3 oz) clear honey
450 ml (¾ pint) water

Wash and carefully wipe the greengages. Pack attractively in a 1 litre (1¾ pint) warmed preserving jar.

Place the sugar, honey and water in a pan. Heat gently to dissolve the sugar and honey, bring to the boil and boil rapidly for 1 minute. Pour over the fruit to within 2.5 cm (1 in) of the top of the jar. Fit the rubber ring around the inside of the glass lid and place on the jar, ensuring that the rubber ring lies evenly all round; do not fix on screwbands or metal clips. Place the jar in the centre of a preheated cool oven at 150°C (300°F, Gas Mark 2) on a baking tray lined with sheets of newspaper and cook for 55 minutes.

Remove from the oven, wipe any excess syrup from the neck of the jar, check that ring and lid are in place, screw on plastic screwbands tightly if used, leave for 2–3 minutes then re-tighten, or secure the metal clips. Label and store in a cool, dry place for up to two years.

Rhubarb Conserve

MAKES ABOUT 1.4 KG (3 LB)

550 g (1¼ lb) rhubarb, trimmed and cut into 2.5 cm (1 in) lengths
350 g (12 oz) tender young carrots, peeled and grated
grated rind and chopped flesh of 1 lemon
water (see method)
100 g (4 oz) chopped mixed cut peel
900 g (2 lb) sugar
50 g (2 oz) raisins
pinch ground ginger

Place the rhubarb, carrots and lemon flesh in a large pan. Add just enough water to cover. Bring to the boil, reduce the heat and simmer until tender, about 15–20 minutes.

Add the lemon rind, peel, sugar, raisins and ginger, blending well. Heat gently to dissolve the sugar, bring to the boil and boil rapidly until setting point is reached, stirring frequently.

Spoon into clean, hot jars. Cover with waxed discs, waxed-sides down, and dampened cellophane rounds. Label and store in a cool, dry, dark place for up to a year.

Plum Conserve

A magnificent blend of plums, oranges and raisins conserved with golden granulated sugar.

MAKES ABOUT 4 KG (8 LB)

1.4 kg (3 lb) plums, halved and stoned
2 oranges, minced (or chopped fine in a blender but not puréed)
1.4 kg (3 lb) golden granulated sugar
450 g (1 lb) raisins

Place the plums and minced oranges in a large pan and cook until softened, about 10 minutes.

Warm the sugar and stir into the plum mixture with the raisins, mixing well. Bring to the boil, reduce the heat and cook gently, stirring occasionally, until very thick, about 1½ hours. Leave to cool for 15 minutes.

Spoon into clean, hot jars. Cover with waxed discs, waxed-sides down, and dampened cellophane rounds. Label and store in a cool, dark, dry place for up to a year.

Apricots in Bourbon

MAKES ABOUT I × 600 ML (I PINT) JAR

225 g (8 oz) sugar
300 ml (½ pint) water
450 g (1 lb) apricots, peeled, halved and stoned
150 ml (¼ pint) bourbon

Place 100 g (4 oz) of the sugar and the water in a pan. Heat gently to dissolve, bring to the boil and boil for 1 minute. Add the apricots and simmer gently until barely tender, about 5 minutes.

Remove with a slotted spoon and arrange attractively in a 600 ml (1 pint) clean, hot preserving jar.

Add the remaining sugar to the syrup, mixing well. Bring to the boil and boil for 5 minutes. Allow to cool, then add the bourbon, blending well. Pour over the apricots to cover. Cover with an airtight, vinegar-proof top (as for pickles). Label and store in a cool, dry, dark place for up to a year.

Salted Cucumbers

MAKES ABOUT 675 G (1½ LB)

4 cucumbers
450 g (1 lb) coarse cooking salt

Thinly slice the cucumbers without peeling. Place in a bowl with half of the salt, blending well. Cover with a plate and weight down for 24 hours.

Drain and pat dry with absorbent kitchen paper. Place a shallow layer of the remaining salt in the base of a large plastic screw-top preserving jar or earthenware jar. Cover with a layer of cucumber slices. Repeat the salt and cucumber layering, finishing with a layer of salt. Cover with waxed paper or the screw-top and seal. Store in a cool, dark place for up to 6 months.

To use, rinse the cucumber and leave to soak in cold water for 1 hour. Drain, rinse again and use as required.

Salted Beans

MAKES 1.4 KG (3 LB)

1.4 kg (3 lb) runner or French beans
450 g (1 lb) coarse cooking salt

String the runner beans, wash and cut into 2.5 cm (1 in) lengths. If using French beans, top and tail and then cut into small lengths if very long.

Place 1 cm (½ in) layer of salt in the base of a large plastic screw-top preserving jar or earthenware jar. Layer about 2.5 cm (1 in) of the prepared beans on top and press down well. Repeat the salt and bean layering, finishing with a layer of salt. Weight down the top of the beans with a saucer to keep immersed in the salt. Cover with waxed paper or the screw-top and leave for 2–3 days. During this time the beans will settle, leaving enough room for another layer of beans and salt.

Add the final layer of beans and salt, pressing down well. Weight again for 2–3 days. Remove the weight, cover with waxed paper or the screw-top and seal. Store in a cool, dark place for up to 6 months.

To use, rinse the beans and leave to soak in cold water for 2 hours. Rinse again, then cook as usual.

Useful Addresses

Organisations

THE HENRY DOUBLEDAY RESEARCH ASSOCIATION (HDRA),
National Centre for Organic Gardening, Ryton-on-Dunsmore,
Coventry CV8 3LG. Tel: 0203 303517
*Britain's organisation for organic gardeners. The ten acres of
demonstration gardens are open daily to the public with free access to
members. Relevant field research is also carried out.*

THE SOIL ASSOCIATION, 86 Colston Street, Bristol BS1 5BB. Tel:
0272 290661.
*The campaigning body of the organic movement. The Soil Association
symbol provides a guarantee of authenticity to fertilisers, sprays and
composts used in organic gardening as well as to food produced
organically.*

ELM FARM RESEARCH CENTRE, Hamstead Marshall, Newbury,
Berks RG15 0RH.
*Organic farming research establishment. Provides a soil analysis service
tailored to the needs of organic gardeners and growers.*

Seeds and Supplies

CHASE ORGANICS (GB) LTD, Coombelands House, Coombelands
Lane, Addlestone, Weybridge KT15 1HY. Tel: 0932 858511.
*Untreated seed of vegetables, flowers and green manures. Books and
sundries including organic potting composts, fertilisers and pest
control products. Some biological control products available.*

HDRA (SALES) LTD, National Centre for Organic Gardening, Ryton-on-Dunsmore, Coventry CV8 3LG. Tel: 0203 303517.
Untreated seed of vegetables, herbs, flowers and green manures, including oriental and unusual types of vegetables and organically raised seed potatoes. Books, publications and a full range of organic gardening sundries including compost bins. Suppliers of biological controls and sole agents for Trichoderma viride. Shop on site or mail order.

SUFFOLK HERBS, Sawyers Farm, Little Cornard, Sudbury, Suffolk CO10 0NY. Tel: 0787 227247.
Specialists in herbs, wildflowers and unusual vegetables and salads, as well as more commonly grown types. Books and general organic sundries.

CUMULUS ORGANICS AND CONSERVATION LTD, Two Mile Lane, Highnam, Glos GL2 8BR. Tel: 0452 305814.
Organic soil treatments, fertilisers, potting composts. Organic pest and weed control products. Booklets.

Index

Index compiled by Peva Keane